New Perspectives on English as a European Lingua Franca

New Perspectives on English as a European Lingua Franca

Heiko Motschenbacher

Goethe University, Frankfurt am Main

John Benjamins Publishing Company

Amsterdam / Philadelphia

™ The paper used in this publication meets the minimum requirements of the American National Standard for Information Sciences – Permanence of Paper for Printed Library Materials, ANSI z39.48-1984.

Library of Congress Cataloging-in-Publication Data

Motschenbacher, Heiko.
  New perspectives on English as a European Lingua Franca / Heiko Motschenbacher.
      pages cm.
Includes bibliographical references and index.
1. English language--Study and teaching--Europe. 2. English language--Europe. 3. English
      language--Influence on foreign languages. 4. Lingua francas--Europe. 5. Languages in
      contact. I. Title.
PE2751.M68   2013
428.0071'04--dc23   2013034840
ISBN 978 90 272 1207 8   (Hb ; alk. paper)
ISBN 978 90 272 7099 3   (Eb)

John Benjamins Publishing Co. · P.O. Box 36224 · 1020 ME Amsterdam · The Netherlands
John Benjamins North America · P.O. Box 27519 · Philadelphia PA 19118-0519 · USA

Table of contents

Acknowledgements

I would like to thank those people who have had an influence on the final shape of this volume. Among these are Will Baker, Jennifer Jenkins, Barbara Seidlhofer and two anonymous reviewers whose comments on the book proposal proved to be extremely helpful. Moreover, I would like to thank Ute Smit for her critical comments on an earlier version of the book manuscript. All remaining insufficiencies remain, of course, my own. My thanks also go out to the team of the English Linguistics Department at Siegen University, Germany, which has been a highly inspiring environment for me and my work during the last couple of months. Finally, I would like to thank the John Benjamins team for its ongoing support.

Country codes

ALB	– Albania	FRA	– France	NED	– Netherlands
ARM	– Armenia	GEO	– Georgia	NOR	– Norway
AZE	– Azerbaijan	GER	– Germany	POL	– Poland
BEL	– Belgium	GRE	– Greece	POR	– Portugal
BLR	– Belarus	HUN	– Hungary	ROM	– Romania
BOS	– Bosnia Herzegovina	IRL	– Ireland	RUS	– Russia
BUL	– Bulgaria	ISL	– Iceland	SER	– Serbia
CRO	– Croatia	ITA	– Italy	SLK	– Slovakia
CYP	– Cyprus	LAT	– Latvia	SLO	– Slovenia
CZE	– Czech Republic	LIT	– Lithuania	SUI	– Switzerland
DAN	– Denmark	LUX	– Luxembourg	SWE	– Sweden
ESP	– Spain	MAC	– Macedonia	TUR	– Turkey
EST	– Estonia	MAL	– Malta	UK	– United Kingdom
FIN	– Finland	MOL	– Moldova	UKR	– Ukraine

Other abbreviations

AME	– American English	ESC-PC	– ESC Press Conferences Corpus
AUSE	– Australian English	ESL	– English as a Second Language
BNC	– British National Corpus	EU	– European Union
BRE	– British English	IRE	– Irish English
EBU	– European Broadcasting Union	LLC	– London-Lund Corpus
EFL	– English as a Foreign Language	NZE	– New Zealand English
ELF	– English as a Lingua Franca	SBC	– Santa Barbara Corpus
ELT	– English Language Teaching	VOICE	– Vienna-Oxford International Corpus of English
ENL	– English as a Native Language		
ESC	– Eurovision Song Contest		

Chapter 1

Introduction

It is generally accepted that the use of English has spread around the world. This spread is a result of two major strands of expansion. Historically, British colonisation efforts have led to English being transported from Britain to territories around the globe. A second, more contemporary motor to this spread is the growing use of English as a lingua franca in contexts where people of different linguacultural backgrounds meet and communicate. It is this latter development that has spawned a great deal of research on English as a lingua franca (henceforth ELF) as of lately. The current book seeks to make an innovative contribution to this enormously growing field, which is currently in the process of separating itself from more traditional approaches to the linguistic variation one finds under the umbrella term "English".

At the moment of writing, ELF research shows two continental centres of gravity: Asia (cf. Baker 2009a; Cheng 2012; Kirkpatrick 2011; Murata & Jenkins eds. 2009) and Europe (cf. Berns 2009; Breiteneder 2009; House 2008a; Seidlhofer 2010). This is, of course, not surprising if one considers that English has played a prominent role as a lingua franca in both contexts. Still, it needs to be acknowledged that these two regional macro-contexts reflect (at least partly) different histories in relation to the use of English. While certain regions of Asia were part of the British Empire (Brunei, Hong Kong, India, Jordan, Malaysia, Myanmar, Pakistan, Singapore, Sri Lanka, to name but a few), mainland Europe has not been subject to the same colonial, Anglophone influences, with British colonial areas being restricted to small territories located at the geographical fringes of Europe (i.e. Cyprus, Gibraltar, Malta). Moreover, Europe is, historically speaking, widely considered to be the cradle of nationalism and therefore possesses a longer and more entrenched tradition of making "languages" central ingredients in nation building processes.

Even though this book does not provide a direct comparison between ELF in Asia and Europe, it is based on the premise that the way ELF manifests itself in Europe is not necessarily the same as in Asia or other parts of the world. This, in turn, means that the findings that are presented cannot be automatically transferred to other geographical areas, even though some aspects clearly do have a wider currency. In fact, it will be argued that even a generalisation of the findings that goes beyond the community of practice studied here is a difficult task that needs to be handled with due care. The use of the phrases *English as a European lingua franca* and *European ELF* in the present book should be understood accordingly: the subject matter is ELF as it manifests itself in transnational European contexts or, more locally, in a specific community of practice of particular European significance, namely *Eurovision Song Contest* (ESC) press conferences.

It needs to be stressed from the start that the label *English as a European lingua franca* does not imply an internally stable and homogeneous entity. By contrast, this book sets out to explore European ELF as a hybrid, internally heterogeneous formation, even within one particular community of practice. To arrive at a comprehensive picture of this hybridity, European ELF is studied on various linguistic levels in the empirical sections of this book. Four levels will be discussed in detail: the code choice level (Chapter 4), the metalinguistic level (Chapter 5), the pragmatic level (in the shape of complimenting behaviour; Chapter 6), and the structural linguistic level (more specifically, relativisation; Chapter 7). These four levels are not analysed for their own sake but in relation to an ethnographic description of ESC press conferences as a usage context. This combination of perspectives is meant to yield a multidimensional, holistic picture of the hybridity of European ELF.

Beside the central goal of documenting the hybridity of European ELF on various levels, this study also has other (related) aims. In studying a community of practice of particular European significance, it also seeks to shed light on how "Europeanness" is performed via ELF as a medium of construction. It contributes to debates on how to conceptualise ELF (in Europe) and documents how ELF – as the epitome of linguistic practices in the postmodern age – clashes with some traditional and highly influential (socio)linguistic concepts that are based on notions of internal homogeneity and regional (often national) boundedness (such as *language, variety* or *speech community*).

ESC press conferences provide excellent data for the research purposes just outlined. This is not just the case because they represent a transnational, pan-European media context in which English is used as a lingua franca by default. Another interesting aspect is that they constitute a context in which "Europeanness" is a salient issue – a salience that has gained prominence throughout the history of the contest. The ESC is an annually televised media spectacle for which Europeans virtually get together to pick the "European song of the year". At the moment of writing, the preparations of the 57th annual edition of the contest are in full speed, and its success as a (if not *the*) pan-European entertainment show is unprecedented. In the course of its history, the contest has turned into a European institution in its own right, and one that – in contrast to more directly political efforts to unite Europe – has been successful in uniting Europeans from across the continent in front of their TV sets. As it is today watched by about 110 million viewers Europe-wide,[1] the contest continues to be an

---

1.   Viewing figures given by Schweiger and Brosius (2003:273) for the ESC 2002 bear witness to the high popularity of the contest in many participating countries, with market shares of 40.4% for DAN, 39.1% for SWE, 32.5% for ESP, roughly 50% in EST, 40.6% for SUI and 38.2% for GER. In GER, the ESC 2011 was awarded the *German Television Prize* in the category "Best Entertainment Show".

important driving force for European integration and identity formation. Through-out its history, the competitive element of the contest has increasingly shifted to the background, which today makes the ESC an event that celebrates European together-ness through popular music. Each participating country pre-selects a pop music act that will then represent the respective nation by giving a musical performance on the Eurovision stage. The contest is televised live. While the winning performance was in earlier times decided through nation-based jury voting, the viewers across Europe have become actively involved in picking the winner by public televoting since 1998. Historically, the contest developed from a largely Western European phenomenon to a truly pan-European event in the 1990s, when more and more Eastern European countries joined the Eurovision family after the fall of the Iron Curtain. Today, the annual event stretches over three nights (two semi-finals and the grand final) and hosts approximately 40 participating national delegations. The press conferences that these national delegations gave during the preparatory phase of the 2010 edition of the contest are used in the present book as data for studying European ELF.

The use of English in contexts where speakers from various national cultures get into contact with each other is certainly not a new phenomenon. However, the greater visibility of such contacts, for example as an outcome of increasing "Europeanisation", has recently caused many linguists to devote a great deal of their attention to such transnational uses of English. This has led to a greater institutional recognition of uses of English that widely depart from more traditional notions of nativeness and standard-orientation. A result of this development is that scholars' reasoning about the status of English in Europe has taken on various shapes, ranging from more tra-ditional to more innovative approaches. It is essential to be aware of these theoreti-cal discussions before moving on to the empirical analyses of transnational uses of English in Europe later in this book. The four major perspectives on English in Europe will therefore be outlined in the four initial sections of the following chapter. Among these four positions, there are two traditional approaches that have lost ground as of recently and can therefore be described as largely historical phases in the treatment of English in Europe. This is the case for the linguistic imperialism approach to English in Europe (Chapter 2.1) and the Euro-English debate (Chapter 2.2). The two remaining strands, the English as a lingua franca approach (Chapter 2.3) and the postmodern-ist reconceptualisation of English (2.4) have become more prominent in recent years and accordingly play a major role in contemporary discussions of English in Europe. Chapter 2.5 motivates the title of the book in explaining which new perspectives on European ELF are to be presented.

Chapter 2

Differing views on the status of English in Europe

2.1 English in Europe and linguistic imperialism

When describing the status of English in contemporary Europe, it is essential to take note of the specificities of Europe as a multilingual macro-context. In contrast to the multilingualism found in other parts of the world, European multilingualism is heavily structured by national orientations to societal monolingualism that are only slowly giving way to alternative discourses. These orientations cause a hierarchisation of languages that generally sees those languages on top which are official national languages, whereas languages that do not fulfil this function are located at the bottom. Ammon (2006b), for example, conceptualises the constellation of languages in Europe in terms of the following hierarchy: 1. English and French as (de facto)[1] EU working languages, 2. the remaining 22 official EU languages (Bulgarian, Croatian, Czech, Danish, Dutch, Estonian, Finnish, French, German, Greek, Hungarian, Irish, Italian, Latvian, Lithuanian, Maltese, Polish, Portuguese, Romanian, Slovak, Slovenian, Spanish and Swedish), 3. national languages of non-EU countries (e.g. Albanian, Bosnian, Icelandic, Montenegrin, Norwegian, Serbian), 4. regional languages with semi-official status in the EU (Basque, Catalan, Galician), 5. acknowledged minority languages (e.g. Scottish Gaelic in the UK, Sorbian in GER), 6. unacknowledged indigenous minority languages (e.g. Romani in many European countries), 7. exogenous minority languages (e.g. Hindi in the UK, Turkish in GER) (Ammon 2006b: 221–222).[2] The status of English at the top of the hierarchy is now unchallenged, as more and more interactions involving speakers from various European linguacultural backgrounds are carried out in English as a lingua franca.

Such traditional descriptions of European multilingualism are centrally based on the notion that European nation states compete for the wider recognition and transnational use of their national languages. Moreover, they are influenced by discussions of linguistic human rights in relation to the spread of English in Europe

---

1. Officially all EU languages are called "working languages" (Ammon 2006a: 321).

2. Ammon (2006b: 222) also includes varieties of debated language status (e.g. Scots) and dialects further down in the hierarchy.

(see Phillipson 1998; Phillipson & Skutnabb-Kangas 1997). The latter approach considers speakers' need to communicate in their L1 as a fundamental human right in need of protection. Such reasoning has proven useful for the recognition of linguistic minorities both on the national and on the European level. However, in transnational European communication, where the use of English as a lingua franca has been gaining ground, an application of linguistic human rights seems much less straightforward. When speakers from various linguacultural backgrounds meet, an insistence on the linguistic human right to use one's L1 turns out a significant obstacle to transnational communication. Trying to establish one's own L1 as a means of transnational communication runs counter to the cooperation-oriented principle of accommodation. It may furthermore be interpreted as an undesirable highlighting of one's national affiliation that carries less prestige and is communicatively less efficient in transnational contexts. In fact, it can be argued that the linguistic human rights discussion shows a tendency to foster nationalist thinking in relation to language and therefore constitutes a serious obstacle to any deeper levels of Europeanisation. The promotion of European multilingualism through foreign language education is unlikely to reduce the problem of these language disputes, because, in practice, people can learn only a small number of (European) languages, meaning that a large number of national languages cannot be covered (let alone the languages that do not enjoy national status).

Supporters of the linguistic human rights approach take issue with the continuing spread of English in transnational communication, which they perceive as a threat to multilingualism and, therefore, as a process of cultural homogenisation as an outcome of British and/or US American linguistic imperialism (the homogeny position; Phillipson 2003a/b; Phillipson & Skutnabb-Kangas 1997; Skutnabb-Kangas & Phillipson 2003). The most ardent representative of this school of thought is Phillipson, whose work has more recently become highly polemic. For example, he describes English as a killer language that endangers all other languages, calling it "lingua frankensteinia" instead of lingua franca (Phillipson 2008a/b). For Europe more specifically, linguistic human rights scholars suggest that English acts as an imperialist force that threatens other European languages and encroaches on their domains of use. However, when recapitulating the last century, one finds, by contrast, that the spread of English in Europe actually coincides with an overcoming of more imperialist-minded structures after World War II and the fall of the Iron Curtain (House 2003:561). This contradiction indicates that the forms of English that are spreading across Europe are, from an anthropological perspective, generally perceived to be less imperialistic than linguistic human rights scholars suggest.

Such polemic moves as relabelling ELF as a "lingua frankensteinia" have lately drawn considerable criticism. Many researchers find the idea that the spread of English today is resultant in a concomitant spread of Anglo-American culture around the globe unconvincing, especially if it is claimed that native speakers of English are the main agents behind this spread (e.g. Dewey 2007; Friedrich 2007, 2009; Grad-dol 2006; Kirkpatrick 2006; Saraceni 2008).[3] From the point of view of ELF, this discussion also has the undesirable side effect of keeping native speakers firmly in their central position as "owners" of English. It is doubtful whether the fact that more and more people around the globe use English is tantamount to their adopting an Anglo-American mindset. Today English can be used to express various cultural models and identity affiliations (Wolf & Polzenhagen 2006: 294). Debates on linguistic imperialism tend to ignore the question why people take up English and how they do it, namely, in local appropriation (Pennycook 2003: 516). It seems that nowadays most people learn English voluntarily. There certainly is an increasing pressure to learn foreign languages in our globalised world, but this pressure is an aspect that relates to foreign languages in general, not just to English. Faced with this pressure, many (if not most) people opt for English, not because they aspire to become British or US American, but simply because choosing English can take away more of this pressure compared to other foreign languages whose degree of efficiency for communication across cultures is more limited. Most people see learning English as an activity that provides them with certain benefits (for example, in terms of communicative reach, on the job market or when travelling abroad). Few people who learn English as a foreign language have the feeling that they are swept over by Anglo-Americanisation or subject to neo-imperialist forces:

> [...] the spread of English has also been a result of an active desire for English [...], which in turn cannot be dismissed as a form of misguided subjection to global hegemony without also bringing into play a heavy-handed notion of ideology that implies that the demand for English is only a superstructural reflection of neo-capital and English infrastructure. (Pennycook 2011: 516)

In short, the top-down goal of EU multilingualism contrasts markedly with the bottom-up drive towards English in Europe, and it is doubtful whether the former stands any realistic chances of successful implementation in the face of the latter.

Gnutzmann (2008: 77) produces evidence that many non-native speakers do not have negative attitudes towards English. In a questionnaire study conducted with the staff and students at the Technical University of Braunschweig (GER), he finds that about 65% of the subjects have positive attitudes towards English, with neutral attitudes amounting to 30% (and negative attitudes to only 5%). Many, if not most, ELF speakers do not perceive their use of English as an instance of being victimised by Anglo-American imperialism (Yano 2009: 253) and creating such an awareness

---

3. As Graddol (2006: 112) points out, the spread of English is still unchallenged despite the fact that the US has significantly lost prestige internationally.

generally leads to nationalist reactions that can hardly be deemed helpful for the "European project".

The strict equalisation of English with Anglo-American culture automatically denies non-native speakers the right to attach other identity values to their use of English. The claim that English can only be used to express an Anglo-American mind-set (e.g. Fiedler 2010) is reminiscent of discussions about linguistic relativism and more extreme readings of the Sapir-Whorf-hypothesis, which are generally no longer viewed as tenable today (Gnutzmann 2008:78; House 2008a:77). Even though language plays an important role in the expression of culture, this does not mean that culture is deterministically linked to language in the sense that the use of a certain language is restricted to an (automatic) construction of a certain national identity.

The argument that non-native speakers are disadvantaged in contexts where they either have to interact or compete with native speakers of English is of greater momentum than that of linguistic relativity in relation to English (Gnutzmann 2008:81–83; Seidlhofer 2012), even though this may be less true than popularly believed (see House 2008a:70). This is an argument that is not specific to English and pertains to all languages that are learnt as foreign languages. Furthermore this argument can easily be turned on its head, because ELF enables speakers to communicate with people from cultures around the world. The use of English for such purposes is therefore a clear advantage that may be said to outweigh the disadvantages non-native speakers have to face (Mukherjee 2008:114). The more English becomes established as a lingua franca, the smaller these disadvantages will become.

An explanation for the fact that English is not a "killer language" that works to the detriment of other European languages is given by House (2003). House takes into account the function of a certain language in people's lives and makes a distinction between "languages of identification" and "languages of communication" (a distinction originally taken from Hüllen 1992). On the one hand, a speaker's L1 serves as a language of ethnic/national identification. English as a foreign language, on the other hand, generally fulfils the pragmatic function of communicating with people outside one's speech community and is therefore a language of communication. As each of these two language types is connected to a different function, they are unlikely to compete and can therefore exist side by side without one encroaching on the domains of the other (Lüdi 2002:8ff). According to this reasoning, ELF as a language of communication does not pose a threat to European national languages, which are considered languages of identification.

Although this functional distinction seems to have great explanatory power (national languages are indeed only marginally threatened by ELF on the national level), there are also some points about this argumentation that need to be viewed more critically (see also Fiedler 2011). It is too simplistic to state that the use of one's L1 is purely symbolic and not also a matter of communication. Conversely, it is implausible to suggest that the use of ELF solely serves communicative purposes and is devoid of identification processes. A clear-cut distinction of these two categories of languages is therefore highly problematic (Jenkins 2006). This view is also shared, on a global scale, by Pennycook:

> This categorization of global and local languages whereby English serves people as a language of international communication while local languages help maintain culture, tradition and identity underlies many current positions on TESOL[4] (strengthening the effective teaching and learning of English around the world while respecting individuals' language rights), bilingualism and language rights. By relegating vernacular languages only to local expression, however, and by elevating English only to the role of international communication, such a view ignores the many complexities of local and global language use.   (Pennycook 2007b: 104)

To transfer this back to the European context: a clear-cut distinction between languages of identification and languages of communication would rule out the possibility that English may also serve identity functions for non-native European speakers. This would seem highly unlikely in the face of abundant evidence that English is seen as a "trendy" language associated with modernity and progress in many contexts in which it is spoken as a "foreign" language (for example, in many Eastern European countries; Braselmann 2005: 165).

One of the fundamental problems associated with the linguistic imperialism approach is its conceptualisation of languages as strictly tied to the nation (or, in the case of minority languages, ethnicity). This seems counterintuitive for transnational communication, where languages are often used by speakers who do not originate from the national background stereotypically associated with a certain language. For English more specifically, such reasoning is tantamount to claiming that its use by non-native speakers in transnational European communication is an expression of speakers' desire to assimilate to Anglophone cultures and works as a promotion of national British or US American interests. Of course, English language teaching is today a lucrative business that provides native English countries with high financial benefits. On the identity plane, however, it is unlikely that most non-native speakers aim at assimilation to Anglophone cultures or see their own national affiliations threatened by their use of English as a European lingua franca.

As has been demonstrated in the preceding discussion, the question of whether the spread of English poses a threat to other European languages cannot be answered in general. The respective macro-context needs to be taken into account. On European soil, English is clearly a threat to minority languages in Anglophone nation states (for example, to Welsh, Scots and Scottish Gaelic in the UK; or to Irish in IRL). Minority

---

4.   TESOL = Teaching English to Speakers of Other Languages

languages in non-Anglophone nation states (German in ITA, Sorbian in GER etc.) are first and foremost threatened by the respective national language(s) in their immediate surroundings, not by English. European national languages are also unlikely to be threatened by English on the national level, where they are typically firmly established and institutionalised. Finally, on the transnational European level, the spread of English indeed works to the detriment of other European languages. However, it needs to be noted that in fact only a handful of languages can be threatened by English in this respect (namely French, German and, to a lesser extent, Italian, Russian and Spanish), simply because most European national languages such as Finnish, Latvian, Polish or Slovenian are not commonly used as languages of wider communication. As pointed out by Ammon (2006a/b), it is mainly the larger language communities that are heard to complain about the growing influence of English on the transnational level. Smaller language communities are less likely to find fault with this situation, because a promotion of languages other than English would mean an extra burden of foreign language learning for them. A concentration on English as the (potentially) sole European lingua franca could help avoid hegemonic multilingualism (i.e. the dominance of a small number of larger languages) and the language-based rivalries associated with it. However, it is clear that such a development cannot take place when a national variety like British English is used as a reference point for transnational communication. This would turn nationally-based hegemonic multilingualism into nationally-based hegemonic monolingualism, since it would clearly privilege the Anglophone nations. The notions of "Euro-English" (Chapter 2.2) and "English as a European lingua franca" (Chapter 2.3) appear to be better candidates to fulfil this function, because they are not nationally based or tied to native English cultures. What speaks against "Euro-English" in this connection is that a conceptualisation of European uses of English as a fixed variety would just as much lead to hegemonic monolingualism as an orientation to British English (though not nationally based). The concept of "English as a European lingua franca", by contrast, is more firmly linked to an internal heterogeneity that is hardly reconcilable with the term "monolingualism".

2.2   Europe and the World Englishes paradigm: Euro-English as a linguistic variety?

From the descriptions in the preceding chapter, it becomes evident that the linguistic human rights approach treats "English" in Europe as a macro-social issue, often without looking at its structural dimension or local interactional practices. The structural level plays a more important role in the "Euro-English" approach, which relates the discussion of English in Europe to the potential identification of a linguistic variety. It needs to be stressed that recently this approach to English in Europe has significantly lost support among researchers. Its discussion at this point therefore has to be seen as a largely historical account of how certain scholars previously conceptualised English in Europe (but see van den Doel & Quené 2013 for a recent investigation along these lines). The approach will here be outlined in its basic assumptions, despite some of them no longer being seriously contemplated. Still, these theoretical discussions represent a crucial step in the (academic) discursive formation of what "English in Europe" means and many of the more recent developments in the field qualify as reactions to them.

Central to the Euro-English debate is the question of whether the non-native English uses across Europe constitute a variety in their own right that may one day acquire the same status as other World Englishes. The main aim of such research is to study Euro-English empirically in order to detect its typical features, which may later be used as a point of reference for codification and/or language teaching (Seidlhofer 2002: 297). In the beginning, the goal of such research seemed to be the creation of an endonormative model for (European) ELF, i.e. raising the English used by non-native European speakers from its norm-dependent to a norm-developing or, in the end, norm-providing status. These motivations, however, no longer figure prominently among current researchers of English in Europe.

The considerations of the Euro-English strand of work are heavily influenced by Kachru's (1985) classic model of the three concentric circles of World Englishes. It categorises Englishes in relation to acquisition patterns, domains, standardisation and, most significantly, by nation. Inner circle Englishes (English as a native language; ENL) are spoken as L1 in countries where English is the default medium for private communication, often by monolingual white speakers as the descendants of the first English diaspora wave coming from the British Isles. These Englishes (e.g. BrE, AmE, AusE, NZE) are well codified and standardised and generally provide norms for foreign language learners of English.

Outer circle Englishes are used as second official languages (English as a second language; ESL) in countries that have a historical relation to the former British Empire (e.g. India, Nigeria, Singapore) and are therefore associated with the second wave diaspora. They usually form a component in speakers' multilingual repertoires and are as a consequence influenced by the speakers' local L1s. Besides education, they tend to be restricted to such domains as administration and government. In multilingual societies, they are often used as an intranational lingua franca, because they are perceived to be neutral in the sense that they do not privilege any of the indigenous ethnic groups. However, from a historical point of view, it is difficult to claim that the use of English, i.e. the language of the former colonisers, is a neutral medium of communication. Outer circle Englishes are typically in a process of developing their own linguistic norms, thereby emancipating themselves from BrE as the normative reference point.

Finally, expanding circle Englishes are said to be spoken in all countries that lack a British colonial past. In these, English is acquired as a foreign language (EFL), i.e. typically through active language learning in formal education. English is here primarily learnt for purposes of international communication (for example, in politics, science or tertiary education) and does not normally fulfil official functions on the national level. Expanding circle Englishes have (so far) not developed local norms and therefore depend on inner circle varieties as exonormative standards. In terms of speaker numbers, expanding circle Englishes are clearly dominant, and this dominance is likely to increase as more and more people around the world learn English as a foreign language. This development raises consequential questions concerning the legitimate "ownership" of the language, which was traditionally seen to be in the hands of the native speakers (Widdowson 1994).

As far as European uses of English are concerned, IRL[5] and the UK belong to the inner circle, whereas MAL is part of the outer circle.[6] MAL is unique in Europe as the only country that shows large-scale bilingualism with English (as opposed to IRL, where English is also co-official but bilingualism is rarer due to the low frequency of Irish speakers). English is spoken by virtually everyone in MAL, but it remains an additional language because it is normally learnt at school. Another point that is special about MAL's bilingualism is that, despite intense language contact, English has hardly had any influence on Maltese and the latter even seems to be slightly on the rise vis-à-vis English (Bonnici 2009; Davidson 1996; Markus 2007). This distinguishes MAL from many European expanding circle countries, where English is only spoken as a foreign language, but has had an extensive impact on the national languages (especially through lexical borrowings; Görlach 2001).

Kachru's circle model has been highly influential and its terminology has proven to be a practical tool for discussing the use of English around the world. However, this very practicality is also an aspect that can easily be criticised in the face of complex local sociolinguistic realities (see, for example, Bruthiaux 2003; Jenkins 2003; Park & Wee 2009; Pennycook 2003; Saraceni 2010; Yano 2009). For example, it is problematic that the three circle categories cover up (often fundamental) intra-circle diversity and that the model does not allow for any flexibility in the handling of the circles, which would be required, for example, for countries that show characteristics of more than one circle category. On the one hand, many outer circle countries today

---

5. IRL could in principle also be placed in the outer circle if one interprets the spread of English in IRL historically as a result of former British occupation (White 2006:222).

6. Another country that may be considered part of the outer circle due to its colonial history is CYP (McEntee-Atalianis 2004; Papapavlou 2001). However, even though English is still a prominent language in CYP, it is no longer a co-official language as in MAL.

have a significant number of native English speakers. On the other hand, immigration to inner circle societies has led to the presence of numerous ESL speakers. A well-known example of a country that cannot be that easily categorised is South Africa (Bruthiaux 2003; Park & Wee 2009), which exhibits a high degree of heterogeneity in the Englishes used, ranging from White South African English (which would actually qualify as an inner circle variety) to Black South African and South African Indian English (which share more characteristics with outer circle Englishes) to EFL (traditionally located in the expanding circle). Furthermore, an approach that divides countries up into three macro circles is not able to deal with the fact that written norms across the three circles differ relatively little from each other compared to spoken usage (Bruthiaux 2003: 162).

It was Kachru's aim to treat varieties of English around the world in a more egalitarian light. As this is of special relevance for postcolonial societies in the outer circle, his approach has also been decribed with the term "liberation linguistics" (while Kachru termed the work of researchers in favour of native standards "deficit linguistics"). Kachru's work can be seen as a reaction to more conservative authorities demanding the use of British or American English as worldwide models. The latter generally view varieties other than inner circle Englishes in terms of deficit, i.e. as learner varieties, foreigner talk or interlanguage.

Another aspect suggested by Kachru's work is that the learning of a foreign language cannot automatically be equalled with a desire to communicate exclusively with native speakers or to assimilate to native English societies. Outer circle varieties were, as a consequence, no longer seen as corrupt forms of inner circle varieties but as the (legitimate) result of nativisation processes. This development has also led to the pluralisation of the notion of English, expressed in the by now common form *Englishes* (turning the non-count noun *English* into a count noun). One is probably safe to claim that nowadays this pluralistic, anti-imperialist stance dominates research on English varieties around the world (Saraceni 2010: 41). As opposed to the homogeny position, which creates the scenario that the spread of English leads to the homogenisation of the world, the World Englishes paradigm may be described as the "heterogeny position" (Pennycook 2007a: 104), which focuses on the development of new national Englishes.

Saraceni (2010: 9) argues that the categories of the circles model are "not only inaccurate and outdated, but [...] also decidedly harmful, as they contribute to erecting psychological and ideological barriers among users of English as well as between them and the English language" (see also Bruthiaux 2003: 174). It is the model's pluralistic view of English, its rigorous form of categorisation and its structurisation as a center-periphery model that has facilitated the formation of a ranking order with inner circle Englishes on top and native speakers as the legitimate owners of the language.

One of the major problems associated with the circles model and the World Englishes paradigm is that they are firmly based on the concept of the nation, i.e. Englishes are named after the nations in which they are spoken, for example Australian English, Indian English, Nigerian English and so on. Such labelling mimics European nation building processes. It is not structural linguistic similarity or difference but rather political boundaries that decide what to call a national variety of English. That such national Englishes exhibit features (in pronunciation and lexicogrammar) that clearly distinguish them from neighbouring national varieties is generally taken for granted. However, transnational similarity and intranational variation are downplayed in such national variety labels, even though they may be extensive (for example, due to a range of different L1 influences in African societies; Pennycook 2004: 28). The national categorisation has made Englishes around the world potential ingredients for the discursive construction of the nation. But a model that is based on the concept of the nation is bound to lose some of its explanatory power in a period in which sub- and transnational identities become more important, as is the case in Europe today. As Saraceni (2010: ch. 4) points out, basing liberationist linguistics on the (originally Euro-centric) concept of the nation contradicts the postcolonial ethos claimed by the World Englishes approach:

> [D]espite having had the merit of bringing to the fore important sociolinguistic issues relating to the worldwide spread of English, the WE [World Englishes, H.M.] paradigm is caught in an ideological conundrum in which while it pursues its anti-imperialistic and egalitarian objectives, it actually replicates, and contributes to reinforcing, a view of the English language which stems directly from those very Eurocentric and imperialistic roots that it wishes to oppose. Thus the WE paradigm is not only unable to achieve its purported aim, but the conceptualisation of English that it articulates actually leads to conclusions that turn that objective on its head.   (Saraceni 2010: 55)

For this very reason, Park and Wee (2009) have set out to reconceptualise the circles model. Instead of treating it as a tool for the description of sociolinguistic realities, they take it to be a model that deals with dominant ideologies in relation to the use of English around the world and stereotypical correlations between a country's sociopolitical history and the local status of English. Moreover, they connect the circles model to Bourdieu's theorisation of the "linguistic market". As a result, inner circle Englishes are said to obtain their high value on the global linguistic market through an indexical association with powerful speaker groups, whereas expanding circle Englishes carry the least prestige. With respect to identity matters, Park and Wee (2009: 397) contrast an essentialist model that assumes a stable, and therefore constraining, relationship between language and (especially national) identity with what they call an "artful performance model", i.e. a model that values crossing and subversions of such normative identity discourses and treats questions of authenticity as irrelevant. The original circles model expects inner circle speakers to be highly proficient and authentic users who construct their (national) belonging through English. In the expanding circle, by contrast, the use of English is expected to be inauthentic, instrumental, of low proficiency and a sign of disloyalty to national affiliations. If one took the actual proficiency of speakers into account, it would be impossible to come up with such a macro-category model as Kachru's, because many speakers would then have to be placed outside of the circle to which their nation has been assigned (see also Yano 2009).

For mainland Europe, Modiano (2009) envisages a future scenario not unlike that of outer circle countries. He even claims that

> [s]upporters of traditional ELT protocols have effectively hindered the L2 English spoken in mainland Europe from going through those processes which lead in the initial stage to the recognition of an emerging local variety, and in a later stage to its subsequent codification and standardization. By maintaining foreign-language status for English, defendants of such positions have been able to define culture-specific linguistic features used by nonnative speakers in continental Europe as errors, as examples of interlanguage. They demand that 'non-standard' features be eradicated from the speech of learners, something which is practiced in class and in the examination processes, but which has considerably less support outside of school.
> (Modiano 2009: 209)

Modiano is one of the most ardent promoters of the establishment of a Euro-English variety which, in its structural divergence from ENL, may serve as a means of constructing a European identity (see also Graddol 2001; Piette 2004). He criticises ELF research (see Chapter 2.3) for "circumvent[ing] the Kachruvian progression of recognition and legitimization, codification, and standardization of local L2 varieties" (Modiano 2009: 211). As a consequence, he explicitly proposes transferring the Kachruvian notion of outer circle English to mainland Europe in order to enable the formation of Euro-English as a local L2 variety:

> [T]he establishment of a mainland European variety of English can be developed along the same lines as second-language varieties have been codified and standardized in Africa and Asia. If one attempts to superimpose postcolonial theory onto a mainland European scenario, much fruitful insight can be gained. Thus, I propose wholeheartedly that it is high time that the postcolonial imagination which championed the rise of second-language varieties across Africa and Asia be imported to Europe.
> (Modiano 2009: 214)

This opinion springs from Modiano's conviction that claiming ESL status for Euro-English entails liberation from native speaker norms and is a powerful means of opposing Anglo-Americanisation. As opposed to most research in the ELF tradition, which is primarily data-driven, Modiano seems to favour a top-down procedure, i.e. he envisages that an official declaration of Euro-English as a legitimate variety will lead to its further systematisation and divergence from native varieties (see also Ferguson 2009: 123). In an earlier article (Modiano 1996), he points out that the English used in mainland Europe is in fact a mixture of BrE and AmE features that he calls "Mid-Atlantic". It seems obvious that ELF in Europe is not to be equalled with either BrE or AmE. But it is doubtful that it is the mixture of BrE and AmE traces that makes

European ELF European. What would appear more plausibly Europe-specific are uses of English influenced by other European languages, i.e. ELF speakers' L1s. Still there remains the problem that European languages may exhibit significant structural differences that are unlikely to result in a homogeneous Euro-English variety.

When dealing with the question of how to implement Euro-English in ELT, Modiano suggests that English be taught in a way that enables Europeans to communicate locally, regionally and internationally, i.e. with speakers from all three circles (Modiano 2009: 211). This goal seems reasonable with respect to the fact that Europe also hosts speakers of inner (IRL, UK) and outer circle Englishes (MAL), who must not be ignored in terms of intra-European communication. However, Modiano does not specify how this inclusive approach is to be reconciled with the formation of a local European L2 variety:

> It is my firm belief that the majority of mainland Europeans are seeking, through their use of English, a middle road here. That is to say, they are collectively gravitating toward a usage which does contain markers of identity, but which is readily understood by users of the English language across Kachru's concentric circles of world Englishes.
> (Modiano 2009: 211)

Modiano (2009: 213) sees the "de-Anglicization"[7] of English as a necessary prerequisite for establishing Euro-English (see also Ammon 2000). Moreover he highlights that the EU has officially adopted the contrary view, namely that English should only flourish as a language of national culture, whereas a loss of its (British/Irish) culture-specificity in its use as a language of cross-cultural European communication is implied to be an undesirable trend. This latter position rules out that something like a transnational European culture may be constructed by means of English.

Modiano's proposal to treat Europe as part of the outer circle has some legitimacy if one considers that the circumstances in many European countries currently approach (and often surpass) those of the original outer circle countries:

> A large percentage of the population is now proficient in English. The younger generations of Europeans are exposed to English, and use English, on a daily basis. No major population outside the Inner Circle has such a large number of competent speakers of English (over 50 per cent of the adult population in mainland Europe can speak English), as well as such a highly developed primary and secondary school English-language program (with approximately 90 per cent of all European children receiving compulsory English-language instruction in upper secondary education.
> (Modiano 2009: 215)

---

7.   Some scholars are of the opinion that such a process has in fact already taken place in Europe (see, for example, Yano 2009: 248).

In a similar way as English serves as an intranational lingua franca between different ethnic groups in multilingual outer circle countries, English is at present likely to be used for communication between Europeans of various national backgrounds or intranationally between speakers of various ethnic backgrounds (e.g. in ESP or SUI; cf. Demont-Heinrich 2005; Dröschel 2011; Reichelt 2006). The acquisition of English, accordingly, is often no longer felt to be that of a "foreign" language in the literal sense of the word. Neither is it invariably motivated by assimilation to inner circle societies.

However, assigning outer circle status to Europe is undesirable in the light of the criticism brought up against the World Englishes paradigm in general (as discussed above). The greatest problem seems to be the strong focus on the nation as a classificatory tool for outer circle Englishes. In principle, there would be two ways in which this could be applied to Europe: (1) claiming a new variety of English for each individual nation (e.g. German English, Finnish English and so forth), or (2) claiming a new variety (Euro-English) for Europe as a whole, i.e. seen as a macro-nation. Modiano's proposal seems to be in favour of the second option. Closer scrutiny, however, reveals that both options are not desirable for Europe.

On the one hand, setting up a myriad of national European Englishes runs counter to the transnational European endeavour, because it places an emphasis on cross-national difference and national independence. On the other hand, European identity is certainly more than merely applying national constructive mechanisms to a larger European level. In other words, an approach to English in Europe that is based on the concept of the nation is hopelessly out of tune with contemporary European identity formation, which is heavily influenced by poststructuralist conceptualisations of Europe as transnational, negotiable, locally enacted, hybrid and internally diverse. Finally, placing Europe in the outer circle may actually have an effect that runs counter to the liberation envisaged by Modiano, because it would then be in the same category as the colonies of the former British Empire. This would unnecessarily strengthen debates of Anglophone linguistic imperialism, even though Europe de facto does not possess such a colonial past. Europe and the outer circle look back on very different kinds of socio-cultural history that also have their repercussions in the different status and prestige of the L1s of bilingual English speakers, which generally enjoy a similar level of prestige as English in Europe (often as sole national languages), but tend to be viewed as less prestigious in the outer circle (where they are at best co-official with English). Related to this, nationalist and standard language ideologies are much more deeply entrenched across Europe than in most former colonies.

Euro-English, in the sense of a European variety of English, has so far mainly been used as a hypothesised concept. On the negative side, sceptics have equalled it with interference-prone learner English or likened it to a Pidgin English (e.g. Görlach 2002: 150ff). Other researchers have been more positive about Euro-English and are of the opinion that, even if the empirical basis is so far at best inconclusive, such a variety is likely to (further) evolve in the future (e.g. Modiano 2006; Yano 2009: 249). Some researchers have tried to find structural evidence for Euro-English as a variety. Potential features are discussed in Jenkins, Modiano and Seidlhofer (2001), among them, for instance, the dropping of third person singular verbal inflections (*she go*), the omission of articles, the interchangeable use of *who* and *which* as relative pronouns, the replacement of gerunds with infinitives (*look forward to see*), or *isn't it?* as a universal tag (see also Seidlhofer 2003: 208).

Mollin's (2006, 2007) work sets out to provide the empirical basis for a discussion of Euro-English. She considers Euro-English to be a candidate for a new variety among the outer circle Englishes and tests whether it can legitimately be called a variety. This is done on three levels that she deems necessary for the formation of an endonormative Euro-English standard: 1. expansion, i.e. use in a whole range of domains such as intranational lingua franca communication, education (as medium of instruction), administration, media, literature etc, 2. nativisation, i.e. the formal linguistic adaptation to the local context of use (for example, through systematic deviation from ENL, L1 influence, fossilisation of interlanguage features), and 3. institutionalisation, i.e. acceptance as a norm (endonormative stabilisation, identity association, labelling as a variety, use in official contexts and teaching, codification etc).

To summarise her findings in a somewhat simplified way, Mollin diagnoses that on all three levels, Euro-English does not yield evidence for variety status. In her opinion, Euro-English has not spread to a significant number of domains in Europe as a consequence of the high vitality of the national languages. The fact that English plays a significant role on the transnational level as an EU working language is not deemed sufficient by Mollin. She tackles the formal linguistic side by means of analysing a corpus consisting of European Commission press conferences and contributions to online discussion groups (400.000 words). Stereotypical Euro-English features such as the use of non-count nouns as count nouns (*two informations*) show relatively low frequencies and are mostly restricted to particular speakers. This induces Mollin to consider such features as idiosyncratic learners' errors rather than legitimate features of a Euro-English variety. Finally, using the findings of a questionnaire study, she points out that an institutionalisation of Euro-English as a norm has so far not made much progress. She concludes that mainland Europe still firmly belongs to the expanding circle, where English is used as a foreign language, mainly for international purposes. Similar studies by Dröschel (2011), Durham (2007) and Rosenberger (2009) on the use of English as an intranational lingua franca in SUI also did not find conclusive evidence for the formation of a Swiss variety of English.

Mollin's work has drawn considerable criticisms (see, for example, Modiano 2007; Seidlhofer 2009b), even though the finding that there is no such thing as a "Euro-English" variety can be considered well received in the research literature on English in Europe. The criticism therefore does not so much focus on Mollin's findings but more on how she has approached the subject theoretically and methodologically. Modiano (2007) reads Mollin's declaration of Europeans' non-native features as "learners' errors" as a homage to a traditional ELT approach that insists on BrE as the unquestionable European standard. He claims that mainland Europeans nowadays do no longer necessarily see their use of English as inferior to native uses. This development may be said to be not only pertinent to the use of English in Europe, but to many ELF contexts around the world, as is also noted by Seidlhofer:

> For ELF speakers, being able to use the language like native speakers and without traces of their L1, is increasingly perceived as unnecessary, unrealistic, and, at least by some, as positively undesirable. Indeed, ELF speakers are beginning to assert their identities and to operate according to their own 'commonsense' criteria, not of externally defined native-speaker norms but of emically perceived communicative efficiency in the current situation [...].   (Seidlhofer 2005a: 164–165)

Another problem (that Mollin also acknowledges herself) is the fact that one does not generally know how much formal divergence has to be documented for the establishment of variety status:[8]

> There are no linguistic criteria for the delimitation of varieties. Language is a continuum in time and space, so what linguists can do is indicate variable features, but they cannot, as linguists, identify the boundaries which demarcate one variety from another [...]. Varieties are social constructs that exist in and through the perception of speakers.   (Seidlhofer 2005a: 162)

If one rules out variety status for Euro-English on the basis of the degree of formal difference, it may well turn out that many outer circle Englishes that have by now reached the status of a legitimate variety may also not qualify as separate varieties if compared to other national varieties of English in close geographical proximity.

Finally, Mollin (2006: 2) claims to be free of any ideological motivation and sees this as a counterpoint to other research on English in Europe that in her eyes is ideologically biased because it aims at empowering non-native speakers. It remains a mystery how Mollin's approach to Euro-English can be seen as any less politically motivated. Whereas a lot of work on English in Europe is driven by a motivation to promote the rights of non-native speakers, Mollin's approach clearly supports the status quo of native-speaker authority – otherwise it would not have to be tested whether Euro-English is a "legitimate" variety.

---

8.   Mollin (2006, 2007) sets an arbitrary level of 50% deviance from the native norm for a certain feature.

Recapitulating the two approaches to English in Europe outlined in this and the preceding chapter, one can conclude that neither has succeeded in improving the situation for non-native speakers of English in Europe. By contrast, their building on essentialist, nation-oriented concepts rather further entrenches the dominant discourses that see native speakers as the owners of English.

2.3   English as a European lingua franca

What Mollin's findings demonstrate is that there is hardly any evidence that would support the notion of Euro-English as a variety from a structural point of view. ELF research reacts to this insight by abandoning the search for formal features as evidence for variety status. Instead it views transnational European uses of English as a hybrid formation that emerges in linguistic practices and exhibits a high degree of contextual variability and negotiability, as it is shaped by speakers of different linguacultural backgrounds and proficiency levels. This reconceptualisation entails a shift from linguistic forms and the language system to pragmatic function and language use as central points of orientation (for a recent state-of-the-art article on ELF research see Jenkins, Cogo & Dewey 2011). Compared to "varieties" of English, which are traditionally based on the notion of an underlying language system that is reflected in language use, ELF as a concept shows a stronger leaning towards language viewed as a matter of creative performance guided by the respective requirements of the local context.

In Europe, English is today predominantly used as a lingua franca, i.e. a "language which is used as a means of communication among people who have no native language in common" (Trudgill 2000: 132). This definition has been understood in two ways: (a) as involving non-native speakers only (i.e. an exclusive definition), and (b) as potentially also involving native speakers (i.e. an inclusive definition). Considering that today many lingua franca interactions involve both native and non-native speakers from all of Kachru's circles, the second definition is more relevant for Europe. However, including native speakers does not automatically mean a concomitant adoption of native speaker norms as the model for lingua franca communication. In prototypical ELF interactions, i.e. those that involve more non-native than native English speakers, such native normative mechanisms tend to be of secondary importance:

> The crucial point, however, is that when Inner Circle speakers participate in ELF communication, they do not set the linguistic agenda. Instead, no matter which circle of use we come from, from an ELF perspective we all need to make adjustments to our local English variety for the benefit of our interlocutors when we take part in lingua franca English communication. ELF is thus a question, not of orientation to the norms of a particular group of English speakers, but of mutual negotiation involving efforts and adjustments from all parties.   (Jenkins 2009: 201)

The term *lingua franca* (as opposed to *variety*) does not denote a certain structural configuration but rather refers to language use for a certain communicative purpose, namely intercultural communication. It is not associated with particular groups of language users and, therefore, leaves it open who the legitimate "owners" of a language are or whether it can in fact be owned by anybody. The term challenges more traditional thinking, according to which the native speakers of a certain variety are considered its only authentic users.

As native speakers regularly form the minority in ELF communication (if they are involved at all), it is questionable whether ELF should be measured against a native-speaker norm. Compared to other terms describing the use of English around the globe (*English as an International Language, International English, Global English*), which are associated with a privileging of inner and outer circle Englishes, the relatively new designation *English as a lingua franca* according to Jenkins (2007: 3–4) has significant advantages. It suggests communication between speakers of different L1s and a tolerance of L1 influence on the use of English. Furthermore, it places greater emphasis on commonalities rather than inter-variety differences and views non-native speakers as the driving force behind developments in contemporary uses of English. ELF is shaped in use by transculturation processes, obtaining its hybridity from what has traditionally been called L1 substrate influence as well as mechanisms of accommodation and meaning negotiation. In other words, – and in contrast to essentialist claims of Anglophone linguistic imperialism – what is currently spreading around the world is neither BrE nor AmE, but local adaptations of English (Mukherjee 2008; Widdowson 1997: 140).

The study of English as a lingua franca originated in the context of the World Englishes paradigm (cf. Chapter 2.2). As Seidlhofer (2009a) discusses at length, the ELF and World Englishes paradigms have a number of common concerns that may be said to unite them as partners challenging more traditional approaches to ELT, which see native English usage patterns (usually BrE or AmE) as target "standards" (see also Cogo 2008: 59; Jenkins 2007: 17–18). While World Englishes research has fostered the emancipation of outer circle Englishes, the motivation of ELF researchers to empower non-native speakers has not stopped at the outer boundaries of the outer circle. Expanding circle users are also seen as practising a legitimate form of English that neither needs to depend on an exonormative native standard nor does it need to establish its own endonormative standard. In fact, ELF communication weakens the traditional connection between language use and linguistic normativity. Both the World Englishes and the ELF approach celebrate the linguistic diversity within "English" and have generally taken multilingualism as the norm (for example, by favouring bilingual teachers or taking the competent L2 speaker as a role model). Both share a decentralising agenda that questions native speakers as the (only) legitimate owners of English (Saraceni 2010: 5).

Even though the ELF paradigm and especially the World Englishes paradigm have gained greater currency on a theoretical level in discussions of English around the world, it needs to be noted that their practical implications have so far not influenced applied linguistic research to a significant extent. In other words, despite their gaining momentum the two paradigms have not led to repercussions in language teaching, where native Englishes still count as the most legitimate models and the native speaker is seen as the ultimate authority (Jenkins 2012).

There are also important aspects in which the two approaches differ (see also Berns 2008; Pakir 2009). These go well beyond the obvious differences in the sociocultural histories of the outer and expanding circles. Whereas outer circle Englishes are nowadays firmly located on the agenda of linguists studying varieties of English, ELF is still largely viewed in terms of learners' errors and deficits. According to Seidlhofer (2009a: 237), this can only be changed if it is accepted that ELF is nobody's mother tongue (a de-anglicised English) but still represents a legitimate research object. While the World Englishes paradigm has put tremendous effort into demonstrating how national outer circle Englishes differ from each other and from inner circle Englishes on a formal level, often resorting to the quantification of features in (decontextualised) corpora, ELF research has given primacy to functional descriptions and qualitative analyses of contextual language use. Establishing variety status is not a central question among ELF researchers. By contrast, ELF scholars commonly stress the interdependency of form and function and have adhered to the credo that form regularly follows function in ELF (Berns 2009; Canagarajah 2007; see also Breiteneder 2009 on 3rd person singular inflection in ELF talk):

> Rather than limiting itself to the identification of particular linguistic features, this research has tended to take a much more processual, communicative view of ELF, of which linguistic features constitute but a part and are investigated not for their own sake but as indications of the various functions ELF fulfils in the interactions observed. So the crucial challenge has been to move from the surface description of particular features, however interesting they may be in themselves, to an explanation of the underlying significance of the forms: to ask what work they do, what functions they are symptomatic of.   (Seidlhofer 2009a: 241)

In empirical studies of ELF such as those done on the *Vienna-Oxford International Corpus of English* (*VOICE*), the dominance of non-native speakers is ensured quantitatively by keeping native speakers in the minority (only 87 out of 1,260 speakers in *VOICE* are native English speakers).[9] ELF research has documented the fluidity of norms in such encounters, a "let-it-pass" attitude, collaborative talk construction,

---

9.   The website of the *VOICE Corpus* under the auspices of Seidlhofer can be found here: http://www.univie.ac.at/voice/page/index.php (last access: 20 October 2013)

an egalitarian consensus orientation, few misunderstandings (compared to less egalitarian interactions between native and non-native speakers), convergence, a smaller repertoire of tokens used, shorter turns and a higher reliance on non-verbal means of expression (e.g. Firth 1996; House 2003; Kordon 2006; Meierkord 1996; Prodromou 2008). Meierkord (2002: 120ff) highlights the interactants' desire to seek peace, which makes them collaboratively construct a hybrid "inter-culture" via ELF. This is notably different in interactions involving native and non-native speakers that are numerically dominated by native speakers. In these, native speakers may employ gatekeeping strategies that render communication uncooperative and asymmetrical in terms of power (Ehrenreich 2011: 22–23; Knapp 2002; Ushioda 2006: 152–153).

Despite the fact that many features that occur in ELF talk do not orient to native usage patterns or normative grammar rules, they do not normally impede communicative efficiency or draw participants' attention. Error-spotting and other-repairs are rare. What speakers seem to orient to instead is the cooperative construction of "normalcy" (Firth 1996). Therefore, advocating native standards as models for ELF communication is "anachronistic at best and patronising or even racist at worst", as Saraceni (2008: 21) remarks. Many non-native speakers do not aim at becoming a member of the English speech community or of an Anglophone national group. Moreover, as Adolphs (2005) has found out, once non-native speakers are exposed to intensive contact with native English cultures, they tend to change their attitudes towards native speaker norms, which are then often viewed in a more critical light and no longer as a necessary target, because they appear unreachable as a learning target and fraught with identity values non-native speakers may not necessarily want to embrace.

ELF does (at least so far) not possess a teaching model. In fact, ELF researchers are careful not to turn the findings of empirical studies directly (and uncritically) into an ELF syllabus (Jenkins 2009: 202). All that has been proposed so far is that for some features which are traditionally assigned considerable portions of time in the native-usage oriented syllabus (namely the non-core features) the high teaching effort may not necessarily be justified with ELF as a target, because their non-native realisation does generally not impede communication (Jenkins 2007: 22). On the other hand, in stressing the importance of core features for intelligibility, ELF research is far from promoting an "anything goes" position, as has sometimes been criticised. For example, Jenkins (2000) has identified the following core features on the phonological level: consonants in general (except [ð], [θ], [ɫ], to which usually much time is devoted in traditional ELT), rhoticity (as in AmE), retention of intervocalic [t] (compare BrE, as opposed to flap allophones in AmE), aspiration of [p], [t], [k], pre-lenis vowel lengthening and pre-fortis vowel shortening, word-initial and word-medial consonant clusters, vowel quantity and tonic stress. These are critical for ELF communication because they ensure intelligibility. Non-core features that allow for a non-native realisation in ELF are the consonants [ð], [θ], [ɫ], word-final consonantal clusters, vowel quality, weak forms and other features of connected speech, stress timing, word stress and pitch movement (see also Jenkins 2005: 146–147).

Examples of non-core features on other linguistic levels are the treatment of non-count nouns as count nouns (e.g. *informations*) or the omission of the 3rd person singular inflection -s (e.g. *he say*; see also Seidlhofer 2004: 215ff for a more comprehensive overview of features). As these do not normally impede communicative efficiency and often are the result of regularisation processes, they are not seen as errors in ELF interactions. Even though the non-core features need not be mastered in a native-like fashion by ELF speakers as far as language production is concerned, it is nevertheless an advantage if they possess the respective comprehension skills for interactions involving (partly) native speakers. More problematic aspects for ELF communication are lexical gaps and culture-specific idioms or proverbs (unilateral idiomaticity). These may lead to communication difficulties in interactions between ELF speakers of various cultural backgrounds (Kecskes 2007; Seidlhofer 2009c).

It is important to note that core and non-core ELF features are neither absolute nor do they form a finite catalogue of aspects that have to be mastered at the minimum to ensure successful communication. Although the association of core features with intelligibility is relevant on a general level, the same association may in concrete ELF interactions not necessarily be relevant. What is contextually intelligible or unintelligible depends significantly on the participants' ability (and willingness) to negotiate meaning, productive as well as receptive accommodation skills, and the degree of overlap of the interactants' linguistic repertoires. Making language learners efficient ELF users, therefore, is not just a matter of teaching the pronunciation, grammar and lexicon of English but additionally of familiarising them with central strategies of collaborative meaning negotiation (independently of notions of grammatical correctness).

Placing only a secondary focus on structural linguistic features (as evidence for variety status) is also a way of questioning the clear separability and countability of Englishes on a formal plane. The primacy of function over form acknowledges that the emergence of formal linguistic systematicity takes place in communication processes – a phenomenon that Seidlhofer (2009b: 41) illustrates with pidginisation and creolisation – and is therefore subject to the functional needs of the speakers. The functional dimension of ELF can more easily be grasped in qualitative study designs, by looking at local interactional practices and paying attention to aspects such as accommodation and communicative efficiency. In fact, there is increasing evidence that innovative language use only seldom leads to misunderstandings in ELF interactions, because such innovations are generally driven by the need to be communicatively successful, whereas a strict adherence to native speaker models is more likely to cause communication problems.

It is, of course, predictable that a departure from traditional approaches to English variability and ELT provokes criticism or at least causes reservations in large parts of the academic audience. In her book *English as a Lingua Franca: Attitude and Identity*, Jenkins (2007: 8–13) provides an excellent overview of researchers who have taken issue with ELF and notes that among these critics are highly authoritative figures (e.g. Gnutzmann 2005; Görlach 2002; Quirk 1985; Trudgill 2005). These scholars show a tendency to locate the ownership of English firmly in the hands of native speakers, often stress that non-native speakers use English only for a restricted range of functions, and generally adhere to the (dubious; see Jenkins 2009: 204) claim that native English varieties are more intelligible around the world. This clinging to native varieties as unquestionable models prevents a conceptual shift towards ELF as the unmarked form of language use and leads to disadvantages for non-native speakers around the world, who are regularly not taken seriously in professional contexts or are viewed as "unintelligent" (Jenkins 2007: 13).

Jenkins (2007) is also concerned with the many kinds of misconceptions that have arisen from the reception of ELF research (see also Seidlhofer 2006). For example, it is false that ELF research has proposed replacing ENL as a teaching model. ELF researchers have merely promoted ELF as a potential alternative to native speaker norms without demanding the abolition of the latter. Their ultimate aim is to put learners in the position to make an informed choice whether they would like to aim at ENL (i.e. as in the traditional ELT approach), which is best suited for communication with native speakers of English, or at ELF, which would be an alternative for those who aim at successful international communication, often with other non-native speakers.

Another frequent misconception is that the ELF paradigm aims at setting up its own standard variety. On the contrary, ELF research does not practice any normative reduction to particular features. It rather considers non-native modifications as legitimate innovations as long as they do not impede communicative efficiency. Divergence from native varieties is not automatically equalled with deficiency. Current ELF research is characterised by a tolerance of these non-native features and is not usually driven by a motivation to foster "neo-standardisation" (Jenkins 2007: 18). This creates a conceptual space for acknowledging that competent ELF speakers can be widely intelligible without sacrificing their sociocultural identifications as speakers from various non-Anglophone backgrounds. Non-native ELF features that are no obstacle to successful communication are accepted as potential indexes of speakers' cultural identities. A fairly recent outcome of this reasoning is demonstrated by the editing policies of the newly founded *Journal of English as a Lingua Franca* (edited by Barbara Seidlhofer, Jennifer Jenkins and Anna Mauranen) and the new book series *Developments in English as a Lingua Franca* (edited by Jennifer Jenkins and Will Baker). For academic publications appearing in these, authors are no longer required to produce manuscripts in native-like or grammatically correct English. Non-native features are accepted as long as they do not impede intelligibility.

The spread of ELF around the world has the side effect that a description of ELF by means of traditional research tools whose origin has pre-dated such developments is ultimately bound to fail. It is difficult to think of ELF speakers as a (regionally bounded) "speech community" in the traditional sense or of ELF as a stable "variety". Similarly, codification and standard language ideologies are not applicable to ELF as a phenomenon that manifests itself locally, in a heterogeneous fashion. Codification in fact supports an outdated model of language that is at odds with current ELF realities. It ignores the fluidity of ELF and would merely create another exonormative linguistic standard that excludes speakers who do not adhere to this norm, in a similar fashion as native standards exclude non-native speakers (Saraceni 2010: 86).

As the traditional variety concept is inadequate for a description of ELF, Seidlhofer (2009b: 42) suggests a reconceptualisation of linguistic variation as a process rather than as a matter of varieties as abstract states of usage. Instead of reintroducing homogeny (a criticism sometimes voiced by World Englishes scholars as representatives of the heterogeny position), the spread of ELF in fact causes linguists to conceptualise linguistic diversity in an alternative way to variety pluralisation, namely as subject to contextual fluidity (Cogo 2008: 58; Otsuji & Pennycook 2010: 251).

2.4   "English" in the postmodern age

Before coming to the last major strand of thought, the postmodern conceptualisation of English, it needs to be pointed out that the boundaries between this approach and the ELF approach are anything but clear-cut. Their separation into two individual chapters may therefore seem somewhat artificial. Still, it is important to note that ELF research was not influenced by postmodernist thinking in its early stages and that it was only more recently that ELF researchers started to find the adoption of postmodernist ideas useful (cf. Cogo 2012a). However, this development corresponds with a central insight of ELF research, namely that ELF epitomises language use in our postmodern world.

A postmodernist conceptualisation of English highlights ELF as a discursive formation in the Foucauldian sense, materialising in locally heterogeneous ways that widely do not correspond to normative English standards. In other words, one can identify a number of competing discourses of what "English" is, ranging from more traditional notions (native-likeness, grammatical correctness, monolingual purity) to less traditional ones exemplified by ELF. In a similar way as the functional turn in ELF research (discussed in Chapter 2.3), a discursive conceptualisation of ELF entails a shift away from linguistic features as evidence for variety status towards more ontologically

oriented questions. ELF itself can be described as a formation resulting from competing, often even contradictory discourses that cause its hybrid shape. The involved discourses are not equally powerful, and their degree of power may change over time.
Traditional discourses revolving around normative standards of grammatical correctness form a powerful ingredient of ELF, because most ELF users can be assumed to have
learned English in formal education. Still it is essential to note that these discourses are
losing ground to alternative discourses that foreground, for example, linguistic inno-
vation or second-language identities. The diversity of the linguacultural backgrounds
and linguistic repertoires of the participants in ELF contexts adds further discourses to
the picture. And other contextually relevant discourses (for example, associated with
certain speech event types or, as in the present study, European salience) also play a role.

The 21st century has witnessed decisive changes that facilitate cross-cultural communication (for example, through easier possibilities of travelling, the internet and
other new communication technologies). It is not surprising that these changes also
affect linguistic practices. Graddol (2006: 58) even proposes that "Global English" in
the postmodernist sense represents a new era in the history of the English language
(after Old, Middle, Early Modern and Modern English). More specifically, these developments call into question traditional, mutually reinforcing conceptualisations such
as *language*, *English(es)* or *native speaker*, which are constructed along national and/
or ethnic lines (Pennycook 2007a: 99). It is obvious that ethnicity and nationality
remain powerful concepts until the present day, but they increasingly have to face the
competition of alternative discourses that militate against the notion of ethnic and/
or national homogeneity and facilitate the formation of transnational identities. As
English is today the dominant lingua franca on a global scale, the latter identities are
inextricably linked to the discursive formation of ELF (James 2008).

The conceptualisation of English in the postmodern age can be seen as a reaction
to modernist theorisations of "languages" as nation-bound, codified and standardised
systems that can be taught as foreign languages to non-native speakers, who in turn
need to orient to native speakers as authorities of correctness (Graddol 2006: 18). In a
world in which national structures increasingly have to face competition from transnational discourses, linguistic concepts that are based on the traditional notion of "a
language" become less relevant for the description of linguistic practices. The recent
strengthening of Europe as a transnational concept as well as of ELF as a language use
that defies variety status can therefore be considered as two sides of the same coin.

The spread of English is accompanied by a certain tension between its supposedly
homogenising effect (one "language" is spreading) and the increasing heterogeneity
exhibited by uses of English around the world. The critique that work in the linguistic imperialism tradition (Chapter 2.1) and in the World Englishes framework (Chapter 2.2) is too essentialist in its handling of the variability contained within the label
"English" culminates in postmodernist discussions of the status of "English". Pennycook

(2003, 2007b) criticises the Kachruvian World Englishes approach because it describes English as a pluricentric language consisting of locally adapted varieties (the heterogeny position). This pluralisation strategy may be empowering for the speakers of the outer circle by giving their Englishes national recognition, but it is blind to the broader political dimension of the global spread of English (beyond the inner and outer circles). The World Englishes paradigm is highly exclusive in character, as it rests on the notion of a stable common grammar and lexicon from which individual Englishes must not diverge too much in order to leave the overarching system ("English") intact. English-based creoles, for example, are not granted any space in such a conceptualisation because they would destabilise the notion of "English" in the traditional sense (Pennycook 2007b: 22):

> The world Englishes paradigm, while attempting to achieve sociolinguistic equality for its varieties, is not epistemologically different from this model of core, variation and exclusion: for a world English to be such, it must adhere to the underlying grammar of central English, demonstrate enough variety to make it interestingly different, but not diverge to the extent that it undermines the myth of English. If we acknowledge creole languages, however, if we refuse to draw a line down the middle of a creole continuum (exclaiming that one end is English while the other is not), if we decide that those 'Other Englishes' may be part of English, then we are not dealing with a language held in place by a core structure but rather a notion of language status that is not definable by interior criteria.   (Pennycook 2007a: 109)

Similarly, discussions of linguistic imperialism in connection with the global spread of English can be criticised for clinging to a modernist conceptualisation: languages are treated as countable, clearly separable and as central means of ethnic or national identity expression that need to be protected.

As Pennycook points out, a theorisation of English around the world today needs to go well beyond such modernist conceptualisations:

> English is closely tied to processes of globalization: a language of threat, desire, destruction and opportunity. It cannot be fully understood in modernist states-centric models of imperialism or world Englishes, or in terms of traditional, segregationist models of language. [...] [W]e need to move beyond arguments about homogeneity or heterogeneity, or imperialism and nation states, and instead focus on translocal and transcultural flows. English is a translocal language, a language of fluidity and fixity that moves across, while becoming embedded in, the materiality of localities and social relations. English is bound up with transcultural flows, a language of imagined communities and refashioning identities.   (Pennycook 2007b: 5–6)

The formation of Europe is clearly related to processes of imagining a community and of re-fashioning identities. It can therefore be argued that the transcultural flows that manifest themselves in European ELF are a central component of contemporary European identity formation.

Postmodernist discussions of the role of English in transcultural flows aim at a reconceptualisation of the notion of "language", or at least at a questioning of its usefulness when it is applied to English. In such discussions, "languages" are considered as discursive formations evolving in language use rather than as abstract language systems (in the Saussurean or Chomskyan sense) that are reflected or instantiated in actual language use. In fact, the very distinction between *langue* and *parole* collapses in the light of poststructuralist thinking, because the latter treats the language system as the result of processes of discursive materialisation (Hornscheidt 1998). Grammatical structures in this view have reached their substance through on-going recitation in language use. It is this substance that grammarians try to describe (and in fact prescribe). However, poststructuralist conceptualisations like these have not yet entered mainstream linguistics to a significant extent, even though procedural approaches to language are not new. Hopper, for example, has proposed a theory of 'emergent grammar' (Hopper 1998; see also Fox 2007), in which the language system is not described as a stable entity in the heads of (native) speakers but rather as taking shape in linguistic practices. The formation of a "language" then takes place performatively through on-going repetition and imitation of communicative acts that finally lead to the sedimentation of those communicative behaviours that have proven to remain in common usage:

> The notion of emergence constitutes a break with standard ideas about grammar that envisage it as a fixed synchronic system. It relativizes structure to speakers' actual experience with language, and sees structure as an on-going response to the pressure of discourse rather than as a pre-existent matrix [...].   (Bybee & Hopper 2001: 3)

Any attempt of describing linguistic systematicity must therefore be considered a perspectivising filter imposed on actual language use that declares some communicative behaviours as regular and other (deviating) behaviours as exceptions to the rules. This has the side effect of conceptualising "language" as a state, i.e. as a particular snapshot that ignores change and variability as fundamental linguistic mechanisms.[10] The notion of "emergence" is also central to anthropological linguistics, where it is used as an explanatory tool for the evolution of culture via linguistic practices. Still, if one transfers this reasoning to ELF as a discursive formation, one has to acknowledge that the degree of sedimentation of linguistic structures is lower for ELF than for other formations that have traditionally been labelled as "languages". The internal hybridity and contextual variability of ELF can be said to prevent those higher degrees of materialisation that would be necessary to speak of a language in the classical sense.

---

10.   Interestingly, Hopper's theorisation has also been fruitfully linked to that of one of the most prominent poststructuralist thinkers, Derrida (Weber 1997), which points to its compatibility with postmodern thinking.

More recently, Makoni and Pennycook (2007) have suggested more explicitly that the notion of "a language" is the product of discursive construction – a phenomenon that is by extension also true for the varieties known as World Englishes (see also Canagarajah 2007:98). They show that much of contemporary linguistics is affected by a metadiscursive regime that treats languages as clearly bounded and therefore countable entities. Labels like "English" or "French", for example, suggest that the entities they denote can be clearly separated. But if one looks at the history of these two "languages", one finds that they are not as separate as would be thought. During the Middle Ages, French extensively influenced English, especially on the lexical level. This has even led some linguists to suggest that Middle English is a French-based creole (see Curzan 2003:48–54). More recently, French (as many other languages) has experienced a strong influx of English vocabulary, which language purists in France had initially tried to curb by proscribing the use of English words in public domains – an attempt that has ultimately failed. After all, both varieties are descendants from one and the same source, namely Proto-Indo-European. Therefore, a representation of French and English as clearly separate entities is too simplistic. An alternative description would be that French is a component of English and vice versa or that French and English share a large part of their resources. Purist language policies such as evident in France aim at making language conform to the dominant nationalised discourse. Language divisions often cut across regional dialect continua and are generally artificially reinforced by national language planning and Ausbau processes (cf. the division of former "Serbocroatian" into Bosnian, Croatian, Montenegrin and Serbian). Indeed, it is in many cases a social or political decision which sets of communicative practices are seen as constituting an autonomous language, which should be called a subvariety of a language and which are denied such a status.

A less static and more processual view of language is expressed in the concept of "languaging" (Jørgensen 2004, 2008; Møller & Jørgensen 2009). There have already been attempts to connect this concept to the theorisation of ELF (Ferguson 2009:129; Seidlhofer 2009a:242), conceiving it as a hybrid formation emerging through the exploitation of linguistic resources that are not necessarily restricted to the material of one "language". In the face of such a conceptualisation, it becomes evident that debates about the variety status of ELF do not make much sense. From a postmodernist perspective, the World Englishes and linguistic imperialism frameworks fall short of questioning the ontological status of "English", i.e. they take for granted that "English" exists as a clearly delineable object and that it is undisputed which linguistic practices belong to this category (Pennycook 2007a:90). ELF users, by contrast, may be described as performing a linguistic activity one could call "Englishing", i.e. they locally renegotiate the traditional boundaries of "English" in their linguistic practices and simultaneously "perform, invent and (re)fashion identities" (Pennycook 2007a:110), typically in transnational communities of practice (Seidlhofer 2009a:238). As noted by James, these aspects render ELF the epitome of language use in the postmodern age:

> Reflecting on the evidence for ELF and its analysis […], the conclusion might be drawn that ELF qualifies well as a [sic] (almost prototypical?) instance of language in a postmodern world. It is fragmented, contingent, marginal, transitional, indeterminate, ambivalent and hybrid in various ways. Its users do not belong thereby to a well defined social group and their subjectivities are indeed diverse. Discourse is construable as a more significant locus for ELF subjectivity than, for example, code type. And finally ELF can certainly be conceptualized as a performative phenomenon.
>
> (James 2005: 141)

English in the postmodernist sense mainly poses a threat to those who have invested in modernist versions of English, i.e. native speakers and those non-native speakers that aim at assimilation to Anglophone cultures (Graddol 2006: 20). The status of the native speaker as the linguistic authority has been questioned in the light of ELF realities (Firth 2009: 151; Graddol 2006: 14). At the same time, views according to which English "belongs" to its native speakers and is only authentically used, controlled and shaped by them, become increasingly suspect. It is not surprising that the monolingually biased native-speaker concept has increasingly drawn criticism, especially with respect to its adequacy for contemporary globalised societies and the transnational uses to which English is put in ELF communication (e.g. Love & Ansaldo 2010; Mesthrie 2010). In any case, it is only when the discursive regimes of native-likeness and grammatical correctness in connection with "English" change that ELF users turn from second-class speakers of English to languagers who exploit their linguistic repertoires in local adaptation and thereby become agents within the discursive formation of what constitutes "English".

2.5 New perspectives on English as a European lingua franca

The empirical analyses in the present book provide a number of new perspectives on English as a European lingua franca. Theoretically, they are based on a combination of the two latest approaches outlined in Sections 2.3 and 2.4, namely the English as a lingua franca approach and the postmodernist approach. However, this theoretical focus will be more explicitly related to Europeanness compared to earlier work using these approaches. The linguistic imperialism and Euro-English frameworks clearly have related English to Europeanness, but in ways that remain unsatisfactory due to their clinging to essentialist discourses of languages as nationally anchored and European English as a potential variety. It is apparent that the two more recent approaches have been relatively silent on the connection between ELF and matters of Europeanness, largely viewing ELF as a global phenomenon. A central aim of this study is, therefore, to explore how these two latter approaches can be reconciled with Europeanness as a concept that actually falls in between the nation as a classifying criteria for "Englishes" and the world at large as a place of manifestation for ELF. More specifically, two central research questions shall be discussed in relation to the empirical findings documenting linguistic practices at ESC press conferences as a transnational community of practice of European salience: 1. how is ELF to be conceptualised more generally (if not as a "variety" or a "language"), and 2. what is the relationship between ELF and Europeanness in the given context.

Readers may find fault with my use of the term "Europeanness" in this context, because it may be thought of as extremely vague. This vagueness is intentional and is the result of an attempt to let the data speak first and then decide in the end what exactly the relationship between ELF and Europeanness is about (Is it a matter of claiming a European identity? Or of signalling a belonging to Europe? Or maybe of creating and shaping Europe in the first place? etc). Still, it should be clear from the start that this relationship is of a relatively complex kind and cannot be captured using the essentialist approaches of linguistic imperialism and Euro-English.

English as a European lingua franca is here conceptualised as a discursive formation that manifests itself in local linguistic practices. The manifestations of ELF on the levels of language choice, metalinguistics, pragmatics and linguistic structures will be analysed in relation to the high European salience of ESC press conferences as a community of practice. The analyses, therefore, firmly build on the assumption that this local significance of "Europeanness" shapes the manifestations and usage conditions of ELF. They aim to shed light on the use of English in a transnational European context in which the traditional connection between "English" and nation states is of little relevance. Even though the challenging of nationalist structures is an aspect surfacing in various parts of the analysis, one also needs to discard the assumption that European ELF is used in a "post-national" (Heller 2011) space. This is clearly not the case. However, the analyses will consistently point to aspects that destabilise the traditional equation of "English" and native English cultures.

It should be stressed in advance that few of the characteristics of European ELF identified in the present study, when viewed in isolation, are specific to a European cultural context. What may be considered Europe-specific is rather their combination, together with their geographical and historical embeddedness in Europe and the linguistic repertoires of European speakers – and these aspects are, in turn, additionally inflected by the local idiosyncrasies of the transnational community of practice studied.

In accordance with the ELF paradigm, linguistic features will not be studied in order to find evidence for variety status (i.e. internal formal homogeneity and formal divergence from ENL and ESL varieties). Instead, communicative function will generally be given priority over linguistic form, and where language structures are studied, this is done in relation to pragmatic function and in order to yield evidence for the structural hybridity (rather than homogeneity) of European ELF.

Another new aspect of the book is the data used in this study. Whereas earlier research on ELF has generally analysed data from academic or other formal professional contexts (e.g. Mauranen 2012; Smit 2010 or the numerous studies conducted using the *ELFA* and *VOICE* corpora), the present study deals with ESC press conferences – a context that may be described as institutional but turns out to be much less formal than most contexts studied so far. The dataset constitutes journalistic language use, i.e. ELF as used by media and music professionals – a form of data that has so far not been systematically studied in ELF research. A more specific description of the data and their interactional context will be provided in the following methodological chapter (Chapter 3).

The book presents a compilation of case studies in which European ELF is approached from various perspectives, using a range of qualitative and quantitative methods. It is the combination of these methods in triangulation that can also be considered an innovative aspect of the study. Furthermore, the analyses rest on an ethnographic basis resulting from in-depth observation of ESC press conferences as a community of practice in which European ELF emerges.

Chapter 4 takes a qualitative look at code choice practices at ESC press conferences. It documents that ELF talk is over wide stretches not purely English but may involve forms or passages traditionally associated with other languages. More specifically, the analysis shows which functions such switches have in the community of practice at hand. Chapter 5 focuses on metalinguistic comments and thereby sheds a folk linguistic light on how the participants themselves conceptualise and motivate their linguistic practices in the light of the Europeanness of the context. Turning to the pragmatic dimension of ELF, Chapter 6 employs a synthesis of quantitative and qualitative methods to examine complimenting behaviour via ELF at ESC press conferences. The internal structural hybridity of European ELF is documented in Chapter 7, which provides a typologically based, quantitative view of the variability exhibited by relativisation patterns in the ESC press conferences data. The concluding chapter (Chapter 8) presents a synthesis of central findings at the various linguistic levels and discusses them with three main aims in mind: to advance the discussion of how to conceptualise ELF, to describe how the use of ELF in the community of practice studied relates to Europeanness, and to make suggestions for ELF-oriented European language policies.

Chapter 3

Methodological framework

The analyses in the present book are framed within the interface of sociolinguistics and discourse analysis and seek to make a contribution to the realm of *socio-cultural linguistics* with its focus on "both the details of language and the workings of culture and society" (Bucholtz & Hall 2010: 18; see also Bucholtz & Hall 2005). In such an approach, the two major meanings of the term *discourse* (i.e. the more narrow linguistic sense and the broader Foucauldian sense) are brought together, as suggested by Cameron:

> The purpose of analysis is to show how discourse in its first sense (language in use) also functions as discourse in its second sense (a form of social practice that 'constructs the objects of which it purports to speak').
> (Cameron 2001: 123)

Transferred to the present research object, this means that the linguistic practices, functions and features observed in the use of ELF at ESC press conferences are treated as contextually embedded, local instantiations of European ELF as a discursive formation. Note that the term *discursive formation* does not per se suggest internal homogeneity. By contrast, it denotes the interplay of competing, at times even contradictory, discourses. It is also important to note that the term *discourse* spans across the traditional dichotomy of language system and language use. From a poststructuralist point of view, both aspects can be considered discursive manifestations, the main difference being that systematic language structures have gained a higher degree of discursive materiality through continued use. Accordingly, Warnke and Spitzmüller (2008: 9), who work with Foucauldian discourse theory, consider structural linguistic analyses as a matter of what they call *innere Diskurslinguistik* ("inner discourse linguistics"), and analyses of language use as a matter of *äußere Diskurslinguistik* ("outer discourse linguistics"). Linguistic practices on both levels can be viewed as a matter of ideologically significant choices whose implications are not necessarily self-evident and need to be exposed by discourse analysis (Cameron 2001: 51).

Various methods will be employed in the empirical analyses of this book. This strategy is widely known as "triangulation" and has proven its value in much discourse analytic work (Wodak 2004: 102–103). The analyses performed range from qualitative to quantitative approaches, at times complementing each other. This eclectic procedure serves to arrive at a holistic picture of the linguistic practices in the community of practice under study. The analyses of language choice practices and metalinguistic comments in Chapters 4 and 5 proceed qualitatively, taking an in-depth, ethnograph-ically based look at the usage conditions of ELF in the community of practice at hand. For the analysis of complimenting behaviour in Chapter 6, both qualitative and quantitative methods are used to shed light on how compliments are performed in ELF interactions and how they relate to certain groups of speakers. The investigation of relativisation practices in the ELF data is done in a largely quantitative manner, based on language typological considerations. The order of the individual case stud-ies, therefore, proceeds from more qualitative to more quantitative approaches. Taken together, the methodology applied here can be described as discourse-ethnographic research, at times supplemented by quantitative methods. Quantification proves to be a valuable tool for identifying the strength of discourses in terms of their linguis-tic visibility, thereby distinguishing dominant from marginalised (or even silenced) discourses. Localised qualitative analyses, by contrast, are particularly important for the study of, from a traditional point of view, non-normative or less traditional dis-courses and identities, which play a crucial role in ELF interactions more generally and European ELF talk more specifically.

A heterogeneous methodological framework as adopted in the present book ensures that no single method is implied to be the best or most adequate for studying ELF. This methodology caters for the fact that different linguistic levels of ELF require different approaches and that one and the same approach cannot be applied to the four levels studied here (namely code choice, metalanguage, complimenting, and rela-tivisation). Instead, the different methods mutually relativise each other (see Wodak et al. 1998: 45; Wodak & Weiss 2005: 124). It is acknowledged from the start that all of these methods have their pros and cons and shed a specific light on the object studied. However, as Bucholtz and Hall note, their combination can achieve synergetic effects, especially when linguistic practices are to be related to identification processes (such as European belonging):

> Different research traditions within socio-cultural linguistics have particular strengths in analysing the varied dimensions of identity […]. […] Although these lines of research have often remained separate from one another, the combination of their diverse theoretical and methodological strengths – including the microanalysis of conversation, the macroanalysis of ideological processes, the quantitative and qualitative analysis of linguistic structures, and the ethnographic focus on local cultural practices and social groupings – calls attention to the fact that identity in all its complexity can never be contained within a single analysis.
>
> (Bucholtz & Hall 2010: 26–27)

Furthermore, the present study aims to negotiate the "tension within ELF research between a system or structure-oriented approach, more characteristic of early ELF research, and a more phenomenological or practice-oriented approach, which is today

perhaps in the ascendant." (Ferguson 2012:177) In accordance with current developments in ELF research, the aim is, therefore, to shift the conceptualisation of ELF as
a stable object towards a more processual conceptualisation which acknowledges its
internal variability and negotiability.

The empirical analyses in Chapters 4 to 7 are based on one particular dataset
documenting the use of European ELF at Eurovision Song Contest (ESC) press conferences. The language data is stored in the ESC-PC corpus (see Chapter 3.2) and
supplemented by video material. The analyses of this corpus material are based on
participatory observation of ESC press conferences as a community of practice. As this
ethnographic, bottom-up perspective on the data represents the overarching methodological framework of the study, it will be discussed at greater length in the following
chapter. Other supplementary methods will be discussed in the respective empirical
chapters (notably Chapters 6.4 and 7.4).

3.1   Studying ELF as community-based practice

The present study provides an in-depth ethnographic description of the linguistic practices exhibited by the participants at ESC press conferences. Apart from Oslo (2010),
the site where the corpus data were collected, the press conferences of two previous
years (Helsinki 2007 and Belgrade 2008) were attended. The participation in these
two earlier editions of the contest served as a pilot phase, in which data collection was
restricted to observation and taking field notes. This phase also served the researcher
to transcend his role as an (uninvolved) observer and to become a member of the
community of practice. The aim of this procedure is to shed light on ELF interaction
from an emic perspective. As "Europeanness" is the salient identity feature of this context, the linguistic practices documented in this community of practice can be deemed
to represent what participants consider to be compatible with (or even desirable for)
communication in a transnational European context.

The concept "community of practice" (Eckert & McConnell-Ginet 1992, 2007;
Wenger 1998) originates from the theory of social learning. It has recently been fruitfully applied to ELF contexts (see Ehrenreich 2009; Kalocsai 2011; Seidlhofer 2007;
Smit 2010), and seems to be particularly adequate for such contexts because it neatly
captures the idea that ELF users outside the foreign language classroom are not learners in the formal education sense but rather lifelong learners in social interaction,
where they learn, among other things, to use ELF. The choice of an ethnographic
methodological framework for the present study is partly motivated by the felt need
to complement earlier studies on large-scale corpora of ELF usage (such as *ELFA*
and *VOICE*). It almost goes without saying that these latter corpora have immensely
advanced empirical ELF research and yielded intriguing findings that have influenced

the current theorisation of ELF. Still, there is one thing that analyses of large-scale corpora tend to miss or at least not grasp in full effect, namely the concrete interactional context and how its specificities shape the use of ELF. This is an aspect that gets lost when a corpus contains material from various, often highly heterogeneous ELF contexts, as also noted by Ehrenreich:

> One of the problems concerning those early studies which were actually based on real ELF data is the fact that, at times, the findings of these studies have been over-generalized beyond their original sociolinguistic and pragmatic contexts, thus generating some myth-like assumptions about the use of ELF and its speakers.
> (Ehrenreich 2009: 129)

The present study, therefore, concentrates on a specific community of practice and studies in detail how this local context shapes the linguistic practices that can be observed. Of course, such a procedure has the drawback of producing findings that are first and foremost relevant for the specific context studied, and it may take quite a while and many more such ethnographic studies to enable researchers to make sophisticated statements about ELF whose relevance extends beyond the local level. The present study aims to be a step into this direction.

Another reason for choosing the community of practice framework is that more traditional linguistic concepts such as "variety" and "speech community" are generally tied to an essentialist and strictly geographical notion of linguistic variability that is unable to capture the more subtle forms of variability occurring within ELF as a per se hybrid formation (cf. Cogo & Dewey 2012; Seidlhofer 2007). The community of practice approach offers a micro-level tool that enables the researcher to study the local linguistic practices of ELF as they become typically manifest among interactants who do not share a common geographical origin but use English as a shared medium of intercultural communication.

As the name "community of practice" suggests, the analytical focus is here less on people's regional background (for example, as ENL, ESL or EFL speakers) but more on the joint activities they carry out while using ELF. A commonly cited definition of the concept can be found in Eckert and McConnell-Ginet (1992):

> A community of practice is an aggregate of people who come together around mutual engagement in some common endeavor. Ways of doing things, ways of talking, beliefs, values, power relations – in short, practices – emerge in the course of their joint activity around that endeavor. A community of practice is different as a social construct from the traditional notion of community, primarily because it is defined simultaneously by its membership and by the practice in which that membership engages.
> (Eckert & McConnell-Ginet 1992: 464)

The definition of a community of practice as a group of people who regularly come together for a certain purpose and, during these joint activities, develop particular behavioural patterns can only make sense in relation to ELF if it is not applied as a macro-concept. In other words, ELF users at large or larger professional subgroups of ELF speakers (businesspeople, academics etc.) do not form a community of practice, even though ELF may be part and parcel of their everyday life (Ehrenreich 2009: 130–131). "Using ELF" is not normally the joint activity or purpose interactants engage in, also because language-related or even linguistic aspects are not usually in the foreground in most ELF interactions. ELF rather represents an efficient medium of communication that community members exploit to perform certain activities (for example, conducting a business meeting, discussing a paper at a conference, or holding a press conference). This central activity, in turn, shapes how ELF manifests itself. There is an infinite number of ELF-using communities of practice at the more local level, i.e. groups of speakers who regularly get together and use ELF (Ehrenreich 2009: 134). Note that this concept can certainly not cover all kinds of ELF interactions. Less stable formations of people meeting only once to do business together cannot be adequately described by means of this tool. It can therefore be argued that the community of practice concept offers a middle ground between the macro-level (for example the speech community, ELF users, or ELF using academics) and the most unstable micro-level of ELF interaction.

In sociolinguistics, the concept "community of practice" has been used to study local interactional practices, largely serving as a de-essentialising instrument that helps researchers to avoid a (mere) correlation of linguistic behaviour with sociodemographic macro-categories. For the present study, the focus will be on how the participants of ESC press conferences discursively construct and negotiate ELF as a situated practice in their interactions. This analytical framework is not meant to suggest that ELF (or, more specifically, European ELF) is to be treated as an internally homogeneous or stable linguistic variety. The focus is rather on how ELF and its internal heterogeneity are enacted in a transnational European community of practice: How do these European speakers "do" ELF on various linguistic levels and how does the Europeanness of the context shape these linguistic practices?

ESC press conferences can be described as a community of practice because participants repeatedly come together with a certain aim in mind, namely that of providing coverage of the famous annual pan-European pop music festival. Two dimensions of continuity are involved in this context. On the one hand, the majority of the participants (journalists and fans) get together every day (and for the entire day) during the two weeks of the preparation phase before the actual contest. The socialising activities, however, extend well beyond the press conference hall and commonly also involve meeting other participants in less official settings, for example in the press working area, during mealtimes at the cafeteria or at one of the numerous delegation parties held in the evenings, to which journalists are invited. On the other hand, there is also considerable continuity of participants across the years, with journalists generally covering the event for many years in a row. This latter form of continuity is also relevant for the interviewees. The national delegations interviewed are represented by the lead artists, accompanied by a varying set of backing singers, composers, lyricists, choreographers, dancers, delegation officials or national media representatives. These national delegates have, in many cases, participated in the contest before. As is typical for communities of practice, ESC press conferences can, therefore, be said to have core members (who are always present) and more peripheral members (who take part less regularly). It is also noteworthy that the three subgroups of journalists, fans and delegation members exhibit a high degree of overlap, i.e. most of the journalists present and many of the national delegates also self-identify as ESC fans. ESC press conferences can be accessed by journalists who are officially accredited to cover the event. In recent years a limited number of fan accreditations (ten per country) has also been granted. Due to the presence of numerous journalists and fans, ESC press conferences are a context in which the production and reception sides of the contest come into direct contact with each other, namely as interviewees and interviewers.

The press conferences are part of the routine schedule that the individual national delegations go through during their preparation for the contest. In the days before the dress rehearsals, all national delegations have two preparatory rehearsals on two different days at their disposal. After the respective rehearsal, each national delegation holds its press conference. It is, therefore, not surprising that performance aspects are a particularly common topic at these press conferences.

Linguistic practices undoubtedly form a central part of the shared repertoire that this community of practice exhibits. In the empirical analyses in Chapters 4 to 7, four levels of these linguistic practices are studied in detail: the code-choice level, the metalinguistic level, the pragmatic level (as surfacing in complimenting behaviour) and the structural level (as manifest in relativisation strategies). All these four levels require contextual negotiation and accommodation on the part of the participants (even though to varying degrees), and therefore yield evidence of how European ELF is enacted by these speakers.

ESC press conferences represent naturalistic talk in the sense that they have not been set up specifically for research purposes and would have taken place anyway (Cameron 2001:20). They are not scripted or rehearsed in advance and are therefore spontaneous. Still, it can be assumed that both journalists and national delegates have invested some thoughts in advance in order to be prepared for asking questions and giving answers that are deemed adequate for the context. The Europeanness of the context necessitates the use of a diplomatic rhetoric that foregrounds transnational needs and tones down national affiliations in front of the pan-European audience. In a similar vein, the consensus-orientation that has generally been documented for ELF interactions seems to be even more intensive at ESC press conferences. Transnational European cooperation clearly stands in the foreground and confrontative exchanges are usually avoided. Expressions of common ground, mutual understanding and appreciation dominate the picture.

As during the press conferences the hall is full of media representatives filming the interaction in order to provide video coverage of the event on the internet, on television or in other media outlets, the additional researcher's camera was unlikely to stand out from the crowd and can therefore be considered only minimally intrusive. To rule out manipulation of the data, the researcher did not actively participate in the conversation at any point during the press conferences.

It should still be noted that these press conferences constitute a form of institutional rather than ordinary talk, and that such a public media context cannot avoid the observer's paradox. Subjects are very well aware that they are being filmed (and one could argue that they in fact want to be filmed in this context). Ethical concerns about recording participants did not arise because press conferences are specifically made for press coverage purposes and presuppose participants' consent to be recorded. Both linguistic practices and identification processes as evident at these press conferences must, therefore, be viewed as catering for a pan-European audience. This audience does not just comprise the participants in the hall, because filmed sequences may be published by journalists on national TV channels or on the internet. However, this is also the particular strength of these data. They enable the researcher to study which linguistic practices are deemed to be adequate for the context, i.e. what is said and how it is said is decisively influenced by the Europeanness of the context.

The distinct Europeanness of ESC press conferences surfaces on various levels. On the geographical level, the 2010 contest took place in Oslo, a capital city on European soil. However, this is probably the weakest link with Europeanness in the transnational sense. When viewed historically, there is much more evidence for transnational exchange in this respect because the contest has been hosted by a substantial number of European countries in the past. The historical dimension of the contest as a European tradition is not to be underestimated. At the press conferences, participants are likely to construct themselves as experts in historical Eurovision knowledge, thereby establishing continuity between the current edition of the contest and its past. Of course, the title of the competition, *Eurovision Song Contest*, already conjures up political associations of Europe as a vision that participants are working on. On the musical level, the ESC is widely known as the annual opportunity to vote for the "European song of the year". Another aspect in which Europeanness is salient in this community of practice is the cultural origin of the majority of the participants. The journalists, fans and delegates at the press conferences overwhelming come from European countries. Linguistically speaking, this entails that the majority of the people present have a European language as their L1. This may matter, for example, on the lexical level, where European languages share a great deal of their vocabulary (MacKenzie 2012: 92), or on the typological level, where they may show certain structural prototypicalities (see also Chapter 7 on relativisation). In other words, the linguistic repertoires of the participants are likely to show a higher degree of overlap compared to intercultural contexts involving European and non-European speakers. Finally, the potential TV audience also stretches across the European continent, and it can be assumed that the press conference participants have both types of audience in mind, the local one and the pan-European one.

Besides the Europeanness of the context, it is evident that the generic conventions pertaining to press conferences as a specific type of professional speech event structure the linguistic practices of this community of practice. The structure of press conferences, however, may differ significantly for various subtypes (see, for example, Bhatia 2006 on political press conferences, or Jacobs 2011 on internet press conferences). It commonly involves rules about who can say what to whom and when. This means that turns are often pre-allocated to certain (groups of) participants and that the order of the turns is, as a consequence, conventionalised.

At ESC press conferences, the greater part of the speaking time is regularly filled by the performing artists and other delegation members. This is only logical because the national delegations are in the center of interest, and it is therefore intentional that they absorb much of the talking time. Even though delegates are not given the right to deliver a speech at the beginning of their press conference (as is common in other press conference types, see Bhatia 2006: 179), they are generally allowed to answer the journalists' questions in lengthy, often monologic turns. The moderator and other press representatives mainly provide comments or ask questions that influence the thematic direction of the delegates' talk. During the first half of the press conference, the moderator talks to the delegates exclusively. Due to the stability of active participants in this phase of the press conference, the exchange is here more typically conversational. In the second half, journalists from the audience have the opportunity to raise their hands and ask questions. As a consequence, the interaction is in this second phase rather a matter of a series of (often thematically unrelated) question-answer sequences. One commonly finds a tripartite structural pattern consisting of (1) the moderator's invitation to journalists to ask questions, (2) a journalist's question or comment to the national delegation, and (3) a delegate's answer or reaction. This structure is illustrated in the extract from the data below:

> KS: *do we have some other questions? (.) yeah please*
> MP4: *yes i'm andy from italy uh about to uh be without shoes on the stage there are some uh eurovision winners who didn't wear shoes on the stage uh may uh sandie shaw in sixty-seven and dima bilan from russia in two thousand nine so do you think this may bring you good luck for this contest*
> FA1: *maybe (.) you never know @@@ (.) let's see* [FIN2][1]

---

1. The press conferences from which illustrations are taken are indicated in square brackets as a combination of the country code plus the numbers 1 or 2 for the first or second press conference of the respective national delegation.

However, this structure is frequently interrupted, for example by a greeting sequence.

ESC press conferences are less prototypical for the press conference genre as a whole, because of their high level of informality. At the venue in Oslo, for example, this was especially visible during the first round of press conferences, for which the moderator and the delegates were seated in a relatively small living room setting erected in a corner of the press conference hall. The informality of the context is further strengthened by the domain of pop music, which is less compatible with formal talk.

3.2   Corpus compilation: ESC-PC

In order to obtain corpus data documenting European ELF, all ESC press conferences taking place in the two weeks before the actual staging of the 2010 edition of the contest were videotaped during a research stay in Oslo. The ESC hosted 39 participating national delegations, which all held two press conferences (i.e. 78 in total).[2] The length of the video material on which the press conference corpus (ESC-PC) is based amounts to 25 hours and 42 minutes. The total number of word tokens in the corpus is 192,856. A list of all press conferences incorporated in the corpus together with details on the date, time, duration and active participants can be found in the Appendix (Chapter 9.2).

For the sake of simplicity, speaking delegation members are abbreviated as A (i.e. FA for female delegates and MA for male delegates) within transcripts.[3] Press representatives asking questions to the delegates are abbreviated as P (i.e. FP and MP accordingly); the moderator *Kristian Strand*, who directed all press conferences, is abbreviated with initials as KS. As ENL and ESL speakers form exceptions in these ELF data, they are specifically marked in the transcript by means of asterisks (e.g. *MA* for a male delegate who is an ENL or ESL speaker). Speakers were assigned ENL/ESL status on the basis of two criteria. Either they identified themselves as coming from an ENL or ESL culture at some point in the press conferences or they were known to come from such a culture, be it because their origins are publicly known (as is generally the case with performing artists) or because the researcher knows them personally (as is the case with some press representatives). If no information on the cultural background of a speaker was available, an (in this context unmarked) EFL

---

2.   The winner's press conference right after the final was not included in the dataset. This ensures a higher homogeneity of the data and avoids the undesirable effect that speakers from one national background contribute more material to the dataset than speakers from the other countries.

3.   The abbreviation A is used because artists de facto form the largest group among delegation members.

speaker status was assumed. As the press conferences involve speakers from 39 nations all over Europe, the data represent (largely non-native) European ELF usage.

The inclusion of ENL and ESL speakers in a corpus that has been set up to study ELF talk is not per se problematic. ELF is an inclusive concept that allows for the participation of ENL and ESL speakers as long as they do not form the majority or dictate communicative norms, which is clearly not the case in this dataset. Even for press conferences at which these speakers contribute the greatest share of the conversation, there is a large audience of journalists from all over Europe in the press conference hall and, therefore, English is indeed used as a lingua franca and cannot be equalled with ENL/ESL.

All 78 press conferences were transcribed employing a transcription system that is in some points similar to the one used for the compilation of the *VOICE Corpus* (Breiteneder et al. 2006; VOICE Project 2007). As *VOICE* is the largest corpus documenting spoken European ELF interactions today, it was deemed a useful point of orientation for the ESC press conference data. The *VOICE* transcription system was adapted to the requirements of the present context.[4] The resulting system employs only a limited range of notational devices commonly used in Conversation Analysis. This is legitimate considering that the focus of attention will not be on conversational structures (i.e. turn-taking, interruptions etc.). The detailed transcription conventions used for ESC-PC can be found in the Appendix (Chapter 9.1).

The verbal behaviour of the participants is generally noted in standard orthography.[5] Non-verbal behaviour is only integrated in the transcript if it conveys information without which a certain passage would not be understandable. Forms that are, from a traditional point of view, non-English or not in accordance with standard English are specifically tagged (e.g. ⟨*French*⟩ *bonjour* ⟨*/French*⟩; ⟨*pvc*⟩ *accompinated* ⟨*/pvc*⟩). This is done to capture the linguistic creativity of ELF users and the fact that ELF may show rather obvious forms of linguistic hybridity. Passages that are acoustically unintelligible are marked as ⟨*un*⟩ *xxx* ⟨*/un*⟩ with the number of x's corresponding to the number of syllables heard. A similar notation convention applies to laughter, which is indicated in the running text by using @ symbols. Overlapping speech is marked by number tags (e.g. ⟨*1*⟩ ⟨*/1*⟩, ⟨*2*⟩ ⟨*/2*⟩ etc.)

---

4.   Some aspects that seemed less relevant for the press conference data have been omitted. For other aspects, the notation is less fine-grained. New aspects have been introduced for phenomena that seemed particularly salient at ESC press conferences (for example, short musical performances during press conferences or laughter in the audience).

5.   Unlike *VOICE*, which deliberately uses a mixture of AmE and BrE spelling to symbolically dissociate ELF from native standards (Breiteneder et al. 2006: 177), BrE spelling is used throughout in ESC-PC. Spelling conventions are merely part of the notation system and therefore do not impose normative standards on spoken ELF data.

The data were transcribed using the transcription software *F4* (created by researchers at the University of Marburg, Germany). In contrast to the programme *VoiceScribe*, which has been used by Seidlhofer and colleagues to transcribe ELF data for the *VOICE Corpus*, F4 provides a wider range of functions. For example, it allows for the integration of video (as opposed to audio) files. Other useful facilities include the automatic insertion of time marks, which make navigating to certain points in the transcript easier, automatic rewinding for self-selected time intervals by pressing "F4" (hence the name of the programme) or the possibility to slow down the speed of the video file, which proves to be helpful when passages are hard to understand in normal speech tempo.

Press conferences have not been transcribed in full. Certain passages have been left untranscribed because they stand out from the normal conversational interaction and are less likely to yield evidence of the discursive construction of European ELF. Two kinds of activities fall into this category. Firstly, musical performances, which are part and parcel of ESC press conferences, have not been transcribed in detail but were noted in curly brackets together with the song title (where known) and the duration in seconds (e.g. {*FA1 performs "my dream" (67)*}). The second activity type that remains untranscribed is the "Norwegian quiz", in which the moderator jokingly tested the participants' knowledge about Norway during the first set of press conferences. The quiz consists of a fixed series of question-answer sequences (e.g. *What is the name of the capitol of Norway? – Oslo!*) and is therefore only noted in square brackets together with information on its duration (e.g. {*Norwegian quiz (55)*}.

As the major focus of analysis is here on ELF, other parts that may remain untranscribed are those spoken in languages that the transcriber is not sufficiently familiar with. All non-English language items that the transcriber was able to decipher are included in the transcript and marked accordingly (e.g. ⟨Spanish⟩ hola ⟨/Spanish⟩). Where a language other than English or German was used for a longer stretch of speech, the data are left untranscribed. This occurs sometimes when artists do not see themselves in a position to answer questions in English. In such cases, another delegation member normally translates the journalists' questions into the artist's L1 and the artist's answer into English for the audience. As such translations immediately follow the non-English passages, the loss of conversational content is negligible.

For the linguistic aspects studied in Chapters 4 to 7, the entire corpus was searched manually to identify all occurrences of a certain feature. This was necessary because all features studied do not show a neat form-function correspondence that would have made the use of corpus tools feasible without ignoring a significant part of the relevant tokens. On the basis of the tokens thus identified, quantitative and qualitative patterns are retrieved.

Chapter 4

Code choice practices and European ELF talk

4.1 Introduction

ELF communication is never purely English communication. As ELF interactions typically involve multilingual participants from various linguacultural backgrounds, it is not surprising that features traditionally associated with languages other than English may surface in talk. However, research adopting a puristic stance on this issue and bracketing out such features from the analysis fails to capture an integral part of ELF communication. ELF constitutes a discursive formation that is not restricted to English language material in the traditional sense, and it may suffice at this point to note that even traditional notions of "English" such as ENL contain substantial admixture from non-English sources (Old Norse, French, Latin, Greek, to name but the most extensive influences historically) and that established loans from other languages typically also started as nonce borrowings in language contact situations, i.e. in lingua franca contexts. Excluding ELF from what counts as "real English" can therefore hardly be legitimated on the basis of "foreign" influences, because they form an integral part even of the most traditional, normative and restrictive notions of "English".

The hybridity of European ELF surfaces decisively in the influence of non-Anglophone European linguacultures in local adaptation. Still it needs to be noted that this influence is highly heterogeneous and therefore unlikely to result in a discursive formation that can be described as a "variety" in any meaningful way. The occurrence of traditionally non-English language material is not random in the ELF talk at ESC press conferences, but rather seems to be governed by certain pragmatic principles that make the surfacing of such material more likely. It is the central aim of the present chapter to shed light on these mechanisms.

In a context with a high European significance in which speakers from nearly all European nations participate, it is self-evident that the non-Anglophone influences that surface within ELF talk stem from European national or, to a lesser extent, ethnic linguacultures, i.e. from a particular set of linguistic influences. It is essential to note the powerful role that "languages" have traditionally played within nation building processes on the European continent since the 18th century. This role is still vibrant today and forms a crucial aspect in discussions of European language policies (cf. Chapter 2.1). The de-nationalised use of ELF in a transnational European context clearly challenges such traditional, normative discourses. At ESC press conferences, for example, it is self-evident that community members use English by default for transnational communication and that only few of them (those from IRL, MAL and the UK) may potentially attach a national identity value to it. Ironically, this makes ENL and ESL the odd ones out at ESC press conferences – on the quantitative level in terms of speaker numbers and on the qualitative level because the traditional association between English and certain national affiliations carries less prestige in a transnational European community of practice in which participants are otherwise normatively required to avoid overt expressions of nationalism.

Before observations concerning the code choice practices at ESC press conferences are made, Chapter 4.2 presents an overview of central aspects relating to Europe as a multilingual space. This is in order to provide a background for the qualitative empirical analyses of code choice patterns in the chapters that follow.

The notion of "switching" is here invoked as an ethnographically motivated concept, i.e. it captures the fact that ESC press conference participants tend to view their linguistic practices in a traditional fashion, namely in terms of switching between "languages" as bounded linguistic entities. However, from a less traditional point of view, switching practices can be seen as integral resources within participants' (multilingual) linguistic repertoires. This latter kind of conceptualisation is clearly more relevant to ELF communication contexts, in which speakers may use linguistic resources traditionally associated with languages that cannot be said to form language systems in their minds (for example, in tokenistic non-English greetings; cf. Chapter 4.4.3).

Practices of switching between material from different languages range on a continuum. On the one end, one finds occurrences in which English and the other language alternate in larger blocs, which makes them relatively easy to separate, their contact being only minimal (for example, when the switch coincides with a speaker switch or sentential boundary; "alternational switching", MacKenzie 2012:85). Such practices are discussed in Chapter 4.3 as instances of macro-switching. The continuum ranges down to instances in which the non-English language material is small in size and/or relatively well integrated within an otherwise traditionally English sentence or utterance ("insertional switching", MacKenzie 2012:85). These types of switches are analysed more closely in Chapter 4.4, which identifies asking for assistance, creating the Eurovision experience and greetings as three central functions for which the participants at ESC press conferences commonly use switching.

4.2   English and European multilingualism

The slogan *unity in diversity* is particularly pertinent to the constellation of languages in Europe. Intranational and international multilingualism are considered a core feature of European culture (Extra & Gorter 2008; Naglo 2006:29). Individual as well as societal monolingualism are the exception rather than the rule in today's Europe.[1] What is special about Europe's relation to multilingualism is its heavily nationalised history that has propagated monolingualism as the national ideal – a matter that current designers of European language policies still have to struggle with (compare discussions in Ammon 2006a/b, 2008; Christiansen 2006; Gubbins 2002; van Els 2001, 2006 and many more).

As languages are never neutral entities, Europe also has to face identity-based (i.e. ethnically or nationally motivated) and economy-driven conflicts of interest. The official EU language policy tries to counter such conflicts by granting official status to one national language of each of its member states (today 24 languages in total). Speaker numbers are of no relevance to this practice. The EU languages Irish and Maltese, for example, have clearly lower speaker numbers than Catalan, which has only semi-official status (besides Basque and Galician).

Immediately, one finds a fundamental contradiction in this regulation. How can a language policy foster multilingualism (which after all is its declared aim) if it allows each country to choose only one of its languages as an official EU language? In doing so, the EU actually reinforces national structures as hardly any other international organisation (see also Brumfit 2006). One encounters another contradiction when looking at which languages are chosen for which purposes in EU institutions. Even though all EU languages are officially equal in their status, such an equality turns out to be a utopian vision. All EU languages are only used in more public and formal contexts (i.e. the European Parliament and the European Council of Ministers), whereas in the more informal contexts of internal bureaucracy only a small number of languages are actually used: English in first position, French in second position (but already far behind, with a decreasing tendency), and German, Spanish and Italian used only marginally (Ammon 2006a; de Swaan 2001: 145). A similar situation pertains to the European Commission, where officially all EU languages should be used, but de facto only a limited number of working languages are employed (Krzyżanowski 2010: 137). To summarise, even though it seems unlikely that English will replace national languages on the national level (leaving aside the influence of English on these languages), there are clear signs of this happening on the transnational European level.

In the early years of the European Economic Community (EEC), it was the French language that dominated the European scene. French enjoyed a history as a language of diplomacy (for example, as the sole official language of the European Coal and Steel Community) and was a national language of three of the six EEC founder states (BEL, FRA, GER, ITA, LUX, NED). But after the joining of DAN, IRL and UK in 1973, English started to gain ground, which resulted in FRA adopting a heavily purist stance

---

1. *Eurobarometer 243* documents that linguistic minorities exist in all EU countries (European Commission 2006: 2).

against the spread of English and the influence of English on French (Braselmann 2005: 156ff).[2] Later accessions of non-Francophone countries further promoted the use of English as an EU working language (de Swaan 2001: 152ff; Kraus 2004: 142–143; Nic Craith 2006: 46ff). Despite the fact that German is the language with the largest number of native speakers in the EU, it has never played a significant role in the fight for becoming Europe's main lingua franca.[3] Although English dominates inofficially as an EU working language, on-going rivalries revolving around language choice between member states (Ammon 2006a: 330ff) are likely to preclude an official English-only policy for the EU. In the absence of a "neutral" language that could be used as a lingua franca, the implementation of translation services is a price the EU has to pay (Kraus 2004: 144–145). The official protection of linguistic diversity also has to be seen as a strategy to differentiate the EU from another major global player – the US and its (former) "melting pot" ideology.

The EU has in recent years increasingly promoted the learning of European languages as foreign languages. This caters for both multilingualism as a European cultural value and efficient intra-European communication. The decision to promote European multilingualism can further be legitimised on democratic (linguistic human rights), economic (language competence as a form of capital), and ecological grounds (countering language loss and linguistic domain loss; Lüdi 2002: 15ff). The envisaged goal is for all EU citizens to have three languages at their disposal: their L1 for national communication, a language for regional intra-European communication, and a language for wider international communication (Brumfit 2006: 37ff). However, it has to be viewed critically that the official EU language policy (and the work of sociolinguists who promote European linguistic diversity) seems to be driven by a motivation to foster peaceful coexistence. This may be a positive goal as such, but it is unrealistic, as has been amply demonstrated at the EU level, where attempts to promote European multilingualism have often resulted in individual member states adopting nationalist positions vis-à-vis their European neighbours, frequently trying to promote their own national languages to the detriment of others (cf. Pennycook 2007b: 20). Debates over which languages should be promoted regularly lead to rivalries between EU member states, because not all official EU languages can be promoted to the same extent. Moreover, the top-down approach of dictating that Europeans should be able to speak three languages ignores that it is usually economic and identity-oriented considerations that are responsible for individuals' language learning choices (Ammon 2006b: 220). An uncritical promotion of multilingualism is biased in the sense that it seems to take the

---

2.   This purist stance was also directed against minority languages spoken in FRA (Fenet 2004).

3.   According to Eurobarometer 243, 18% of EU citizens have German as their native language, followed by English, Italian (both 13%) and French (12%) (European Commission 2006: 4).

social milieu of cosmopolitan, European intelligentsia (i.e. the researchers' own social background) as a point of orientation and extends it to other populations who may be much less inclined to learn (several) foreign languages (Wright 2000: 237). Finally, the promotion of European multilingualism de facto boils down to a promotion of a handful of larger languages which are popularly learnt as foreign languages (English, French, German, Italian, Spanish). The learning of other European languages remains at best marginal.

Much work remains to be done if the three-languages goal is ever to be achieved. According to the *Special Eurobarometer 243 "Europeans and their Languages"* (European Commission 2006), only 28% of the EU citizens consulted said that they can speak at least two foreign languages. 56% stated that they could speak at least one foreign language, which also means that 44% do not see themselves in a position to hold a conversation in any foreign language (the Anglophone countries IRL and UK showing the highest figures with 66% and 62% respectively). English remains the dominant foreign language across Europe, with 38% of the EU citizens saying that they can speak it. In 2004, more than 90% of European students in secondary education were learning English (Modiano 2006: 224). On average, more foreign languages are learnt in smaller countries (whose national languages are not usually languages of wider communication) and in the north of Europe compared to the south. The typical multilingual European is young, well-educated, resident in another country than the one he or she was born in, and uses foreign languages in his or her profession. Only one out of five EU citizens is an active language learner. However, the benefit of foreign language learning is generally recognised. Foreign languages are overwhelmingly acquired at school, increasingly as early as on the primary education level. 77% of the subjects name English as their first foreign language. French is popular in the natively Anglophone countries (IRL, UK) and in countries with a Romance language tradition, German has a stronger presence as a foreign language in Eastern Europe (for example in CZE and HUN), Russian in the Baltic states.

However, European multilingualism does not just involve those languages that enjoy national or EU language status. Ammon (2003) states that in Europe about fifty autochthonous minority languages (e.g. Breton, Sorbian) and an indefinite number of exogenous (immigrant) languages (e.g. Hindi, Turkish) are spoken. Minority languages are protected by the *European Bureau for Lesser Used Languages* (EBLUL) and the *European Charter for Regional and Minority Languages* (ECRML; see Kraus 2004: 129ff; Nic Craith 2006: 75ff). The growing influence of the EU as a transnational body has in many contexts led to a strengthening of regional issues, for example in the form of institutional support for minority language communities (Caviedes 2003: 260; Wright 2000: ch. 8). This makes EU efforts to increase multilingualism more convincing because its official commitment to multilingualism on the European level is from a logical point of view incompatible with a promotion of monolingualism on the national level (Wright 2000:175). Since the 1990s, the protection of minorities has also been taken as a prerequisite for EU accession (for those countries that have joined the EU since 2004) and for accession talks with TUR, CRO and MAC (Schreiner 2006:109). However, immigrant languages do not normally receive any EU support despite the fact that there are, for example, more speakers of Turkish than of Danish in the EU. This makes the EU's commitment to multilingualism a highly selective business (Ammon 2003:394–395). Both European transnationalism and intra-/crossnational regionalism can be thought of as having taken away power from the nation state.

English has become the dominant European language despite the fact that its spread is generally considered to privilege the Anglophone member states. The smaller non-Anglophone language communities are not often heard to protest against this situation. They are unlikely to promote their own languages to the status of languages of wider communication. Supporting other languages would mean an extra burden of foreign language learning for them. Protests mainly come from larger European language communities, which want to prevent their languages from losing their lingua franca function (Ammon 2006a:323).

Even though the continuing spread of English as a lingua franca across Europe is often lamented, it must be acknowledged that the use of English as a foreign language by Europeans is neither automatically in opposition to multilingualism nor a threat to it, especially not if one takes seriously the widely propagated goal of the EU that citizens should have access to three European languages. If one accepts the L1 and EFL as two such languages, there is still space for one more European language (in the case of English native speakers even for two).

Many of the problems in connection with European language policies as we know them today can be traced back to the dominant nation-equals-language discourse. Much could be gained in this respect from a shift in the way "English" is conceptualised. In the Europe of the 21st century, English is de facto used both as a national language (in IRL, MAL and the UK) and in transnational communication, and it is not difficult to predict that it is the latter use that will gain even greater prominence in the future. Language policies and ELT regimes that cling to ENL as the only legitimate form of English in Europe must therefore appear somewhat out of tune with current sociolinguistic realities.

If one foregrounds the transnational and, as a consequence, de-nationalised uses of English in Europe today, it becomes hard to substantiate the claim that European users of English project national (British, Irish, Maltese) identities or aim at an assimilation to Angophone nations by means of their linguistic practices. It is even more implausible to argue, in line with a linguistic human rights approach, that these speakers are swept over by Anglophone neocolonial forces. As soon as one conceptualises English in Europe in terms of ELF rather than ENL and acknowledges that ELF is a linguistic resource that nobody speaks natively (or, by extension, nationally), it becomes possible to leave some of the nationalist baggage behind that has turned out to be an impediment to European language policies.

It is, of course, self-evident that ELF is not the L1 of the majority of European speakers who reside outside Ireland and the UK. But even British and Irish ENL speakers cannot be claimed to be "native speakers of ELF" (a phrase that is contradictory), because they generally have acquired English in communication with other ENL speakers and are therefore not automatically well equipped for transnational communication via ELF. They may be said to have an advantage in terms of the acquired ENL structures that are part of their linguistic repertoire, but these cannot automatically enable them to be successful ELF communicators. By contrast, native structures (for example, unilateral idiomaticity or native regional accents etc) may in some cases even turn out to be obstacles to efficient communication with or among speakers from non-Anglophone backgrounds. As a consequence, ENL speakers also need to familiarise themselves with the practices of meaning negotiation and accommodation across linguacultural boundaries when they wish to become successful ELF communicators.

ELF communication is different from ENL in that it draws on the (normally) multilingual linguistic repertoires of ELF users. This repertoire does not consist of several clearly separable linguistic systems of which one is switched on when a person is speaking while the others are switched off. It is rather the case that all linguistic resources within the repertoire are constantly activated and interact (MacKenzie 2012: 84–85). Notions of linguistic purity and of English as a language system are irrelevant for ELF communication.

Contemporary sociolinguistics has come up with a range of (mutually related) concepts that move away from a nationalist, purist and systematic conceptualisation of "English" and highlight the mixed character of communicative practices. These include concepts such as superdiversity (Blommaert & Rampton 2011), crossing (Rampton 1999), languaging (Jørgensen 2004), metrolingualism (Otsuji & Pennycook 2010) or transidiomatic practices (Jacquemet 2005). Current sociolinguistic studies on the use of English in Europe suggest that ELF can be very fruitfully linked to such concepts (see Cogo 2012a). On the code-choice level, the linguistic hybridity of ELF becomes manifest in codeswitching (cf. Klimpfinger 2007, 2009), but also in more subtle transfer mechanisms (such as cognates; cf. Hülmbauer 2011), i.e. phenomena that would, in traditional English language teaching, be attributed to lexical gaps, negative transfer, L1 interference or fossilisation. In ELF contexts, by contrast, where these features are often used to facilitate communication, these can be considered a matter of positive L1 transfer and of a goal-oriented exploitation of a speaker's multilingual repertoire (Jenkins, Cogo & Dewey 2011: 284).

4.3   Code choice at the macro-level

Even though the dominant part of the ESC press conference data is in English, it is obvious that this data does not represent monolingual English usage. This is the case because ELF communication per se involves predominantly multilingual speakers whose linguistic repertoires include English. By the same token, European languages other than English are regularly used at ESC press conferences, sometimes in code switching, sometimes as the source for English translations provided by interpreters, and sometimes out of the reach of the microphone. Chapters 4.3 and 4.4 aim at a description of the main functions of these switches. As will be shown in Chapter 5, ELF is the ritualised default choice in this community of practice, whereas the use of other languages is considered as a marked choice. Although the analytical focus is here on language material that is not traditionally considered to belong to "English", the analyses nevertheless provide insights into the internal hybridity and the typical usage conditions of European ELF. Moreover, the functional analysis of code choices at ESC press conferences yields evidence of the functional borders of ELF by highlighting at which points English does not seem to be a feasible choice for the participants.

In the present chapter, the descriptive focus is on the macro-level of code choice, i.e. a level at which the "languages" involved are relatively easily separable because the switching coincides with a speaker change or a sentential boundary. Although English is the default choice for speakers holding the conversational floor at ESC press conferences, there are certain press conferences at which a relatively high degree of non-English co-presence is found. These fall into two (overlapping) groups: those press conferences in which the national delegation is accompanied by an interpreter and those held by the "Big 5" countries. The Eurovision-internal designation "Big 5" countries is adopted here as a cover term for the four big national broadcasters (ESP, FRA, GER, UK) and the host country of 2010 (NOR), which are automatically qualified for the ESC final.

Of the 39 participating countries, seven national delegations were accompanied by an interpreter. In all of these cases, the lead artists generally answered questions in their L1 and the interpreter translated both the English questions to the delegates and the delegates' answers into English for the audience. Apart from ESP and FRA (two "Big 5" countries), the five remaining countries adopting this strategy (AZE, BLR, BUL, SLK and UKR) are all found in the Eastern parts of the Eurovision territory, which points to the well-known continuum of decreasing English proficiency ranging from Western to Eastern Europe. Interestingly, the use of national languages at the press conferences by these artists is not necessarily paralleled by a use of national languages in their ESC performances: AZE, BLR and UKR performed their 2010 ESC entries completely, BUL partly in English on the ESC stage. This, in turn, indicates that the presentation of a song in English on the ESC stage, which does not require any higher-level ELF conversational skills, is deemed an important way of appealing to the pan-European audience and may be viewed by these national delegations as a means of passing as European. Whereas language choice is free on the ESC stage, speaking English (or at least providing English translation) is obligatory at ESC press conferences – otherwise communicative efficiency would be endangered.

Moreover, a look at the data shows that even those artists that do not speak English during the press conferences still use short, tokenistic English utterances (such as greetings at the beginning of the press conference). As insignificant such utterances may appear at first glance, they serve the important function of downplaying the speaker's national affiliation and signalling openness to the wider European public. They are necessary to demonstrate that the artists' use of their L1 is neither perceived as a means of boosting their own national identities nor as a sign of ignorance concerning the communicative needs of the wider European public. This is illustrated by Extract 1. (In the following, underlining is used to highlight particular features for the analysis. Note that underlining was not part of the transcription conventions.)

> (1)
> KS: welcome (.) please sit down
> FA1: <u>hello everybody how you're (.) feeling? (.) oh it's okay</u>
> {applause}
> KS: yeah i think the press is really great (.) it's a great day and since you are here (.) uhm (.) i think you can sit down if you want to
> FA1: <u>hey guys uh</u> {FA1 speaks Ukrainian (9)}
> MA1 (translates): first of all i would like to thank you for coming and i would like to thank for your attention [UKR2]

In this extract, the Ukrainian lead artist (FA1) greets the audience twice in English at the beginning of the press conference (hello everybody how you're (.) feeling?; hey guys), before she switches to Ukrainian. The function of these short English passages is clearly phatic, i.e. the artist tries to establish a connection with the audience. For the rest of the press conference, her Ukrainian utterances are translated into English by the interpreter (MA1).

Another example comes from the French press conference:

> (2)
> MP3: uh are you listening the other songs? uh (.) you know the other songs? of eurovision song contest and (.) uh yo- your favourite songs what do you believe
> {MA3 translates for MA2 (5)}
> MA2: ⟨French⟩ uhm ma chanson favorite pour pour la eurovision c'est la grèce ⟨/French⟩ (.) <u>the greece uh song</u> [FRA1]

In this excerpt, a journalist (MP3) asks the French lead artist (MA2) in English about his favourite Eurovision songs in the 2010 contest. After the question has been translated to the artist, he answers in French that he favours the Greek song. This is not remarkable because the artist uses French throughout the press conference and another delegation member translates. However, in this particular passage, the artist ends his utterance with an English phrase: *the greece uh song*. This minimalist use of English is particularly important in the case of the French delegation because it is widely known that FRA had in the past adopted a strongly anti-English (and pro-French) stance, for example at the EU level. Apparently the lead artist feels that a French-only strategy is not compatible with the Europeanness of the context, as it could be read as an overtly nationalistic construction. It is not surprising, then, that such a move is made in response to a question about ESC participants other than the French, which surely makes transnationalism a salient issue.

In the case of ESP and FRA, the greater use of Spanish and French at the press conferences may not just be due to a lack of English proficiency. Two other "Big 5" countries, GER and NOR, also show a higher presence of their national languages at their press conferences, even though these national delegations were not accompanied by a translator and the lead artists indeed spoke English. Not surprisingly, at the press conferences of the remaining "Big 5" country, the UK, English clearly dominates the picture with hardly any other languages surfacing and code switching being restricted to a minimum. This is similar at the other press conferences in which English is predominantly used as a native and/or national language (i.e. CYP,[4] IRL, MAL). These press conferences represent less prototypical examples of ELF communication, because in them the majority of the active participants are ENL speakers and code switching is rare.

The greater use of national languages at the press conferences of the "Big 5" countries is clearly connected to issues of power. ESP, FRA, GER and the UK represent the largest broadcasters within the EBU, which provide most of the funds for carrying out the ESC. A linguistic correlate of this circumstance is that their respective national languages, English, French, German and Spanish, are languages of wider currency that are more likely to fulfil European lingua franca functions than the national languages of other European countries. Viewed from this perspective, using these languages at ESC press conferences is more compatible with cross-European communication than using other languages such as Finnish, Latvian or Serbian.

The country hosting the ESC (NOR) can also be said to be in a position of power relative to the other European countries. Whereas the "Big 5" countries are permanently in a better position to enforce the use of their national languages, this powerful position is only a temporary privilege for the host country NOR. However, the use of national languages at the press conferences of ESP, FRA, GER and NOR is in most

---

4.   The band members of the group *Jon Lilygreen and the Islanders*, which respresented CYP in the ESC 2010, mainly come from the UK.

cases not initiated by the national delegations themselves. The delegations either speak English (GER, NOR) or systematically provide translation into English (ESP, FRA). The use of national languages is almost invariably initiated by press representatives who ask questions to the artists. This often makes the delegation members use their national language in return. In other words, the delegates are well aware of the fact that it is less well received when they as national representatives initiate the use of their own national language. The common pattern, therefore, is that national languages (other than English) are preferably only employed in this transnational European community of practice when their use is initiated by somebody from outside the respective national delegation.

If one looks at which press conferences contain at least one passage in which a journalist asks a question in a language other than English, the four non-Anglophone "Big 5" countries dominate the picture: ESP1, ESP2, FRA1, FRA2, GER1, GER2, NOR1 and NOR2 all contain such passages. Another country whose press conferences contain such passages is RUS. This finding is compatible with the power factor identified above. RUS is certainly one of the major players on European soil and Russian still serves as a lingua franca in certain Eastern regions of the Eurovision territory (even though this function is decreasing).

Besides the press conferences of these more powerful countries, there are only four other press conferences at which questions in the respective national language occur: BLR1, ALB2, GRE2 and SUI2. All of these four press conferences show exactly one such question, whereas those held by the more powerful countries usually contain several of them. Moreover, in the Greek case, the journalist first asks in English for the permission to use Greek, which also points to a less self-confident stance towards using Greek in this transnational European context. Another qualitative difference can be seen in the fact that in the few instances in which the press conferences of the less powerful countries contain a question in the national language, it is immediately translated, either by the journalists themselves or by a member of the national delegation. This procedure is illustrated by the following extract from the Swiss press conference:

(3)
MP4: ⟨French⟩ bonjour stéphane de paris ⟨/French⟩
      [hello stéphane from paris]
MA1: ⟨French⟩ bonsoir stéphane ⟨/French⟩
      [good evening stéphane]
MP4: ⟨French⟩ bonsoir (.) uh je voulais savoir si vous avez uh si cette version c'que l'on vient de voir était la version définitive ou si il y a des surprises qui viennent après ⟨/French⟩ (.) uh english (.) uh do you have any other surprise that would (.) be added to your current act or if it is definitive like that
[good evening (.) uh i would like to know whether you have uh whether this version that we have seen was the definite version or whether there are surprises that will come later] [SUI2]

In this passage, the use of French is initiated by a journalist from FRA (MP4), who first greets the Swiss lead artist (MA1) and introduces himself. Afterwards, he asks a question in French and translates it immediately into English. The initial use of French by this journalist is probably motivated by the fact that French is one of the Swiss national languages and can therefore not primarily be counted as an instance of the journalist projecting his own national identity. It enables the journalist to create a language-based, transnational form of solidarity between himself and the artist. However, a French-only strategy would not generally be well received in this community of practice, because it can be assumed to exclude a substantial number of participants, thereby threatening communicative efficiency. The code choice practices of the journalist in Extract 3 therefore enable him to cater for two functions: creating solidarity with the artist and ensuring cross-European intelligibility.

At the press conferences of FRA, GER, NOR and RUS, by contrast, non-English passages are sometimes left untranslated.[5] In some such cases, certain participants intervene and demand a translation. Especially the moderator does this several times, as in the following extract from the German press conference (translations of non-English passages are in the following noted in square brackets):

> (4)
> MP3: ⟨German⟩ *hallo lena* ⟨/German⟩
>   [hello lena]
>
> FA1: *hi*
> MP3: ⟨German⟩ *ähm heute gibt es eine aufzeichnung beim zweiten rehearsal und die juries kriegen diese aufzeichnung* ⟨/German⟩
> [uhm today there will be a recording at the second rehearsal and the juries will get this recording]
> FA1: ⟨German⟩ *ja* ⟨/German⟩
>   [yes]
> MP3: ⟨German⟩ *und dann entscheiden die schon mal was die zuschauer erst morgen entscheiden* ⟨/German⟩
> [and then they will already decide what the viewers will decide not until tomorrow]
> FA1: ⟨German⟩ *ja* ⟨/German⟩
>   [yes]
> MP3: ⟨German⟩ *wie fühlst du dich dabei* (2) *also heute ist auch=* ⟨/German⟩
>   [how do you feel about that (2) so today is also=]
> FA1: ⟨German⟩ *=normal* @@@ (.) *ähm* ⟨/German⟩
>   [=normal @@@ (.) uhm]

---

5.   The Spanish press conferences represent an exception in this respect. In these, either the translator of the national delegation or the journalists themselves translate the Spanish passages into English.

> *MP3: ⟨German⟩ wirst du noch etwas ändern? ⟨/German⟩*
>   [will you still change something?]
> *FA1: ⟨German⟩ nein ach was (.) ich mach das was ich immer mache (.) ä:h ich geb*
> *immer mein bestes (.) und deswegen ähm (.) wird das so wie immer (.) nichts neues*
> *langweili:g ⟨/German⟩*
>   [no come off it (.) i do what i always do (.) u:h i always give my best (.) and therefore
>   uhm (.) this will be like always (.) nothing new bori:ng]
> *KS: could you translate for us lena?*
> *FA1: uhm i just said that i don't change uh i'm i'm not going change anything in my*
> *performance uhm because he asked about the jury today (.) uhm and i said that i'm gonna*
> *do my performance like every time and nothing special (.) kind of boring @@@ [GER2]*

It is only after ten turns between the lead artist (FA1) and the journalist (MP3) have been completed in German that the moderator (KS) intervenes and asks the artist to provide an English translation (*could you translate for us lena?*). The English passage uttered by the artist in response to this request is logically not a literal translation of the preceding conversation but rather a summary of it. The phrase *kind of boring* at the end of her account is ambiguous. It may refer to what she said before, namely that her performance will not change. On the other hand, it may also be read as an excuse for the long German exchange preceding her English turn, i.e. a translation was not immediately provided because the content of the conversation was *kind of boring* and therefore deemed less relevant to the wider European audience.

A power factor may also be involved when national delegates make jokes that are not translated into English and, therefore, mainly target a national sub-audience rather than the pan-European audience. Such passages are rare in the data as a whole, but a closer look at them can shed light on the functional division between ELF and the national language as it evolves in the community of practice at hand. As can be seen in Extract 5 below, such jokes may even be directed against other national delegations. It is doubtful whether similar jokes could as easily be voiced in English, simply because the wider European audience (including audience members affiliated with the nation targeted by the joke) would be able to understand. Conversely, it is clearly naïve to believe that the participants in ESC press conferences are generally unable to understand languages other than English – and this may also be the reason why such a strategy is hardly ever used in this context.

The passage given in Extract 5 took place after the German delegates had been asked how they felt being the favourites to win the competition. Stating that one sees one's own national delegation as a favourite would probably not be seen as particularly positive in this community of practice, as it would likely be interpreted as an overtly nationalistic statement (especially when uttered in the respective national language). On the other hand, it is the general purpose of these press conferences to promote one's own entry, and explicitly rejecting the compliment that one is among the favourites or saying something negative about one's own national team is generally not feasible either. Faced with this ideological dilemma, one delegation member (MA1) resorts to humour, initiating a joking sequence about the Dutch entry by declaring it in German to be *the* favourite:

> (5)
> MA1: ⟨German⟩ *die favoriten sind holland* ⟨/German⟩
>   [the favourites are holland]
> {*audience applauds (7)*}
> FA1: ⟨German⟩ *willst du's vielleicht kurz anstimmen?* ⟨/German⟩
>   [would you perhaps like to start singing it?]
> MA1: ⟨singing⟩ *shalali shalala shalali shalala* ⟨/singing⟩
> FA1: ⟨German⟩ *und alle klatschen mit* ⟨/German⟩
>   [and all clap their hands]
> MA1: ⟨German⟩ *ich finde aber auch dass äh dass ich mein ich mein das wirklich ernst weil ich finde dass dieser titel ist so reaktionär revolutionär reaktionär ähm (.) damit hätte keiner gerechnet und äh äh dass sich das noch jemand traut ist äh hat meine vollste würdigung und äh der titel ist nummer eins in holland und das hat seinen grund* ⟨/German⟩
> [but i also think that uh that i mean i mean this really seriously because i think that this title is so reactionary revolutionary reactionary uhm (.) nobody would have thought of that and uh uh that someone dares to do this is uh has my full appreciation and uh the title is number one in holland and that is for a reason]
> [GER1]

Taking note of the local communicative context at the press conferences, designating the Dutch entry a potential winner may already be taken as a joke, because the journalists' betting odds for the Dutch entry, which were published in the press centre before the competition, were relatively low and the performance was generally not judged to be among the favourites to win the contest. The utterance is met with a relatively long applause (seven seconds) from the audience, which indicates that many of the journalists and fans present understood what was said in German. This applause is not just generated by people in the audience who took this as a joke. Despite its low betting odds, the Dutch entry was highly celebrated as a piece of Eurovision nostalgia by the fans in Oslo, firstly because it was sung in Dutch (after a long stretch of years in which NED was represented by English songs), and secondly because the performance reflected a camp approach to Dutch national identity (by exploiting Dutch stereotypes such as a huge barrel organ with puppets on stage). One journalist even thanked the Dutch entrant *for bringing* ⟨German⟩ *schlager* ⟨/German⟩ *back to eurovision* (NED2).

After the applause, the lead artist (FA1) continues the joking sequence by suggesting that MA1 should sing a passage from the song (which he does immediately) and asks everybody to join in clapping their hands. At the end of this passage, MA1 takes a relatively long turn in which he explicitly orients to the predominance of the humourous reading of the preceding utterances by stating that he is being serious (*ich mein das wirklich ernst*). Moreover, he describes the Dutch song ironically as a reactionary and revolutionary piece (*dieser titel ist so reaktionär revolutionär reaktionär*), which clearly contrasts with the fact that the genre of the song is rather traditional and schlageresque. Moreover, he states that he feels great respect for people who still dare to bring such a song to the ESC in 2010 (*dass sich das noch jemand traut ist äh hat meine vollste würdigung*). The implied message is, of course, that the song is anything but revolutionary and indeed rather old-fashioned, and that it is a courageous act to bring such a performance to the ESC stage today.

The entire joking passage targeting the Dutch entry is uttered in German and, therefore, intended for the German-speaking part of the audience (most of whom are German nationals). This is evidence for the fact that joking about the Dutch entry may have a certain prestige with respect to national German identity construction, but it certainly does not support a transnational European construction, which is incompatible with both making fun of one's European neighbours and using one's national language to exclude certain parts of the pan-European audience.

It is interesting to note that at the second German press conference, which took place after the two semi-finals, the delegation members again alluded to the original joking sequence by saying (this time in English) that they were *tired that the netherlands didn't do it* (GER2), i.e. disappointed that the Dutch entry had failed to qualify for the final. Moreover, MA1 said that he tried to contact the Dutch delegation after the semi-final in order to invite them to his TV show but he could not reach them. The continuation of this joke in English only works for those people in the audience who also witnessed and understood it at the first press conference. For other journalists who may not have a good command of German, the sarcasm of this passage at the second press conference is more difficult to retrieve. In other words, the delegates make here use of a double indexicality in relation to various audience types. For one, voicing their disappointment about the result of the Dutch delegation in English is compatible with showing concern for other participants across national boundaries. At the same time, it enables the speaker to allude to the earlier (German) joking sequence about the Dutch entry, which is certainly less compatible with European transnationalism.

Overall it is important to stress that the use of languages other than English for longer stretches of speech (without translation) is generally avoided at ESC press conferences. This has two main reasons. On the one hand, the use of languages other than English is generally viewed along national lines and, therefore, carries little prestige in this context. On the other hand, such practices are also likely to exclude large parts of the pan-European audience. This latter mechanism may be negligible when performances are given in a language other than English on the ESC stage, because musical pleasure may also be derived from performances one does not fully understand. By contrast, journalists need to understand what is said at the press conferences in order to be able to cover the event. Switching to languages other than English on the macro-level is, therefore, the exception rather than the rule.

A similar point can be made about the language use of some ENL speakers at ESC press conferences who seem to be less inclined to accommodate to their pan-European audience (for example, by retaining their regional accent in ELF communication). Such linguistic practices are also viewed critically in the community of practice at hand, because they can be read as a projection of a national (rather than transnational) affiliation and may, in some cases, even work to the detriment of communicative efficiency.

4.4   Micro-switching in ELF talk

The following chapters take a closer look at practices of code choice on the micro level, i.e. cases in which a language other than English is not used for a longer stretch of speech but only in the form of short instances of (often intrasentential) code switching. As ELF speakers prototypically are multilingual speakers for whom English is an L2, L3, L4 and so on, such code switching is particularly likely to occur in ELF interactions. However, if one takes the form follows function principle into consideration, code switching has to be described as a dispreferred move in ELF talk, simply because in many cases interlocutors cannot automatically be assumed to possess a command of the code that is being switched into. This entails that where code switching does occur in ELF talk, it will usually be employed to improve rather than restrict communicative efficiency or at least in a way that does not threaten communicative success.

Research on conversational micro-level code switching has come up with various taxonomies for the description of its functions. For example, Mahootian (2006:516) identifies the following functions of code switching: 1. quotation, 2. addressee specification, 3. interjection, 4. reiteration (for clarification), 5. message qualification (additional information), 6. personalisation vs. objectification (speaker involvement or distancing vis-à-vis the message). Still others could be added such as emphasising in-group solidarity, excluding out-group members, or raising speaker status by creating authority and expertise. The salience of these functions varies with actual communication contexts. For this purpose, only those functions considered salient within the present community of practice will be discussed.

The three major practices of micro-switching discussed in the next three chapters (Chapters 4.4.1 to 4.4.3), i.e. asking for assistance, creating the Eurovision experience and greetings, do not constitute an obstacle to efficient communication. In accordance with ELF theorisation, they need to be considered as legitimate deviations from native English usage patterns that possess identity indexing potential (i.e. they are about constructing transnational European identities rather than assimilation to native Anglophone cultures). The three mechanisms mentioned can easily be related to the functions of code switching that have been shown to operate in other studies of ELF talk. Klimpfinger (2007), for example, identifies four major, often overlapping functions of code switching in her *VOICE Corpus* data: specifying an addressee, appealing for assistance, introducing another idea, signalling culture. Asking for assistance corresponds neatly to Klimpfinger's category "appealing for assistance". Creating the Eurovision experience is a practice that can be related to "introducing another idea" in the sense that switches to languages other than English may be topic-dependent and motivated by using the professional jargon associated with a European pop music event. Greetings serve as an important means of addressee-specification in ELF talk. Finally, the "signalling culture" function may be said to cut across the three other functions. The ESC press conference data may be considered "special" in this respect because national self-stylisation is only of restricted prestige in this European community of practice. In other words, when culture is signalled in these interactions, an emblematic construction of the speaker's own national identity is not normally the primary motivation. However, other forms of signalling culture may well be salient in this context, especially those that transcend traditional language-equals-nation discourses and are employed by speakers to convey transnational messages, which in turn are well compatible with the Europeanness of the context.

4.4.1   Asking for assistance

Languages other than English may be used at ESC press conferences in situations in which communication has in fact broken down or runs the risk of breaking down. This may occur when the participants reach a point where their communication in ELF is unsuccessful, either because they were not able to understand their conversational partners or because they lack the English words to communicate a certain meaning to the audience. In the first case, the switching that takes place may border macro-switching because it may involve longer stretches of talk. For example, when artists have been asked a question that they have not understood, they may consult other members of the national delegation and ask them in their L1 what the question was about. After this has been explained to the artists in their L1, they can continue with the conversation in English. Such instances of L1 use do not directly occur in the transcribed talk because questions for clarification are not normally asked through the microphone but are often just whispered to the person sitting next to one.

Speakers may also ask for assistance in a language other than English if they lack certain lexical items or have difficulty in finishing their utterances in English. Such examples are given below:

> (6)
> *FA1: yeah uh like in finland we have these uh white dresses but now we have one our main sponsors noolan uh we uh (.) designed with uh susan and maria ⟨un⟩ x ⟨/un⟩ who is owner this beautiful dresses and this mater- material is be- ⟨talks to other group members in Finnish (3)⟩ @@@ like natural very natural*
> *FA2: linen*
> *FA1: linen* [FIN2]

> (7)
> *KS: how do you think about being one of the favourites*
> *FA1: i understand i understand (.) uh well (2) maybe somebody will (.) be (.) how to say ⟨talks to FA2 in Russian (9)⟩*
> *FA2: she says uh maybe somebody would give a big uh importance to this fact* [ARM2]

In Extract 6 from the Finnish press conference, FA1 apparently cannot think of an English word to describe the material of which the artists' costumes are made. Therefore she briefly talks to the other delegation members in Finnish, then laughs and provides a vague paraphrase of the kind of material used (*like natural very natural*). After her turn has been finished, FA2 comes up with the missing English word *linen*, which is then repeated by FA1. In Extract 7, the moderator (KS) asks the Armenian lead artist (FA1) how she feels as one of the favourites in the competition. FA1 responds first by confirming that she has understood the question and then starts phrasing an answer in English. However, in the middle of her utterance she realises that she lacks the linguistic means to express her thought and therefore turns (in Russian) to another delegation member for help, who then translates the passage into English.

In some cases, the speaker first uses a non-English word to elicit the corresponding English form from other participants:

> (8)
> *MA1: [...] and uh no (.) not at all uh i didn't knew the song and uh if you know you like also pop music all of you and you know we ha- we don't have uh th- thousand notes to co- uh compose a song (.) so uh sometimes it reminds at something other people said that this song uh (.) uh ⟨French⟩ ressemble ça uh ressemble ⟨un⟩ xx ⟨/un⟩ uh ⟨/French⟩ ⟨German⟩ gleicht wie sagt man's ⟨/German⟩*
> *FA1: sounds=*
> *MA1: =sound thank you (.) sounds like ⟨French⟩ voulez-vous ⟨/French⟩ from abba? (.) it don't sounds like ⟨French⟩ voulez-vous ⟨/French⟩ fro- from abba [...]* [SUI2]

In this excerpt, the Swiss artist (MA1) talks about the fact that some people have accused the Swiss entry of being a case of plagiarism because it contains passages that resemble those from other previously existing songs. Apparently, he lacks the English word *resemble* and uses first the French cognate verb *ressembler* (*ressemble ça uh ressemble*) and then the German verb *gleichen* (*gleicht wie sagt man's* "resembles how do you say it") in order to make the other participants provide him with a corresponding English form. Another delegation member (FA1) does not provide a literal translation of these French and German verbs, but rather resorts to a semantically more specific form (*sound [like]*), which is in the end taken up by the lead artist.

Sometimes speakers use a non-English word first and then supply the corresponding English form themselves, as can be seen in the following extract:

> (9)
>
> *MA1: uh it it's it's a a big difference actually the the cameras uh are are are good because i i has i had some e- experience wi- with the camera and uh that that's a great uh (.) ⟨Dutch⟩ voordeel ⟨/Dutch⟩ uh that's a great uh advantage (.) [...] [BEL1]*

In this excerpt, the Belgian artist arrives at a point at which he apparently lacks the linguistic means to express his thought in English. First he hesitates (compare the use of the filler *uh* and the short pause), before he resorts to using the Dutch word *voordeel* "advantage". However, he then comes up with the English form *advantage* himself. A similar example comes again from the Swiss press conference:

> (10)
>
> *MA1: no it was uh just uh (.) if i would uh have uh the last number uh i will be so nervous and so i i ⟨pvc⟩ choosed ⟨/pvc⟩ (.) number five it it came spontaneously ⟨makes sound of a bullet⟩ (.) from ⟨German⟩ bauch raus ⟨/German⟩ from the bottom of my my uh stomach [SUI2]*

In this extract, the Swiss artist, whose L1 is German, uses the German idiomatic expression *aus dem Bauch raus*, which literally means "out of the stomach" and is used to indicate that somebody did something on the spot without much reasoning. This meaning is also communicated non-verbally by the artist's imitating the sound of a bullet. The switch to German occurs within the idiomatic phrase. The initial preposition is rendered in English (*from*), the definite article in the German original phrase is dropped and the remaining part is in accordance with the German idiom (*bauch raus*). Straight afterwards, the artist provides an English rendition of the German idiom: *from the bottom of my stomach*. This latter phrase is not a native English idiom. Similar native English idioms expressing the same meaning normally use the word *gut* (e.g. *on a gut level; a gut reaction*) instead of *stomach*. Nevertheless the speaker seems to model his idiom on other English idioms such as *from the bottom of my heart*. Using the online interface BNCweb,[6] one finds that the query "from the bottom of _DPS" (in which _DPS stands for any possessive pronoun) yields 25

---

6. Link to BNCweb: http://bncweb.lancs.ac.uk (last access: 20 October 2013).

hits in the *BNC*, of which 17 are completed with the form *heart(s)*. The remaining eight hits do not include the word *stomach*. Idioms have been demonstrated to be a notorious troublespot in ELF talk (Seidlhofer & Widdowson 2007; Seidlhofer 2009c) because they are generally associated with culture-specific meanings that make a literal translation into English impossible, at least from a normative point of view. As Extract 10 illustrates, however, such literal translations of idioms may occur in ELF talk and do not necessarily lead to communication breakdown (despite their non-nativeness).

The examples discussed in this chapter illustrate how ELF speakers exploit their multilingual repertoires in situations in which their English skills do not seem to be sufficient to convey a certain message. Non-English language material is here used in ELF talk to keep up communicative efficiency, be it as an incentive for other participants to provide the missing forms or as a device to help speakers to come up with a translation themselves. These mechanisms are most likely candidates for features that are common in intercultural communication and ELF talk in general. They merely receive a European twist through the type of language material that is inserted, which invariably stems from European languages in this community of practice.

4.4.2   Creating the Eurovision experience

The functional category "creating the Eurovision experience" refers to practices that help the participants to construct themselves as professional artists, delegates and journalists involved in a pan-European pop music competition. English is widely perceived to be the language of pop culture. It is therefore remarkable, and potentially a European characteristic, that code switching with non-English material from other European languages figures prominently at ESC press conferences. Many of the non-English items used by the press conference participants have to do with the larger field of music and/or television. Their use is therefore clearly topic-related. Besides references to national preselection shows, which tend to occur at the press conferences of the respective countries (e.g. *Eesti Laulu* in EST1/2, *Melodifestivalen* in SWE1/2, *Festivali i Këngës* in ALB2, or *Melodi Grand Prix* in NOR1), many of the non-English items represent examples of intra-European crossing in the sense that the language material inserted is not associated with the speaker's L1 but with another European language (cf. Rampton 1999). Artists often mention that they have attended international music festivals in other European countries. For example, the Russian artists said they would also attend the Austrian *Stimmen* ("voices") festival, while the Macedonian lead singer stated that he had participated in the *Slavjanski Bazar* festival in BLR. TV shows mentioned by delegation members include, for example, the Italian *Festival di San Remo* (in ALB1) or the Turkish show *Beyaz* (in GEO1).

Non-English material may also be involved when journalists introduce themselves as working for a particular media outlet in their home country. For example, the following national media are identified in the dataset: the Norwegian newspapers *Aftenposten* (e.g. in NOR1/2) and *Dagbladet* (e.g. in BLR2), the French TV channels *France Deux* and *France Trois* (in FRA1/2), or the German magazines *Prinz* (e.g. in ISR1) and *Vorwärts* (e.g. in RUS2).

Some artists highlighted that they have played roles in famous musicals whose names may be French (e.g. *Les Misérables* in POL1 and MAL1, *La Cage aux Folles* in UK2, *Le Soldat Rose* in FRA2) or Italian (*Mamma Mia* in ESP1/2). Furthermore, the names of musical genres are also commonly expressed with non-English material, as the following extracts illustrate (non-English genre names underlined):

(11)
MA1: […] and then we talked about uh uh that ⟨Hebrew⟩ milim ⟨/Hebrew⟩ is very uh ⟨French⟩ chanson ⟨/French⟩ very french s- uh song […] [ISR1]

(12)
MA1: the song ⟨French⟩ il pleut de l'or ⟨/French⟩ it's called uh in english it's raining gold or in uh german uh ⟨German⟩ es regnet gold ⟨/German⟩ it's about love of course uh it's a a a ⟨French⟩ hym- hymne á l'amour ⟨/French⟩ (.) yes after a storm [SUI1]

(13)
FA1: [..] we wrote the lyrics and we feel the song even though ⟨Croatian⟩ zovi ⟨/Croatian⟩ call me is our like uh ⟨Croatian⟩ himna ⟨/Croatian⟩ (.) […] [CRO1]

(14)
MP2: hi from the ⟨spel⟩ uk ⟨/spel⟩ schlagerboys uhm thank you for bringing ⟨German⟩ schlager ⟨/German⟩ back to eurovision […] [NED2]

By far the most common practice of creating the Eurovision experience is by means of references to Eurovision songs of the past and the present. It is logical that the data contain many references to titles of songs that competed in 2010: for example, *Työlki ellää* (FIN1/2), *Legenda* (POL1), *Opa* (GRE1/2), *Je ne sais quoi* (ISL1/2), *Milim* (ISR1/2), *Il pleut de l'or* (SUI1/2), *Algo pequeñito* (ESP1), *Allez, ola, olé* (FRA2), *Ovo je balkan* (GER2), *Narodnozabavni rock* (SLO2). However, references to former Eurovision entries are also frequent and have the important function of creating a continued Eurovision history. Demonstrating that one possesses historical ESC knowledge carries high prestige at ESC press conferences and highlights a long tradition of European popular music since 1956. Former non-English Eurovision songs mentioned at the press conferences include the following entries: SUI 1969 – *Bonjour, bonjour* (in SUI2); LUX 1973 – *Tu te reconnaîtras* (in ISR1); ISR 1979 – *Hallelujah* (in ISR1); GER 1988 – *Lied für einen Freund* (in ROM2); TUR 1988 – *Sufi* (in TUR1); NOR 1995 – *Nocturne* (in MAC2); BOS 2005 – *Zovi* (in CRO1); BOS 2009 – *Bistra voda* (in BOS1). The following passages illustrate how such song titles are used by participants to conjure up Eurovision history:

> (15)
> *MA1: okay i think anne marie david (.) is is a wonderful woman she's very smart and very funny and uh our connection is so good and we talk on skype on the internet and i see her and she's very beautiful i think (.) and she uh i think that her song ⟨French⟩ tu te reconnaîtras ⟨/French⟩ is is the best eurovision song ever (.) […] [ISR1]*

In this excerpt, the Israeli artist talks about his ties to former Eurovision winner *Anne Marie David* (LUX 1973). He says that he admires her and her winning song, which he judges to be the best Eurovision song ever. This must seem even more remarkable considering that the Israeli artist was born in 1981, well after *Anne Marie David* participated in the ESC. However, aligning oneself with this Eurovision past is a highly valued practice at ESC press conferences, especially when it is done across national boundaries, as is the case in Extract 15.

A similar example occurred at the Macedonian press conference:

> (16)
> *MA1: i'm always ready for singing i i must say now that uh we are now in norway and uh the norway song that won uh i don't know which year was uh goes uh ⟨Norwegian⟩ nocturne ⟨3⟩ nocturne? ⟨/Norwegian⟩ and i ⟨/3⟩ that's that is my favourite ⟨un⟩ xxx ⟨/un⟩ song of all uh in eurovision it's going like uh ⟨sings melody (13)⟩ it was something like that KS: ⟨3⟩ oh yeah secret garden ⟨/3⟩ [MAC2]*

In this extract, the Macedonian artist talks about his favourite Eurovision entry of all time. In homage to the host country NOR, he designates the winning Norwegian song of the ESC 1995 as his favourite song and even sings a passage of its melody. Picking a song from 1995 may also seem remarkable in this case because the first time that MAC participated in the ESC as an independent country was in 1998. This bears witness to the fact that the contest was nevertheless watched in MAC in the mid-1990s, maybe in continuation of Yugoslavia's ESC history (1961–1992).

We have seen in the examples discussed in this chapter that code switching involving non-English material serves an important local function in the present community of practice, namely that of enabling participants to construct themselves as ESC experts and musical or media professionals participating in a pan-European pop music event. As many of these switches linguistically transcend national boundaries, they furthermore have the effect of creating a transnational European space. Clearly, these switching practices do not impede communicative efficiency. In fact, most of them involve language material that de facto cannot be readily expressed in English (names of TV shows, song titles, names of musical genres). They can be said to fill a functional gap and therefore represent a type of switching that facilitates cross-European communication.

4.4.3   Greetings

Greetings are the third major function of micro-switches at ESC press conferences. The use of greetings in European languages other than English is in accordance with the form-follows-function principle of ELF because the respective lexical items represent forms with which participants are generally familiar, even if they have never acquired or learnt the respective language. For two reasons, intelligibility is unlikely to be affected by the use of non-English greetings. For one, such greetings are widely known across Europe as lexical items stereotypically connected to a certain language or national culture. Secondly, as phatic elements, they typically occur at the beginning of an interactional exchange and can therefore easily be decoded as greetings. However, non-English greeting formulas constitute more than just a legitimate deviation from native speaker norms. In a transnational European context, they are employed in clearly strategic ways, namely as an essential means of symbolic convergence to the interlocutor. The default use of English in this community of practice generally rules out any possibilities of macro-level switching as a form of symbolic convergence to a conversational partner whose L1 is not English. However, non-English greetings allow the speaker to temporarily switch to the addressee's L1 – a move that signals good will and respect for the conversational partner. Again this can be viewed as a crossing strategy because speakers perform speech acts in a language that is neither their L1 nor English. By doing so, the greeting persons tone down their own national affiliations, pay attention to the interlocutor's positive face, and signal a transnational form of intra-European solidarity.

Thanking formulas show a similar but weaker trend to be voiced in languages other than English at the press conferences. This is not a coincidence, because they share central characteristics with greetings. They are also widely known, occur in specific places within a conversational exchange, are unlikely to cause communication difficulty and enable speakers to accommodate symbolically to interlocutors of other linguacultural European backgrounds. It is therefore evident that the relevance of the form-follows-function principle to micro-switching is a more general mechanism in ELF talk that is not restricted to greetings as a specific speech act type.

Kelly-Holmes (2005) has studied similar cases of minimal or token bilingualism in advertising texts, showing that such practices assume only a limited competence of the respective language on the side of the audience and exploit the symbolic rather than the informational function of language. The use of foreign languages in advertising is particularly frequent where products are to be associated with a certain national identity (for example, watches as Swiss, cheese as Dutch and so on) – a phenomenon that Kelly-Holmes describes as a matter of linguistic fetishisation. By contrast, the symbolic value of non-English greetings at ESC press conferences is not primarily one of national stylisation. The majority of the non-English greetings in the present data are instances of intra-European crossing and therefore carry transnational European indexical potential.

Greetings as manifestations of intra-European crossing are most likely to occur at ESC press conferences during the phase when journalists ask questions to the national delegations, namely as prefaces to the actual questions. The most common pattern in the data shows media representatives accommodating to the national delegates by greeting them in their national language. This is illustrated by the following extracts:

> (17)
> MP1: ⟨Hebrew⟩ shalom ⟨/Hebrew⟩ i'm ⟨6⟩ simon ⟨/6⟩ from poland uh you know that there are some contests […]
> MA1: ⟨6⟩ ⟨Hebrew⟩ shalom ⟨/Hebrew⟩ ⟨/6⟩ [ISR1]

> (18)
> *MP4*: ⟨Azerbaijani⟩ merhaba ⟨/Azerbaijani⟩ safura
> FA1: ⟨Azerbaijani⟩ merhaba ⟨/Azerbaijani⟩ @@
> *MP4*: ⟨un⟩ xxx ⟨/un⟩ from london (.) uhm azerbaijan seems determined to win the contest (.) […] [AZE2]

> (19)
> MP5: ⟨French⟩ bonsoir jessy bonsoir bruno ⟨/French⟩ (.) uh my qu- my hilmar from germany uh my question goes to uh your own uh memories about eurovision song contests in the past […] [FRA1]

Extract 17 shows a Polish journalist (MP1) greeting the Israeli artist (MA1) in Hebrew (*shalom*), while in Extract 18 a media representative from the UK (*MP4*) greets the Azerbaijani artist (FA1) in her L1 (*merhaba*). A French greeting (*bonsoir*) is used by a German journalist in Extract 19 while addressing the French delegation.

In some cases, journalists use an English greeting first and then add a greeting in the delegates' L1. This is illustrated by Extract 20, in which a journalist from LUX (MP1) greets the Portuguese artist first in English (*hi, how are you*) and then in Portuguese (*olá*):

> (20)
> KS: […] yeah eric from from luxembourg
> MP1: hi
> FA1: hi
> MP1: how are you (.) ⟨Portuguese⟩ olá ⟨/Portuguese⟩ @ (.) uhm yeah well then tell us please uh why do you think portugal has never managed to (.) win the trophy [POR1]

Another example comes from the Croatian press conference:

> (21)
> MP2: hello sören from german radio ⟨Croatian⟩ dobar dan ⟨/Croatian⟩
> FA2: ⟨3⟩ hello ⟨/3⟩
> FA1: ⟨3⟩ oh ⟨/3⟩ ⟨German⟩ guten tag ⟨/German⟩
> MP2: @ ⟨German⟩ guten tag ⟨/German⟩ i have a question about the ⟨spel⟩ cd ⟨/spel⟩ […]
> [CRO2]

In this excerpt, a German media representative (MP2) first uses an English greeting (*hello*) and then a Croatian greeting formula (*dobar dan*) while addressing the Croatian artists. The latter (FA2 and FA1) in turn reciprocate this with an English (*hello*) and a German greeting (*guten tag*). The German greeting is probably used because the journalist has introduced himself as working for a German radio station. So both parties are here seen to accommodate symbolically to their interlocutors via intra-European national crossing. It is only after one of the Croatian artists has used the German greeting that the German journalist also uses a German greeting formula in return. A greeting in one's own national language without such other-initiation would generally be less well received, as it runs the risk of being perceived as a privileging of national over European affiliations.

As has already been seen in Extract 21, crossing via greeting can also be initiated by the national delegates. However, this move is only possible when the journalists have first introduced themselves with their name and national origin – a fairly common practice at ESC press conferences. This puts the delegates in a position to symbolically converge by using a greeting in the journalist's national language, as is also shown in the following extract:

> (22)
> *MP3: hi hello*
> *MA1: hello*
> *MP3: my name is ⟨un⟩ xx ⟨/un⟩ and i'm from turkish delegation*
> *MA1: ⟨Turkish⟩ nasılsınız ⟨/Turkish⟩*
>   [how are you]
> *MP3: oh @ ⟨Turkish⟩ iyi ⟨/Turkish⟩ thank you (.) uh how are you*
>   [fine]
> *MA1: thanks i'm fine ⟨Turkish⟩ iyi ⟨/Turkish⟩*
>   [fine]   [BUL2]

In Extract 22, a Turkish journalist (MP3) and the Bulgarian lead artist (MA1) first exchange English greetings (*hi hello*; *hello*). After the journalist has disclosed that he is a member of the Turkish delegation, the Bulgarian artist uses a Turkish greeting (*nasılsınız* "how are you"), to which the journalist responds in Turkish (*iyi* "fine"). Then he thanks the artist in English and uses a corresponding English greeting (*how are you*) in return. This in turn is answered in both English and Turkish by the artist (*thanks i'm fine iyi*).

A special type of crossing is constituted by accommodative greetings to the host country Norway. These generally occur at the very beginning of the press conference, when the artists arrive at the press conference hall. However, the use of Norwegian in homage to the host country may also occur at later stages in the press conference and is not restricted to greetings. For example, at the Bosnian press conference, the artists performed a Norwegian version of their Eurovision song, and at the Swiss press conference, the lead artist asked the moderator to teach him how to say "I am from Switzerland" in Norwegian.

The following extract shows the Polish artist greeting the audience in Norwegian (*god dag*) at the beginning of his press conference. Additionally, the artist congratulates the Norwegians present in the hall in Norwegian on their national celebration day:

> (23)
> *KS: so how are you*
> *MA1: ⟨Norwegian⟩ god dag uh gratulerer uh med dagen ⟨/Norwegian⟩ @@@@*
>   [hello uh congratulations on your birthday @@@@]
> *KS: thank you so much*
> *MA1: i know it's yo- it's it's your day so national day so uhm i wish you the best* [POL1]

As illustrated by some of the extracts discussed in this chapter, speakers will not usually use a greeting in their own national language, except when the greeting sequence is initiated by a person from another country. The basic ritualised rule that surfaces in these greeting-cum-crossing practices is that the national identity of the addressee takes precedence over one's own national identity, which cannot normally be foregrounded. Apparently it is deemed appropriate within the transnational European context of ESC press conferences to tone down one's own national affiliation and at the same time to show respect for the addressee's national affiliation.

There are only few exceptions to this pattern in the press conference data. Most of them represent cases in which journalist and artist share the same national and/or linguistic background. In such cases, the use of a certain language in greetings is more likely to be perceived as accommodation to the national delegation than as a projection of the journalist's own national identity. This is illustrated in Extract 24:

> (24)
> *FP1: hello?*
> *MA1: hello=*
> *FP1: ⟨German⟩ =guten abend ⟨/German⟩*
>   [good evening]
> *MA1: ⟨German⟩ guten abend ⟨/German⟩ ⟨2⟩ ⟨French⟩ bonsoir ⟨/French⟩ ⟨/2⟩*
>   [good evening]   [good evening]
> *FP1: ⟨2⟩ anke ⟨/2⟩ from germany*
> *MA1: ⟨German⟩ hallo anke ⟨/German⟩*
>   [hello anke] [SUI2]

In this passage, a German media representative (FP1) first greets the Swiss artist (MA1) in English (*hello*) and then in German (*guten abend*). The latter greeting is likely to be understood as a form of symbolic accommodation to the Swiss artist, because German is a national language of SUI and the Swiss artist's L1. Both greetings are reciprocated likewise by the artist, but he adds a French greeting (*bonsoir*) after the German greeting, maybe as a reminder that SUI has several national languages, of which French and German form the largest speaker groups. In the next turn, the journalist introduces herself by name and specifies her national origin as German. This move finally makes the Swiss artist use a last German greeting (*hallo*), with which he can symbolically converge in return.

Cases in which the code choice in a non-English greeting is not motivated by the national affiliation of the addressee form clear exceptions in the data. One such example is the following, in which an Austrian journalist uses a Spanish greeting (*hola*) to address the French delegation:

> (25)
> MP2: ⟨Spanish⟩ hola ⟨/Spanish⟩ (.) ⟨un⟩ xxx ⟨/un⟩ *from austria pride magazine i have a uh question to the producers or maybe to to french television* [...] [FRA2]

There is in fact only one instance in the entire dataset in which a journalist projects his own national identity while addressing a delegation member (see Extract 26).

> (26)
> MP6: ⟨French⟩ *bonjour c'est stéphane de paris* ⟨/French⟩
>   [hello this is stéphane from paris]
> MA1: ⟨French⟩ *bonjour* (.) *comment ça va* ⟨/French⟩
>   [hello (.) how are you]
> MP6: ⟨French⟩ *tres bien merci et toi?* ⟨/French⟩
>   [very good thank you and you?]
> MA1: ⟨French⟩ *ça va* ⟨/French⟩
>   [fine]
> {MP6 continues in French (3)}
> MA1: *no no in english* ⟨1⟩ @@@@ ⟨/1⟩
> MP6: ⟨1⟩ *it's okay* ⟨/1⟩ (.) *you spoke french last time that's why* [...] [ISR1]

In this passage a French journalist (MP6) greets the Israeli artist and introduces himself in French (*bonjour c'est stéphane de paris*). The greeting is also reciprocated in French by the artist (*bonjour* (.) *comment ça va*), but as the journalist sets out to continue in French after the greeting exchange, the Israeli artist asks him to use English. That the use of French in this situation is considered a marked choice is also suggested by the fact that MP6 apparently feels the need to explain why he addressed the Israeli artist in French. His utterance *you spoke french last time* seems to refer to an earlier interview that he had conducted with the artist. At the same time, this bears witness to the default status of English, whose use is never explicitly legitimated in the press conference data.

Finally the data also contain one example in which the accommodation pattern initiated by the journalist is not reciprocated by the artist addressed:

> (27)
> *MP6*: *liam whelan from west midlands radio*
> *FA1*: *hello sir*

MP6: hello (.) uh ⟨Irish⟩ tá tú go hiontach agus tá amhrán go hiontach agat (.) go raibh
míle míle maith agat ⟨/Irish⟩ uh you have given us many many eurovision memories and
i know there are many more (.) in your words moments of ⟨un⟩ xxx ⟨/un⟩ to come?
[You are wonderful and you have a wonderful song. Many many thanks.][7]
FA1: yeah
MP6: and i want to know what your first eurovision memory is please could you share
it with us?
FA1: okay but first of all i'm really grateful you didn't continue that the whole way in
irish cause i was i was feeling the pressure to respond to that uhm (.) [...] [IRL1]

Here the journalist (*MP6*) first introduces himself as working for a British radio station. The Irish artist (*FA1*) then greets him in English (*hello sir*), and he greets back in English (*hello*). The accommodation pattern is in this case not initiated by a greeting, but by the journalist's following utterance in (non-native) Irish, which he uses as a preface for his following question in English. The Irish artist clearly distances herself from the use of Irish at the press conference and explicitly thanks the journalist that he did not continue in Irish. This can be interpreted as an indication that the artist's proficiency in Irish is lower than her English proficiency. At the same time, it can be seen as a mechanism of toning down her national Irish affiliation, which is more likely to be made apparent by the use of Irish (as a symbolic language) than by the use of English. It is interesting to note that this strategy differs from the one adopted by IRL on the EU level, where it has recently chosen to promote Irish to the status of an official EU language – a move that can be characterised as motivated more by national than by European considerations.

To sum up, code switching in greetings serves important identity-related functions at ESC press conferences and is almost invariably done in the shape of transnational linguistic crossing. Such greetings are widely used in a strategic fashion, in order to tone down a speaker's own national affiliation and to practice symbolic convergence across national boundaries – a phenomenon that carries high prestige in this pan-European community of practice and that cannot be performed in English. Although crossing via greeting can potentially be treated as an aspect common to many forms of intercultural communication, it can be assumed that both the languages involved and the regularity with which the national identity of the addressee is acknowledged are more typical of Europe as a linguacultural sphere with a heavily nationalised history.

4.5   Conclusions: The embedding of ELF in European speakers' multilingual repertoires

The analysis of code choice patterns at the macro- and micro-level has shown that European ELF is never purely English talk, because it invariably takes place in a

---

7.   Translation of the Irish passage by Helen Kelly-Holmes (personal communication)

multilingual environment between speakers from various linguacultural backgrounds who make creative use of their linguistic repertoires. These repertoires do not just consist of full language systems but also contain traces of linguistic material associated with languages the participants have never acquired. Still, this language material may be used in ELF contexts for important social functions for which English is not equipped (for example, tokenistic accommodative greetings). European ELF as manifest at ESC press conferences, therefore, turns out to be an integrative phenomenon that is open for numerous "foreign", non-English influences as it emerges in interactional practices (cf. Cogo 2012a: 295).

Linguistic material that is traditionally associated with European languages other than English regularly surfaces at ESC press conferences. The occurrence of such material is never considered problematic by the participants. It is rather part of the ritualised practices of this community. Accordingly, such switching practices should rather be viewed as legitimate indexes of the hybridity of European ELF talk and as a matter of non-native European speaker identifications. When non-English material is used within ELF talk, this is done in ways that do not impede communicative efficiency (form-follows-function principle). By contrast, one could argue that the types of switching found generally facilitate communication, because they are used to make amends for lexical gaps (asking for assistance), to contribute to community-specific matters of identity construction (creating the Eurovision experience), or to save the positive face of interactants from other countries (greetings). In other words, switches into languages other than English are, in this community of practice, not used to exclude participants who do not have a command of the respective language.

The usage conditions evident in the code-switching practices within ELF talk also tell us something about the functional borders of ELF in this transnational European community of practice, because it can be assumed that other languages are particularly likely to surface in functions that cannot be sufficiently fulfilled by English. For example, due to its unquestioned lingua franca status in Europe, English cannot normally be exploited for intra-European linguistic crossing practices, because its use is perceived to be largely de-nationalised (at least for non-ENL/ESL users of ELF). Crossing as a solidarity-creating device is, therefore, more effectively performed with languages that possess a stronger national association. With crossing, the language switched into must clearly be felt to be not a language of the respective speaker. This mechanism is only weakly (if at all) present with English, which is commonly used by speakers from all European nations. Furthermore, the co-occurrence of English and other European languages is an effective means of constructing a specifically European popular music context which contrasts with other pop music events where English is more likely to be used exclusively. As trivial as non-English references to musical genres, events, media and Eurovision songs may appear, they are an integral component of the ritualised linguistic practices involved in the formation of ESC press conferences as a community of practice.

The use of languages other than English over longer stretches of talk constitutes clearly marked behaviour and is generally less well received at ESC press conferences because it amounts to an exclusionary practice and can easily be interpreted as a means of highlighting national affiliations, which carries only little prestige in this transnational community of practice. The use of ELF, i.e. the use of English as a non-national and primarily non-native medium, by contrast, is deemed more adequate for intra-European transnational communication because it fulfils two central functions: it ensures pan-European communicative efficiency and enables participants to tone down their national affiliations. This is deemed more adequate in a context where the construction of transnational European affiliations is perceived as central. The analyses in the following chapter will complement the evidence gathered in connection with the actual code-switching practices at ESC press conferences as outlined in the present chapter. More specifically, an investigation of participants' metalinguistic comments will shed light on how speakers motivate their linguistic practices in front of the pan-European audience.

Chapter 5

Metalinguistic comments on the use of English

5.1 Introduction

The preceding chapter has provided an emic perspective on the most prevalent code choice patterns at ESC press conferences, highlighting the pragmatic functions in which traditionally non-English language material is likely to occur within ELF talk. The current chapter aims to complement this picture by taking an in-depth qualitative look at how the participants at ESC press conferences talk about linguistic practices and their use of English. Note that Chapter 4 and 5, in principle, deal with two separate levels of analysis. What participants say about their own linguistic behaviour does not necessarily coincide with their actual linguistic practices, but this does not render comments about language use less interesting as data. On the contrary, in the present research context it can be assumed that such metalinguistic comments are affected by the Europeanness of the context, i.e. one can expect that participants describe (their) linguistic practices in a way that they feel is appropriate for a transnational, pan-European context. In this sense, Europeanness may be said to shape the usage conditions of ELF in this community of practice.

Chapter 5.2 presents a short outline of the theorisation of metalanguage within folk linguistics. It is followed by three empirical chapters that deal with central categories of metalinguistic comments as found in the dataset: general comments on code choices at ESC press conferences (Chapter 5.3), and more specific comments on English proficiency (Chapter 5.4) and non-native English accents (Chapter 5.5).

5.2 Metalanguage

The term "metalanguage" is used in a number of ways in linguistics and has figured prominently in applied linguistics and sociolinguistics (e.g. Berry 2005; Cameron 2004; Jaworski, Coupland & Galasiński 2004). When used in a broad sense, the term can be found to cover a number of phenomena, ranging from technical linguistic terminology to quotation and reporting practices in everyday conversation. What is of interest for the present study, however, is the narrower definition of the term in the sense of linguistic practices with which speakers comment on language in an overt and conscious fashion. This kind of metalanguage has been called "metalanguage 1" by Niedzielski and Preston (2000), who contrast it with more covert and unconscious forms of making comments about language such as presuppositions ("metalanguage 2"; see also Berry 2005:9, who makes a terminological distinction between "micro-metalanguage" and "macro-metalanguage").[1] As the people talking about language are in many instances not linguists, "metalanguage 1" is of central interest to the field of folk linguistics (e.g. Niedzielski & Preston 2000; Preston 2004; Wilton & Stegu 2011). It needs to be noted that the metalanguage used by linguists is not per se better or more adequate than that used by laypeople (even though the former may be associated with a higher level of authority; Coupland & Jaworski 2004:24). Systematically studying contexts in which speakers make conscious comments about linguistic choices enables the analyst to make statements about shared beliefs concerning linguistic practices in the community at hand (Niedzielski & Preston 2000:314). Metalinguistic comments are, therefore, expressions of speakers' metalinguistic awareness. Such awareness is usually more pronounced in multilinguals (Jessner 2006), who typically form the majority of interactants in ELF contexts more generally and in the community of practice studied here more specifically.

Folk metalanguage yields evidence of the social evaluations connected to linguistic practices. Such evaluations can be seen as traces of (often dominant) discourses which influence people's linguistic behaviour in a certain society or, on the local level, in a certain community of practice. For example, Nakamura (2009) has shown that metalinguistic comments tend to support dominant gender discourses connected to linguistic practices in Japanese ("women's language" vs. "men's language") while at the same time suppressing more subversive practices. A similar point is made by Jaworski, Coupland and Galasiński:

> When we approach language use as discourse and social practice, we naturally view language as a form of social action. But it is in the interplay between usage and social evaluation that much of the social 'work' of language – including pressures towards social integration and division, and the policing of social boundaries generally – is done. This is one of the reasons why metalanguage matters to sociolinguistics.
>
> (Jaworski, Coupland & Galasiński 2004:3)

The "pressures towards social integration and division" mentioned above can easily be viewed in terms of European vs. national affiliations and are therefore also relevant for the present study. In fact, a prioritising of one or the other of these two types of affiliation is likely to result in metalinguistic comments of a largely different quality. Whereas a national affiliation is typically associated with the privileging of national

---

1.   Note that the analysis of "metalanguage" in the present study needs to be distinguished from the study of "metadiscourse" in ELF (e.g. Penz 2011). The latter is a cover term to describe linguistic features that language users employ to organise their text or talk.

languages, a transnational European affiliation shows a higher tendency to promote the use of lingua francas.

Contrary to most other professional ELF contexts, in which language issues are relatively unlikely to surface as a topic in interactions, ESC press conferences represent a context in which speakers are likely to comment on linguistic practices. This indicates that the European prominence of the context may in fact shift questions of code choice to the foreground. The metalinguistic comments made provide important insights into the motivations that lie behind the choice of a certain language, either at the press conferences or on the ESC stage. At first glance, metalinguistic comments may be thought to be equally problematic as other kinds of self-report data, i.e. what is said by the participants may not necessarily correspond to their actual behaviour or motivations. But studying them is nevertheless a valuable undertaking for the present project because even if the code choice practices reported on by the participants do not conform to their actual practices, such comments can still be taken as indexes of what is deemed appropriate in this transnational European community of practice.

One example of a dominant language-related discourse that surfaces repeatedly at ESC press conferences is the "one nation – one language" discourse, which forms an integral part of the discursive construction of the nation. In the dataset, several instances can be found in which participants use the name of a country where normally the name of a language would be used. This bears witness to the fact that nation and national language are widely conceptualised as a unity and may even sometimes substitute each other. The following three extracts include passages in which the speakers oscillate between the name of the respective country (or its population) and that of the respective language:

> (1)
> MA1: *uhm thank you very much we uh are really uh proud of of the <u>spanish</u> version and uh <u>their language</u> is uh uh really melodic so uh that's why that version is uh so sweet (.) and uh we were thinking about a lot of uh versions but (.) it's not like you know just to make uh a few versions more we had a lot of uh uh texts on uh lyrics on a on a <u>a lot of uh languages</u> (.) it's good for promoting but at the other hand if you have no uh uh really really good lyrics it it won't be a good promotion <u>in that country</u> especially (.) uh actually we we are uh hoping that the energy and the music is uh uni- universal for for (.) or or all all the countries and uh we count on on th- on that (.) not on the lyrics* [SER1]

In Extract 1, the speaker's description shows two conceptual shifts: one from the Spanish language to the Spanish people (*spanish version – their language*) and one from languages to countries (*a lot of languages – in that country*). These shifts indicate that languages are normatively thought to "belong" to a national group of speakers (note the possessive pronoun in the phrase *their language*) and that languages are normatively associated with particular countries. Of course, linguists are today highly sceptical of such nationalised discourses in relation to language, for which copious counter-evidence could be adduced. The phenomenon of English as a European lingua franca is especially incompatible with such discourses, as it describes the use of a "language" mainly by speakers from outside Anglophone nations for the purpose of transnational communication.

In a similar manner as the preceding extract, the two following extracts bear witness to the language-equals-nation discourse:

> (2)
> MA2: *so (.) we are doing our hits and uh uh play the club uh in ukraine moldova uh (.) russia (.) <u>romanian</u> uh but uh (.) pop music uh (.) need a (.) vocal* [...] [MOL1]

> (3)
> KS: *and then you say* ⟨Norwegian⟩ *jeg er fra sveits* ⟨/Norwegian⟩
> [I am from Switzerland]
> MA1: ⟨Norwegian⟩ *jeg er fra sveits* ⟨/Norwegian⟩ *(.)* ⟨1⟩ *uh but uh* ⟨/1⟩ *sybille she knows a bit uh <u>norway</u>*
> [I am from Switzerland]
> KS: ⟨1⟩ *that's good* ⟨/1⟩
> KS: *you know norwegian?* [SUI1]

Extract 2 shows an example in which the name of a language is used instead of the name of a country (*romanian* instead of *romania*), while in Extract 3 a country's name is used instead of the name of the language (*she knows a bit norway*). Such usages demonstrate that country and national language are in fact perceived to be in such a close relationship to each other that they may become interchangeable concepts. However, it should also be noted that in the present dataset, there is not a single example of a passage in which this language-equals-nation discourse is applied to English, which may be taken as evidence that its national associations are only limited in this community of practice, where English is invariably used for transnational lingua franca purposes.

5.3   Comments on code choice at ESC press conferences

If English really is the default code choice at ESC press conferences, as already suggested by the data presented in Chapter 4, it can be expected that participants also orient to this default status in their interactions. More specifically, it can be expected that divergences from this default choice are felt to be in need of explanation and are, therefore, frequently commented on. However, press conference participants may also directly orient to the default status of English in conversation, often pointing to a clear ranking that places English on top of the language hierarchy. For example on the first day of press conferences, the moderator repeatedly pointed out to the audience that questions should be asked first in English, whereas he allowed questions in the artists' L1 only much later or not at all if the entire press conference time could easily be filled with English questions. Such comments can be found in a number of press conferences (e.g. MOL1, RUS1, EST1, SLK1, LAT1, SER1, BOS1 and BUL1). It is interesting to note that once the moderator has permitted non-English questions, such questions are never actually voiced. In other words, even though the participants are given the opportunity for a national display via language, they apparently feel that this strategy is less appropriate in this transnational context. The only exception occurred at the first Norwegian press conference (NOR1), at which the moderator treated English and Norwegian on an equal footing, stating that questions are allowed in both languages without showing any preference for either of the two. This exceptional status can be attributed to the fact that, as NOR was the host country, more Norwegian media representatives were present at the Norwegian press conferences than at those of the other national delegations. At all other press conferences, English was clearly constructed as the privileged choice. The following excerpts from the Russian and Moldovan press conferences may serve as illustrations:

> (4)
> *KS: i think we will try to open for some questions from starting in in in english and then the mother language so we can go (.) to radio luxembourg right?* [RUS1]

> (5)
> *KS: i think we will (.) i think we will open for some questions first in ENGlish please so if anyone have a question please raise your hand evan will come with the microphone* [...]
> [...]
> *KS: uh we got ⟨un⟩ xx ⟨/un⟩ for a moment (.) uh no she's (.) no she had the same question do we have anyone in the back? (.) if you want you can (.) if you want you can ask in the mother language (.) if if someone got a question (.) no-one? (.) okay (.)* [...] [MOL1]

In Extract 4, the moderator explicitly states that questions should first of all be asked in English, while questions in the artists' mother tongue are accepted only at a later point. Similarly, in Extract 5 the moderator introduces the question-answer section of the press conference by asking for questions in English (with the word *ENGlish* receiving strong emphasis). The second part of Extract 5, in which the moderator asks for questions in the artists' mother tongue, took place about nine minutes later, when the press conference was already drawing to a close. The passage shows that the moderator was, in that particular moment, faced with the difficulty of finding anyone to ask a question. The moderator has two central tasks. On the one hand, he is responsible for the overall structure of the press conferences and determines the order of the journalists' questions. On the other hand, as illustrated in Extract 5, it is also his duty to keep the press conference going and to avoid an early or abrupt ending. It is evident from Extract 5 that the circumstances that make the moderator ask for questions in languages other than English approximate those of an emergency for him. Only when nobody wants to ask a question in English, he also encourages questions in other languages.

The centrality of English is further stressed when press conference participants ask for translations of non-English passages into English whereas English passages are never requested to be translated into other languages for the audience. This is illustrated by the following extract, in which the moderator allows for both English and Spanish questions but at the same time requests an English translation for potential Spanish questions:

> (6)
> KS: thank you (.) uh we will open for question in both english and spanish and if there are any spanish questions will you translate for us thank you so much (.) […] [ESP1]

The default status of English is also demonstrated by the fact that sometimes delegation members ask for the permission to use their mother tongue instead of English, whereas nobody ever asks for the permission to use English:

> (7)
> KS: do we have some questions yeah please stand up (.) in second row (2) you will get a microphone
> MP1: can i speak in greek please?
> KS: of course
> {MP1 speaks Greek (5)}
> MA1: sorry about the greek you know (.) gonna translate [GRE2]

In Extract 7, a Greek journalist (MP1) asks in English for the permission to speak Greek to the Greek delegation, and the moderator immediately grants this request. Despite the brevity of this exchange, it attests to a fundamental ideological dilemma that participants face in this context. For the Greek journalist, it would under other circumstances be the most natural choice to talk to another Greek person in Greek. His asking for the permission to use Greek in the present context indicates that the presence of Europeans from other countries renders the use of Greek a marked choice, because it privileges national over transnational affiliations. On the other hand, using English when talking to a Greek person would normally also be considered a marked choice for him. The dilemma is in this case resolved by privileging the national position, but this is highly unusual for ESC press conferences at large. In fact, this move only becomes acceptable when the permission to do so has been asked for and a translation into English is provided.

Transnational communicative efficiency is at the press conferences usually safeguarded by the use of English. The request of the Greek journalist, therefore, also exposes the moderator to an ideological dilemma: on the one hand, he is supposed to construct English as the preferred language choice; on the other hand, explicitly ruling out questions in languages other than English would constitute an immense threat to the positive face of the present native speakers of these languages. This immanent face threat is apparently felt to be more severe than a breakdown in communicative efficiency, and this is why the request of the Greek journalist is granted. The moderator can explicitly promote the use of ELF, but he is not in a position to explicitly discourage the use of other languages. Both of these aspects are clearly related to the European transnationality of the context. Europe is here constructed as a space where the use of all languages is generally accepted and the use of languages with a lingua franca function (mainly English) is encouraged.

After the journalist's question, the Greek lead artist (MA1) apologises for the fact that the journalist has used Greek and promises to translate the question into English. In other words, he resolves the moderator's ideological dilemma by ensuring communicative efficiency through translating (which is in principle not his job as a lead artist). As in Extract 7, the moderator always allows journalists and/or delegation members to use their L1 when they ask whether they may use it (which is rarely the case). This indicates that an official English-only policy would in general not be perceived to be compatible with the Europeanness of the context. So there is a clash between the public language policy as constructed by the moderator on behalf of the EBU, which allows (but does not actively encourage) the use of languages other than English, and the need for communicative efficiency at ESC press conferences, which rather demands that English be used. However, an identity dimension is also connected to the use of English in this context, because it serves as a way of toning down one's national affiliation.

Judging from participants' metalinguistic comments, the use of English at the press conferences is widely perceived as positive. This is indicated, for example, in the following passage:

> (8)
> MP5: *hello sieneke*
> FA1: *hello*
> MP5: *uh just want to remind you that this is the very first press conference for today*
> FA1: *yes*
> MP5: *in english*
> FA1: *yes*
> MP5: *so congratulations ⟨2⟩ for that ⟨/2⟩*
> FA1: *⟨2⟩ oh thank ⟨/2⟩ you very much*
> *{applause (4)} [NED2]*

In this excerpt, a journalist congratulates the Dutch artist on the first press conference of the day that is held (entirely) in English. This statement is at the same time a criticism targeting the two national delegations which had held their press conferences right before the Dutch press conference (AZE and UKR). At these press conferences, the lead artists had not used English themselves, but their utterances had been translated into English. This clearly shows that there is more at stake than communicative efficiency, which would also be ensured by translation. The criticism rather targets the fact that the delegates themselves did not (even try to) use English. Proficiency levels in the traditional sense (i.e. in terms of correctness or nativeness) are apparently not felt to be relevant, because the journalist's criticism suggests that there is no excuse for using one's national language at ESC press conferences. Accordingly, participants never complain about low proficiency levels of other participants, but they may criticise that no effort has been made to use English. In other words, it does not really matter how native-like or correct the English used is. All that counts is that English is in fact used.

Another aspect that repeatedly surfaces in the dataset is the (naïve) belief that people do not understand languages other than English. This shows, for example, in the constant demand (by the moderator and the audience) for an English translation when other languages are used or in the sensation that is created when participants show that they can speak languages other than English. In addition, one can find passages in which the participants orient more directly to the belief that everybody understands English and hardly anyone other languages:

> (9)
> MP2: hello ⟨6⟩ uh ⟨/6⟩ stefan from germany
> MA1: ⟨6⟩ hello ⟨/6⟩
> MA1: stefan?
> MP2: yes
> MA1: so you can speak german with me
> {laughter (2)}
> MP2: ⟨German⟩ ich schon aber die andern nicht ⟨/German⟩ @
>   [I can but the others can't]
> MA1: okay sorry (.) yes of course [SUI1]

In this excerpt, a German journalist (MP2) introduces himself to the Swiss artist (MA1) and specifies his national affiliation. For the artist, it is apparently not primarily the mentioning of Germany as a country of origin but the (German sounding) first name *Stefan*, which induces the Swiss artist, whose L1 is also German, to suggest that the journalist should speak German with him. The journalist replies in German with the utterance *ich schon aber die andern nicht* ("I can but the others can't"), which implies that they can only be understood when they speak English, while German is believed to exclude large parts of the audience – a belief that is in the end also acknowledged by the artist, who apologises for his temporary privileging of German at the press conference (okay sorry (.) *yes of course*).

At the second Swiss press conference, it is the Swiss artist himself who makes a similar assumption:

> (10)
> MA1: ⟨French⟩ alors si la france ne nous donne- ne nous donnerait pas des points on va le chanter en français bien sûr on va téléphoner uh à elisabeth teissier pour le savoir ⟨/French⟩ (.) uh nobody knows uh of course he asked me if uh ⟨clears throat⟩ (.) uh maybe we we will give a surprise uh if uh we sing the song in english or in german or a mix hh uh (.) […]
> [well if france doesn't gi- doesn't give us any points we will of course sing it in french we are going to call uh elisabeth teissier to find out] [SUI2]

In this passage, the artist replies in French to a question that was asked to him in French by a journalist. He also translates (parts of) his answer into English, after stating that many journalists in the audience are unlikely to have understood his French answer. His comment *nobody knows uh of course* must seem like an exaggeration if one considers that French is a co-official language of the EBU (besides English) and that there are a number of journalists from Francophone countries in the audience, as well as other journalists who have a sufficient command of French to understand. Still it should be noted that the answer the artist gives in French contains pieces of information that are not present in his English translation. This is, of course, a general problem associated with translations. They may, therefore, create scepticism in parts of the audience whether all information conveyed in the national language is also contained in the English translation. In other words, even though a translation may be offered, this does not necessarily preclude certain parts of the audience from feeling excluded.

A similar point is made by the German lead artist during her press conference:

> (11)
> FA1: *uhm (.) i actually don't think so (.) i just answer in english because it's uh more comfortable for everyone else (.) uhm i actually don't think so germany can win in a few years too uhm i'm not god* [GER2]

In response to a question asked in German, the German artist states that she is going to answer in English because using English is *more comfortable for everyone else*, which in turn suggests that using other languages is in fact less comfortable or maybe even uncomfortable in this pan-European context. Note that a similar ideological dilemma surfaces here as in Extract 7. Under normal circumstances, it would be the unmarked choice for a native German speaker to respond in German to a question voiced in German. But the pan-European context overrules this mechanism and induces the artist to use English in return.

A final piece of evidence for the belief that people can only understand English is provided by the following passage, which took place after the Norwegian quiz during the Slovenian press conference:

> (12)
> KS: *well you made uh seven out of nine (.) that's a good one*
> MA1: *which language was that?*
> {*laughter*}
> KS: *you got seven points out of nine*
> MA1: *oh seven points* [SLO1]

Apparently, the Slovenian delegation member (MA1) is, in this situation, not able to understand what the moderator (KS) has said in his preceding turn. This makes him ask which language has been used by the moderator, which suggests a belief that whenever a passage is not understood, it must be because a language other than English has been used (which is not the case in this situation). This shows that the press conference participants adhere to an essentialist and simplified binary discourse that equates English with cross-European understanding and other languages with unintelligibility.

All examples discussed in this chapter yield evidence that English is treated as the default choice at ESC press conferences. Other languages are of secondary importance and their use normally requires explanations on the part of the speaker, both because their national association is apparently perceived to be stronger than for English and because their potential to guarantee successful pan-European communication is judged to be limited. The central role of English in this context can, therefore, be related to at least two factors: 1. the desire to achieve communicative efficiency (based on the belief that only English can be widely understood across Europe), and 2. the need to tone down one's national affiliation in front of the pan-European audience. Having established the default status of ELF in the community of practice at hand, the following two chapters concentrate on how the press conference participants conceptualise their use of English in their metalinguistic comments.

5.4   Comments on English proficiency

Throughout the press conferences, one gets the impression that, even though a native-like knowledge is not demanded, a good command of English is generally taken to be a positive trait, because it is thought to facilitate successful communication in such a transnational context. More specifically, a good command of English is perceived to be an integral skill for professional artists competing in a pan-European pop music event. Some artists even admitted that they had taken measures to improve their English skills in the months before the contest. For example, when the Norwegian artist was asked about the most important thing he had learned since winning the Norwegian national final, he answered that his improved English skills are probably the most important thing:

> (13)
> *FP4: hi uh lynne ⟨un⟩ xxxx ⟨/un⟩ (.) uh first can you tell us about the most important thing you've learned since the national final this winter (.) and second how's your gut feeling after performing now today*
> *MA1: how how my?*
> *FP4: gut feeling how ⟨5⟩ how is that ⟨/5⟩*
> *MA1: ⟨5⟩ oh yeah ⟨/5⟩ yeah okay (.) uh well uh the most important thing i learn uh maybe (.) my english? (.) i don't know (.) what do you think? {laughter} (.) […]*
> [NOR2]

Similarly, the Dutch artist told the audience that she had stayed a week in a monastery before coming to Oslo in order to dedicate some time to improving her English skills:

> (14)
> *FA1: uhm uhm yeah i'm i'm sorry but i uhm i try my best for to speak english so if i made a mistake please apologise me so ⟨1⟩ ⟨un⟩ x ⟨/un⟩ ⟨/1⟩*
> *KS: ⟨1⟩ no ⟨/1⟩ you're very good (.) v- very good*
> *{applause (6)}*
> *[…]*
> *MP5: uhm a technical question why do you keep on apologising cause i think your english is absolutely brilliant and is it true that you spent some time in a monastery?*
> *FA1: yeah that's true @ one week and i choose uh uh of i learnt there uh a lot of things in english specially grammar and uhm yeah it was a heavy week but yeah so if you can see uh @ it's a little bit uhm (.) i'm nervous for for to talk english (.) so yeah (.) i thank you very much*
> *{applause (3)}* [NED2]

What can be seen in this passage is that ESC press conferences generally provide an encouraging environment for speakers with non-native language skills. At first, the Dutch singer apologises for her low English proficiency. It is evident that she conceptualises using English within a context of traditional English language teaching, namely in terms of orienting to native English standards (note her use of the word *grammar*). This may be the case because she is a very young speaker (18 years) who has so far only used English in formal education contexts, in which non-native features would indeed be treated as *mistakes*. It is not surprising that such a conceptualisation renders her a less self-confident user of English. The other participants, however, adopt a stance on English that is more in tune with ELF theorisation. Even though the Dutch artist's language use contains features that would count as errors in the traditional ELF classroom, they repeatedly compliment her on her English. The moderator, for example, tries to reassure her (*no you're very good*), which is also supported by the audience through applause. At a later point at the press conference, a journalist (MP5) also compliments the artist on her English (*i think your english is absolutely brilliant*). There are two ways of reading such comments. On the one hand, they may be seen as merely polite and therefore insincere statements. On the other hand, they can be taken as an indication that English skills are valued in this community of practice even if they are clearly non-native. In other words, non-native English is generally preferred to the (native) use of national languages at ESC press conferences.

Apologising for low English proficiency is a common pattern throughout the press conferences. The participants nevertheless do not seem to face communicative difficulties. This suggests that low proficiency levels are generally understood in terms of native-likeness and correctness rather than communicative efficiency. Another instance of apologising for low English proficiency occurred at the Macedonian press conference:

> (15)
> *KS: do the composer wanna say anything to the to the press?*
> *MA2: uh i'm sorry i don't speak english very well and i will speak macedonian gordana*
> *⟨3⟩ will tran- will translate ⟨/3⟩ ⟨un⟩ xx ⟨/un⟩ @@@*
> *KS: ⟨3⟩ of course of course macedonian ⟨/3⟩*
> *[...]*
> *FA1: we have twelve uh delegations ⟨5⟩ yesterday ⟨/5⟩ all of them were performing (.) and*
> *they were having really great fun they were all satisfied and we had three hours party*
> *and the tension was all the way from the beginning ⟨6⟩ to the end ⟨/6⟩*
> *MA1: ⟨5⟩ yeah ⟨/5⟩*
> *MA1: ⟨6⟩ maybe we ⟨/6⟩ are not that good at speaking but we are good at uh ⟨7⟩ uh*
> *making ⟨/7⟩ parties yeah*
> *KS: ⟨7⟩ @ partying ⟨/7⟩ [MAC2]*

In this excerpt, the moderator (KS) asks the songwriter (MA2) whether he would like to make a statement to the press. The songwriter apologises for his (supposedly) poor English skills, adding that he will speak Macedonian and that a translation will be provided by one of the delegation members. Note, however, that the English utterance of the songwriter consists of several grammatically well-formed English clauses, which indicates that his proficiency (even by traditional standards) cannot be that low after all. At a later point at the same press conference, another member of the Macedonian delegation (MA1) even plays a joke on the supposedly low proficiency level of the delegation members by saying that they, the Macedonian representatives, *are not that good at speaking* [English] *but* [...] *at making parties*. Joking is here employed as a means of reducing the apparent embarrassment of not being able to speak English well enough in front of the pan-European audience.

It needs to be noted that, when speakers state at the press conferences that they have no or only low proficiency in languages other than English, such statements are never voiced as apologies. The following statement from the Russian lead singer may serve as an example:

> (16)
> *MA1: no f- uh further speaking i i don't don't speak italian and french alas {MA2 talks*
> *to MA1 (3)} uh yes i can sing i can sing it on a on a language which i can't sp- speak and*
> *it's no problem (.) [...] [RUS2]*

This extract shows that the fact that one is not able to speak European languages other than English is perceived as legitimate and can therefore be stated without any apologies, whereas insufficient proficiency in English would be viewed as a clear deficit in this context. Note that the delegate apparently is not embarrassed to say that he has no command whatsoever of languages other than English (*i don't don't speak italian and french*). This contrasts with the descriptions in Extracts 14 and 15, where participants apologised already for a (supposedly) low proficiency level of English (and not for not speaking English at all). Still the general value of learning foreign languages such as Italian and French is acknowledged by the Russian delegate, which is indicated by his use of the form *alas*. Another interesting point is that the singer does not see language proficiency as a prerequisite for singing in a particular language – an aspect that is also borne out by some of the artists that performed in English on the ESC stage but used their national language and interpreters at the press conferences.

Overall, the press conferences bear witness to a behavioural pattern according to which participants tend to apologise for their own (supposedly low) English proficiency levels, whereas they generally compliment other speakers on their English proficiency and encourage them to speak English despite their non-native competence. This means that native-likeness is not necessarily something that one would demand from other persons in this community of practice and that the use of English is rather conceptualised in terms of communicative efficiency and the underplay of national affiliations. Speakers' self-conscious apologies about their own proficiency levels, by contrast, orient to wider social norms that are influenced by traditional concepts of English proficiency in terms of native-likeness and grammatical correctness.

5.5   Comments on non-native English accents

Another linguistic aspect that is frequently commented on at ESC press conferences is non-native accents. This is hardly surprising if one considers that language use both on the ESC stage and at ESC press conferences is widely a non-native business and that pronunciation tends to mark even highly proficient speakers as non-native. It is most of the time non-native English accents that are commented on. Such accents form a decisive component of the cultural hybridity of ELF. In line with an ELF theorisation, however, non-native accents are never constructed as problematic by the participants. This shows that they are viewed as a community-specific norm and as a legitimate index of second-language identities.

One may wonder in how far the participants of ESC press conferences take native English pronunciation models as a point of orientation. High proficiency in English is generally viewed as an indicator of high professionality in the international music business. But in ELF contexts, high proficiency cannot automatically be equalled with nativeness. In fact, it can be expected that a non-native speaker's seemingly native American or British English accent is decoded as a sign of divergence from prototypical ELF patterns and therefore as an exaggerated or unnecessary form of assimilation to Anglophone cultures. At ESC press conferences, such native-like accents may, due to their national indexical potential, even be viewed in a negative light. A similar reaction is likely where native English speakers show no sign of accommodation and retain (often non-standard) native English pronunciation patterns.

The comments on English accents made by the press conference participants explicate the role native models play for European L2 speakers of English. However, they also attest to a less rigid adherence to these models, even though their influence can clearly be felt. This is illustrated by the following extract from the Norwegian press conference:

> (17)
> *MP2: alexander ⟨un⟩ xx ⟨/un⟩ ⟨spel⟩ tv ⟨/spel⟩ two norway uh i can ask you this question in english because it's quite funny uh when and why did you decide to go from an american accent to a british accent singing*
> *{audience laughs (3)}*
> *MA1: u::h well hh (.) i got some complaints (.) actually so uh (.) that's the reason (2) i i and (.) i like to improve so (.) yeah (.) it's just that*
> *MP2: don't you think it sounds better? (.) you sing that's why*
> *KS: i don't think the uh the foreign press knows about the story cou- could you (.) please tell us a little bit about the story behind the question?*
> *MA1: oh yeah uhm it was uhm (.) f- uhm after the norwegian final uhm (.) it uh was uh (.) some newspapers in norway that uh (.) pointed out that i sang heaRt instead of heart*
> *KS: and the way you pronounced heart ⟨1⟩ right? ⟨/1⟩*
> *MA1: ⟨1⟩ yeah ⟨/1⟩ uhm (.) and uh for me there was no news uhm (.) me and my boys made fun of that for a long time but uhm the way it came out of the media we (.) oh yeah you guys do something about it so well (.) we did*
> *KS: and now it sounds fantastic (.) […] [NOR1]*

In this passage, a Norwegian journalist (MP2) asks the Norwegian singer (MA1) why he chose to switch from an American English accent in the Norwegian national final to a British English accent in his performance during the rehearsals for the ESC final. This switch is constructed as a positive development by all three speakers. The artist describes the change to BrE as an improvement (*i like to improve*). The journalist points to a similar evaluation with his suggestive question *don't you think it sounds better?*. The moderator then explains to the pan-European audience that there have been discussions in the Norwegian media about the accent of the Norwegian singer. These discussions are conceptualised by the artist as *complaints*. He furthermore specifies that a certain Norwegian newspaper had pointed out to him that his use of non-prevocalic /r/ in the chorus of the song (*My heart is yours*) represented an AmE accent. However, the artist also says that he did not really take these comments seriously, although he has indeed changed his pronunciation. The moderator in the end praises the artist's new (non-rhotic) pronunciation (*and now it sounds fantastic*).

This episode indicates a number of interesting aspects. The journalist's question about switching from an AmE accent to a BrE accent explicitly orients to two traditional reference varieties of English. It leaves no space for alternative conceptualisations of the Norwegian artist's English: it must either be AmE or BrE. An ELF conceptualisation does not seem to play a role. Furthermore, the question shows that AmE is in this context of high European salience generally not seen as an adequate role model for European speakers of English. The insistence on a British target accent on the European scene is highly remarkable if one considers that pop music is a business in which AmE dominates (in part even with British pop musicians; cf. Trudgill 1980). It may therefore also be read as a means of distancing oneself (as Norwegians and Europeans) from US culture. It is remarkable that the Norwegian public obviously frames the accent of the singer in terms of a competition between two native models. As non-rhoticity is not a common feature of Norwegian, one could also have taken the singer's rhotic accent as an instance of L1 transfer, which is in accordance with the notion of rhoticity being a core feature facilitating intelligibility in ELF communication (Jenkins 2000). However, this possibility is apparently not taken up by the media. Moreover, it is interesting to note that these accent complaints surface on the national level, while they seem to have only little bearing on the pan-European level, where they are even made fun of.

The winning song in 2010 also drew a lot of media attention because of the idiosyncratic English accent of the German singer. Not surprisingly, her accent was topicalised at both German press conferences. The following extract is taken from the first press conference:

> (18)
> *MP4*: [...] (.) *where does your wonderful english accent come from we think it's so cute (.) it's quite different of all the other germans i know how how did you learn to speak english or to sing at least in english that way?*
> [...]
> *FA1: the accent (.) uhm (.) okay i will answer in english because (.) you questioned in in english ⟨un⟩ xx ⟨/un⟩ so (.) uhm i don't know where my accent come from it's just german school english my english teacher taught me to speak like it and you like it other persons don't like it and say wa:h this (.) this (.) this is so ugly what is she talking uh uhm so uhm the opinions are different and it's okay because i'm i i didn't train to have any accent it's just coming (.) and i let it out*
> *{applause (4)}* [GER1]

In this passage, an Australian journalist (*MP4*) asks the German singer (FA1) about the origin of her accent, which he describes as *quite different of all the other germans* he knows. This positions the singer's accent as a non-native accent from a native speaker's point of view and, at the same time, as departing from typically German non-native English accents. However, her non-native accent is in this context not described in a negative fashion or as something that needs to be corrected but rather in a positive light (as *wonderful* and *so cute*). It is noteworthy that the native speaker (who is traditionally supposed to be the authority in terms of English) does not see himself in a position to judge where this accent comes from. The artist then answers that she has learnt to speak like this in her English classes at school. She also expresses an awareness that her accent causes mixed reactions in the audience. In her answer, she clearly juxtaposes a more liberal, ELF-compatible view on her accent with views associated with traditional ELT (*you like it other persons don't like it and say wa:h this (.) this (.) this is so ugly what is she talking*). In the end, she states that she did not specifically train to get this accent and that it just came naturally (*it's just coming (.) and i let it out*), which does not index an assimilationist stance towards native models but a self-confident, positive evaluation of her own non-native accent. The singer's last statement is also followed by applause from the audience, which seems to appreciate that the singer does not use a contrived, more native-like accent which would be considered inauthentic.

The following passage is taken from the second German press conference at which the German singer (FA1) was again asked about her *german english accent*:

> (19)
> MP8: *uhm (.) there were much discussions about your english uh german english accent and you have uh listened to many different accents here now in in oslo (.) uhm do you have plans to change or prove improve your english?*
> FA1: ⟨slow⟩ *uhm these question comes so often and i'm tired to answer it* ⟨/slow⟩ (.) ⟨imitates snoring⟩
> KS: *oh she's sleeping now*
> FA1: @@
> MA1: *but then we can answer with a song (.) what do you think?*
> KS: *yeah*
> MA1: ⟨imitating German accent⟩ *i i don't think so* ⟨7⟩ *that the (.)* ⟨/7⟩ *i don't think so that the uh german a- accent is very obvious you speak* ⟨/imitating German accent⟩
> FA1: ⟨7⟩ @@@ ⟨/7⟩
> {laughter}
> [...]
> MA1: *we have a song we have a song that explains everything*
> KS: @@@@ [GER2]

In this excerpt, the journalist (MP8) talking to the German singer first mentions the numerous different accents that can be heard at the ESC press conferences in Oslo and thereby orients to a prototypical feature of transnational European ELF communication, namely its hybridity in terms of pronunciation (*you have uh listened to many different accents here now in in oslo*). The word choice in the journalist's following question echoes traditional ELT norms, because it suggests that the German singer should *change* or even *improve* her English. It seems as if the delegation had anticipated this question because another delegation member (MA1) suggests answering it with a song that must have been prepared in advance. Moreover he says jokingly that he does not think that the singer's non-native accent is obvious. In his utterance, he humorously imitates a stereotypically German accent, for example by replacing dental fricatives ([θ] and [ð]) with alveolar fricatives ([s] and [z]). FA1 and MA1 then perform a parody of the *Boyzone* song "No matter what" in which they make fun of the entire discussion revolving around the singer's accent. The lyrics they use are given below:[2]

> (20)
> {*MA1 plays the guitar, FA1 performs humorous version of "no matter what", audience repeatedly bursts into laughter*}
> FA1: ⟨*makes noises imitating the song intro*⟩ *go on* (.) ⟨*singing, imitating German accent*⟩ *no matter what they tell you* (.) *no matter what they say* (.) *we germans have good humour* (.) *and can good music play* (.) *if you don't like my accent* (.) *i try the best i can* (.) *and if you still don't like it* (.) *I SING THE SONG AGAIN* ⟨*/singing, imitating German accent*⟩
> {*applause and cheering* (8)} [GER2]

While singing, the artist mimics a stereotypically German accent. Some of the notes she sings are clearly out of tune, which supports the humorous message of the song. Besides stereotypical accent features, the lyrics contain structures that are reminiscent of stereotypically German interference patterns. The sentence *we germans have good humour* (.) *and can good music play*, for example, shows the typically English SVO order in its first half, but the syntax of the second half is more typical of German main clauses, with the auxiliary verb preceding and the main verb following the direct object (Vaux – A – O – V; as in the German translation *und können gut Musik spielen*). The adverb form *good* formally resembles the German adverb *gut* rather than the form *well*, which would be prescribed by normative grammar.[3] The content of the lyrics plays with popular stereotypes of Germans having no sense of humour and being only moderately successful musicians (at least in the ESC). At the end of the performance, the lyrics express the singer's self-confident attitude towards her own

---

2.   Performance link: http://www.youtube.com/watch?v=YkrlIRxyVTw (last access: 20 October 2013).

3.   Alternatively, a reading of *good* as an adjective premodifying *music* is also possible (parallel to German *und können gute Musik spielen*). This analysis results in a Vaux – O – V structure that is also not in accordance with standard English grammar.

accent, because she sings that she will sing the song again, even if the audience does not like her accent.

After the performance, MA1 jokingly reminds the audience that the *Beatles* also used to sing some of their songs in German and that their accent was also clearly non-native:

> (21)
> *MA1: hey hea- i heard the beatles sing in german*
> *KS: oh really?*
> *MA1: and THEIR accent their their german english english german accent was so far away from a clean german accent like the british soccer team is away from w- winning the world cup*
> *{applause (3)} [GER2]*

The delegate uses the *Beatles* as an example to make the point that a non-native accent does not necessarily pose an obstacle to a singer's success. Interestingly, this foreshadows that the German singer in the end won the 2010 contest, despite her accent. Moreover, the delegate's teasing comment on the (supposedly unsuccessful) British football team once more indicates that these ELF speakers are far from aiming at an assimilation to native English cultures, even though they use English by default in this context. It is apparent from these episodes that the participants display a self-ironic and self-confident attitude towards their non-native accents. This is an outcome of the European transnationality of the context and the fact that non-native speakers constitute the majority of the participants in this community of practice.

Questions surrounding the accent of the German singer also surfaced at other press conferences. The following passage, for example, is taken from the Cypriot press conference:

> (22)
> *MP3: i just want to know have you heard the german song (.) because in uh in the german press there is a discussion going on about the accent of uh the german singer (.) whether it's (.) well good english or not or or whether it's what kind of english is it it is (.) so have you heard it and what do you think*
> *FA1: we've heard it (.) it's it's very much uhm it's quite lily allen-esque so it's it's ⟨5⟩ it's an homage to ⟨/5⟩ british yeah very very ⟨pvc⟩ catchys catchit ⟨/pvc⟩*
> **MA5*: ⟨5⟩ it's a very good song ⟨/5⟩*
> *{laughter}*
> *FA1: don't ask the norwegian ask the english woman*
> **FA2*: i li- i like the song and uhm yes it's it it's it's great very very catchy so uh (.) yeah and her accent's very good yeah*
> **MA5*: yeah i mean who (.) it's difficult to answer because we are from the united kingdom so obviously (.) we're gonna sound very english @@@*
> **FA2*: i think it has a slight sort of cockney lilt to it i would say so yeah (.) but very much in the style of lily allen and (.) ⟨un⟩ xxx ⟨/un⟩ [CYP1]*

In this passage, a German journalist (MP3) talks to the group representing CYP and informs the artists about the discussion that had taken place in the German media on the accent of the German representative. In a similar way as the Norwegian press had initiated a normative debate on the accent of the Norwegian artist (cf. Extract 17), the media in the German national context also had sparked a discussion on whether the accent of the German singer was *good English*. The journalist directs this question to the Cypriot delegation, which mainly consists of native BrE speakers, who would (in principle) qualify as linguistic authorities in the traditional sense. FA1, who is originally from NOR and not a native speaker of English, replies that the accent of the German singer reminds her of the British singer *Lily Allen*. However, she immediately disempowers her own judgement as a non-native speaker and passes the English accent question on to the native speakers in the delegation (*don't ask the norwegian ask the english woman*).

The two native speakers involved in this passage (*MA5* and *FA2*) first respond with more general comments on the quality of the German song, stating that they like it and find it *good* and *catchy*. When *FA2* finally starts talking about the singer's accent, she begins with a rather careful, fairly general statement expressing a positive evaluation: *her accent's very good yeah*. *MA5* then seems to realise that the group is in the awkward position of not having satisfactorily answered the journalist's question so far. As a consequence, he adds that the question is difficult to answer for native speakers of English (*it's difficult to answer because we are from the united kingdom so obviously (.) we're gonna sound very english*). This, however, begs the question who should be the authority to judge English accents when the English native speakers obviously do not see themselves in a position to do so. Note that the delegate's statement *we are from the united kingdom so obviously (.) we're gonna sound very English* in fact orients to the traditional native-speaker-as-authority status. His essentialist construction of speakers from the UK obviously sounding *very English* implies that residents of the UK sound native when they speak English and speakers from other cultural contexts generally sound "less English" (or maybe even not English at all). It is also interesting to note that the delegate's utterance is not an answer to the question about the German singer's accent but rather a statement about native speakers' accents, which may be read as a means of avoiding to say something negative about one's European fellow contestants in front of the pan-European audience. It is doubtful whether the native speakers' judgement on the German singer's non-native accent would have been equally positive had they been in a context where native speakers form the majority.

It is remarkable that the non-native group member (FA1), judging from the speed with which she answers, felt the most competent to answer the accent question, whereas the native English speakers were reluctant to provide any meaningful comment. This phenomenon is partly an outcome of the Europeanness of the context, i.e. native speakers seem to be aware that they are not supposed to play the role of normative authorities in a context that is otherwise dominated by European non-native speakers of English. Only at the very end of Extract 22, *FA2* provides a more specific characterisation of the accent of the German singer. However, even in her last statement she rather echoes the description of the Norwegian group member by saying that the accent is similar to that of *Lily Allen* and has a *Cockney lilt* to it.

Another point that evolves from this stretch of talk is that the nativeness vs. non-nativeness distinction is not always useful when describing concrete English accents and how they are perceived. *FA2*'s description indicates that judging accents in terms of nativeness may not always be a straightforward task: even a German speaker's non-native accent may show native-like traces (being *quite lily allen-esque* or having *a slight sort of cockney lilt*). Furthermore, a particular accent may sound native-like for certain non-native speakers (as suggested by FA1), whereas native speakers may vary in their judgement of the same accent, with some describing it as non-native and others as influenced by native accents. In this sense, the accent of the German singer was also (at least to some people in the audience) an instance of crossing, because it incorporated elements of native non-standard accents, which traditionally cannot be seen to "belong" to a German speaker. A standard BrE accent is clearly not the most influential model for the German singer, even though she claims that she has acquired her accent at school (see Extract 18), where native standard accents are hitherto unchallenged models. Given that the German singer has always publicly admitted that she is a fan of *Lily Allen* (and also did so at her second press conference), this non-standard native influence is not surprising and would in fact be a more plausible explanation.

Another instance in which the issue of non-native accents received attention took place at the Icelandic press conference. In the following extract, the discussion of accent is even more remote from any associations with native standards. The Icelandic ESC entry 2010 contains mainly English lyrics, but its title, which is repeated throughout the song in the chorus, is in French: *Je ne sais quoi*. At the beginning of the following excerpt, the singer (FA1) announces that she is going to perform an entirely French version of her song at the press conference together with her backing singers:

(23)
FA1: we actually have been uhm we want to take a little uh piece of it in french
KS: oh really? (.) do we have some french press here? (.) ⟨1⟩ yes we have (.) yeah french press is here ⟨/1⟩
FA1: ⟨1⟩ ⟨French⟩ oui oui (.) allô allô? ⟨/French⟩ ⟨/1⟩ aha (.) because uh we actually uh (.) prepared in france (.) uh even though uh i don't speak it (.) ⟨mimicking French accent⟩ but i speak uh fluent france uh uh english with france accent so uh that's really really difficult (.) so i always speak like this when i'm in france in the nice ⟨un⟩ xxx ⟨/un⟩ i speak like this and i get everything i want uh ⟨/mimicking French accent⟩ (.) ⟨French⟩ oui? ⟨/French⟩ (.) so (.) here is the song in france and uh kristján is gonna give us the key {FA1 sings a few notes in advance}
MA2: the ethnic sound of iceland
FA1: @@@@@ [ISL2]

The announcement that an (entirely) French version of the song will be performed makes the moderator (KS) ask whether there are any French journalists in the audience, which is confirmed. Again we witness here a stereotypical language-equals-nation discourse, because it is assumed that a song performed in French must target the French nationals in the hall – a statement that ignores both speakers from other countries in which French is an official language (BEL, LUX, SUI) and the numerous speakers of French as a foreign language present. Of course, the entire passage documents a tongue-in-cheek attitude towards speaking English with a French accent and the "camp" quality this is sometimes perceived to possess (see Harvey 2002). The lead singer uses minimalist French greeting tokens (*oui oui* (.) *allô allô?*) and exhibits instances of nation-equals-language confusion throughout her talk (e.g. *we actually uh* (.) *prepared in france* (.) *uh even though uh i don't speak it* or *but i speak uh fluent france uh uh english with france accent*). Large stretches of her talk humorously mimic a stereotypically French accent of English. The comment of another delegation member (MA2) right before the performance of the song, in which he jokingly declares the French version of an otherwise largely English song to be *the ethnic sound of iceland*, also points to a less than serious attitude of the performers. It highlights a de-essentialised approach to music and language choice as a matter of national identity construction. Despite the joking tone of the lead singer's utterances, it is interesting to note that she seems to refer to accommodative processes that are considered typical of ELF talk (i.e. using a French accent of English when she is in FRA and presumably involved in ELF talk with French non-native speakers of English).

In sum, the metalinguistic comments on accents in the data have shown that in this pan-European context standard English accents are no longer invariably perceived as the models non-native European speakers need to aim at. There is an increasing awareness that accents are not automatically tied to particular speaker groups, that they can be faked, played with and strategically employed and that they need not stand in the way of communicative efficiency or musical success. Non-native ELF communication is widely constructed as the norm in this transnational European community of practice – a norm that does not carry the stigma that non-native features traditionally possess in ELT or native-speaker dominated contexts.

5.6   Conclusions: ELF norms superseding traditional ELT norms

Metalinguistic comments are at the heart of what has been termed folk linguistics. For linguists, such comments provide important insights into shared beliefs about linguistic practices in a given society (at the macro-level) or in a particular community of practice (at the micro level). As a consequence, metalinguistic comments possess an intrinsic applied linguistic dimension because speakers' beliefs about linguistic practices need

to be taken into account in the creation of effective foreign language teaching strategies or language policies. More specifically, metalinguistic comments yield evidence of
the usage norms which have an impact on people's concrete linguistic behaviour. Even
though what participants say about their linguistic practices may not be an exact representation of their actual linguistic beliefs and practices, their metalinguistic comments
tell us something about which linguistic practices they believe to be appropriate for a
given context, in the present study in a context of pan-European prominence.

One central insight that the analyses of metalinguistic comments in the preceding chapters provide is that participants in ESC press conferences generally need to
negotiate between more traditional ELT-related discourses in connection with their
use of English and more ELF-oriented discourses that treat nativeness and correctness
as secondary to communicative success, authenticity and transnational orientation.
The evidence furthermore suggests that these latter discourses are gaining ground,
at least in this transnational European community of practice. This became particularly evident in ELF speakers' attitudes on their own accents as reflected in the present
dataset.

The predominant use of ELF at the press conferences is due to the participants'
concrete local requirements. The highlighting of national affiliations via national languages carries little prestige in this context and is generally viewed as an impediment
to successful intra-European communication. In this respect, ELF provides the participants with a medium that facilitates cross-European understanding and at the same
time enables them to tone down their national affiliations, which would otherwise
be perceived as too salient in a competitive environment like the ESC. The default
status of ELF at the press conferences can be considered a phenomenon typical of most
contemporary contexts in which Europeans from various linguacultural backgrounds
communicate. The metalinguistic comments show that participants regularly orient
to English as the preferred medium of communication, while other languages clearly
possess a marked status (which is, for example, evident in requests for the permission
to use these languages and for translations into English) and are regularly associated
with a highlighting of national affiliations that are usually deemed inappropriate for a
transnational European context.

The default status of ELF in this community of practice is potentially problematic
if one takes into account that English plays a national role in three of the participating countries (IRL, MAL, UK). A traditional interpretation of this situation (for
example, along linguistic imperialism lines) would probably highlight that the three
Anglophone nations are privileged, because (one of) their national language(s) is used.
However, such reasoning is not evident at ESC press conferences. This can only be
explained by the fact that ELF is today perceived to be to some extent distinct from
native and national forms of English and that the advantage that Anglophone cultures

have in ELF communication is therefore minimal or negligible. In fact, what the meta-linguistic comments of the native speakers at ESC press conferences demonstrate is an increasing insecurity when it comes to judging uses of English that depart from native models or standards. In other words, it seems as if it is the native speakers that are disempowered in ELF communication contexts.

ELF as used by speakers from non-Anglophone cultures at the press conferences is judged to be, if not completely neutral, at least less nationally loaded than the use of other European national languages. This property of ELF makes it an important means of denationalisation in this transnational European community of practice. One can also witness a process of de-anglicisation of ELF in the data: even though participants use something that has traditionally been called "English", they do not necessarily see this as a means of expressing or assimilating to Anglo-American identity values. There is rather a general awareness that ELF as a hybrid can potentially take on many different identity indexing roles, among them those associated with popular culture, profes-sional artists and transnationality. This finding contrasts with the reasoning of scholars criticising the spread of English across Europe as an instance of linguistic imperialism. The ESC press conference data contain no evidence that participants view the role of English as problematic, let alone imperialistic. What is viewed as problematic is rather the use of national languages.

English language skills are generally expected (and encouraged) in this trans-national European context. However, while speakers apologising for their own (supposedly low) English proficiency levels orient to proficiency in terms of nativeness and correctness, not adhering to these normative influences in one's linguistic practices is not normally considered as problematic by the other participants. ESC press confer-ences represent a context in which it is obvious that the notions of "proficiency" and "nativeness/correctness" in many cases do not go together. Many participants exhibit a relatively high proficiency level in terms of communicative efficiency but do not necessarily approximate or aim at native standard usage. Even though traditional ELT discourses are not absent in this community of practice, alternative discourses that see non-native English accents as legitimate indexes of L2 identities are increasingly apparent. This development is clearly connected to the fact that non-native European speakers form the majority in this community of practice and that native speakers from IRL or the UK are, therefore, not in a position to enforce native standards as targets. This eliminates a central mechanism that renders non-native uses of English deficient in other contexts. The following chapter moves on to explore this phenomenon on the pragmatic level of European ELF communication by investigating complimenting behaviour at ESC press conferences.

Chapter 6

Compliments in European ELF talk

6.1 Introduction

Chapters 4 and 5 have taken a qualitative look at the linguistic practices exhibited by participants of ESC press conferences as a Europe-focused community of practice. This qualitative approach will be continued in the present chapter, which also discusses the pragmatic linguistic level and studies complimenting behaviour at ESC press conferences. However, this qualitative view on how participants perform and negotiate compliments will also be complemented by quantitative analyses, which are used to describe the structural make-up of compliments and their sociolinguistic relation to certain speaker groups. We have seen in the preceding chapters that European ELF speakers do not necessarily orient to traditional notions of linguistic purity, nativeness and grammatical correctness in the way they use English or comment on their use of English. At the pragmatic level, one would therefore also expect a certain degree of divergence from native usage conventions as a sign of the internal hybridity of ELF. Crucial questions in this respect are whether this hybridity stands in the way of efficient communication and whether the heterogeneity of cultural influences is perceived as problematic by the participants, which in turn would mean that ELF communication is (partly) pragmatically deficient.

Compliments are important solidarity-creating devices. A common function of compliments is orienting to the positive face of one's interlocutors. In intercultural communication, their use particularly foregrounds expressions of solidarity across national or cultural boundaries. An in-depth analysis of compliments, as carried out in the present chapter, captures the interface of pragmatic function, linguistic structure and sociolinguistic patterns at which ELF is discursively located in the transnational European community of practice at hand.

As a theoretical background to complimenting in ELF communication, compliments are first discussed on a theoretical level, reviewing central findings of studies on complimenting behaviour in Western Anglophone cultures (Chapter 6.2) and on the sociolinguistic dimension of compliments (Chapter 6.3). Chapter 6.4 discusses additional methodological issues that go beyond the basic methodological framework outlined in Chapter 3. The four following sub-chapters present a range of analyses of complimenting behaviour at ESC press conferences, namely in terms of compliment frequency (Chapter 6.5), the structural make-up of the compliments (Chapter 6.6), compliment functions (Chapter 6.7), and the sociolinguistic relationship between complimenting, gender and sexuality (Chapter 6.8).

6.2   Compliments in Western Anglophone cultures: Form and function

ELF research has – in accordance with the form-follows-function principle – often concentrated on pragmatic phenomena. The present chapter focuses on a pragmatic phenomenon that has so far not been studied in ELF talk, namely compliments. Compliments play a significant role in ELF communication contexts in which speakers want to present themselves in a cooperative light. A common definition of the term *compliment* is provided by Holmes:

> A compliment is a speech act which explicitly or implicitly attributes credit to someone other than the speaker, usually the person addressed, for some 'good' (possession, characteristic, skill, etc.) which is positively valued by the speaker and the hearer.
>
> (Holmes 1986: 485)

Complimenting behaviour has figured prominently as an object of study in the pragmatic research literature since the 1980s and has been shown to differ cross-culturally (e.g. Biancolini Decuypère 2000; Cordella, Large & Pardo 1995; Duttlinger 1999; Golato 2005; Grein 2008; Herbert 1991; Lubecka 2000; Mironovschi 2009; Mulo Farenkia 2005; Nicolaysen 2007; Norrick 1980; Probst 2003; Wieland 1995; Wolfson 1981; see Chen 2010 for a recent synopsis of research on compliments from a cross-cultural point of view). Because of their cross-cultural variability, compliments are an interesting aspect to study within the framework of the present project. When European ELF speakers from various cultural backgrounds communicate, this necessitates a high degree of pragmatic negotiability because they are likely to transfer the pragmatic norms of their own culture to their use of ELF, thereby causing a certain degree of internal pragmatic hybridity (Wolfson 1989: 227). Pragmatic aspects related to politeness and/or facework (such as compliments) have been demonstrated to vary even across European cultures, despite their geographical proximity (see Chen 2010: 82–86 and contributions in Hickey & Stewart 2005). In particular, it is doubtful that patterns of complimenting behaviour observed in (native) Anglophone cultures can be mapped one-to-one onto compliments in European ELF talk (cf. Holmes & Brown 1987).

Interestingly, patterns of complimenting behaviour have been found to be remarkably similar across (native) Western Anglophone cultures. This conclusion can be drawn from research on cultures such as the US (Knapp, Hopper & Bell 1984; Manes & Wolfson 1981; Wolfson 1983; Wolfson & Manes 1980), Australia (Cordella, Large & Pardo 1995; Milinkovic 2010) and New Zealand (Holmes 1986, 1988, 1995). Patterns surfacing across such studies, namely the structural formulaicness of compliments,

the similarity of compliment topics and the typically gendered distribution of compliments are outlined in more detail below. With respect to native European Anglophone
cultures, one finds (with the exception of Creese 1991) a lack of research on British,
Irish and Maltese compliment data. There is no study on compliments in IrE and
Maltese English.[1] Judging from research on other politeness phenomena, one would
expect a higher leaning towards negative politeness strategies (showing deference,
not imposing on the addressee) for Britain (Bousfield 2008:38; Stewart 2005). As
compliments are a prototypical example of a positively polite speech act (showing
addressees that they are socially accepted), this would point to lower frequencies in
BrE (Lewandowska-Tomaszczyk 1989:75). Research on compliments in the US has
demonstrated that they are used in higher frequencies there than in other cultures.
The apparent excessive use of compliments may cause recipients from other cultures
to decode such compliments as trivial and dishonest (Herbert 1989:7).

Complimenting in Britain has been investigated by Creese (1991), in a study that
contrasts complimenting behaviour in Britain and the US. For this study, Americans
and Britons were interviewed about differences between the US and Britain in terms of
the realisation of a range of speech act types (including compliments). Subjects drew a
highly stereotypical picture: "English people are polite, indirect and cold as opposed to
the Americans who are loud, direct and pseudo-friendly" (Creese 1991:43). For compliments more specifically, subjects remarked that Americans use them more often
and phrase them with stronger appreciative terms (Creese 1991:46). In the second
part of the study, Creese observed complimenting behaviour in two teachers' rooms
on both sides of the Atlantic. On the one hand, she found similarities between the two
cultural contexts in terms of lexical predictability and compliment responses. However, she also noted two differences. As far as syntactic formulas were concerned, the
US subjects favoured the "I (really) like/love NP" pattern (42.4%), followed by the "NP
is/looks (really) Adj" pattern (34.2%). The latter pattern was most common in the BrE
data, where the second most frequent category (35.5%) was "miscellaneous". In other
words, the British subjects were much less formulaic in their complimentary syntax
than the US subjects. The second difference involved compliment topics. Whereas in
the US context appearance compliments were the most frequent category (65.8%),
ability compliments (54.3%) were favoured in Britain.

Across Europe, most cultures have been shown to be less fond of compliments
as positive politeness strategies compared to the US (see, for example, Herbert
1991:386 and Lewandowska-Tomaszczyk 1989:75 on POL; Kallen 2005:130 on IRL;
Keevallik 2005:209 on EST; Nekvapil & Neustupny 2005:259 on CZE; Nicolaysen
2007:84 on SWE; Sifianou & Antonopolou 2005:265 on GRE, Wieland 1995:809 on

---

1.   Schneider and Schneider (2000) only study compliment responses in IrE.

FRA, Ylänne-McEwen 1993 on FIN), with ESP being a notable exception (see Hickey 2005:320). It may therefore well be the case that, with respect to complimenting behaviour, the three European Anglophone cultures (IRL, MAL, UK) pattern more with their European neighbours than with other native English cultures such as the US, Australia or New Zealand. It is mainly the US and New Zealand that have been extensively studied in this respect. Due to the absence of similar BrE, IrE and Maltese English data, the results from these studies will serve as a (tentative) point of comparison for the ESC-PC data (but see Chapter 6.4 for a discussion of the potential problems of such a comparison).

From a conversation analytic perspective, complimenting behaviour prototypically exhibits the structure of an adjacency pair consisting of the compliment and the following compliment response. Compliment responses represent an equally interesting pragmatic phenomenon and have also been extensively studied to date (see, for example, Holmes 1995; Nixdorf 2002; Pomerantz 1978; Schneider & Schneider 2000; Werthwein 2009). As has been noted early on by Pomerantz (1978:81–82), compliment responses are subject to two conflicting constraints: the need to agree with the complimenter and the need to avoid self-praise. Accordingly, researchers have come up with a tripartite set of terms to classify compliment responses: acceptance (i.e. the need to agree with the complimenter takes priority), rejection (i.e. the need to avoid self-praise prevails), and deflect/evade (an outcome of the attempt to adhere to both constraints at the same time; Holmes 1995:139–141). Among these options, compliments have preferred responses that are culture-specific. For example in Western Anglophone cultures, acceptance has been found to be the preferred response type (Pomerantz 1978).

(Native) English compliments are formulaic in the sense that a restricted number of evaluative lexical items and syntactic structures accounts for the majority of the compliment tokens. Adjectives used in compliments are commonly positive degree adjectives, especially those of general appraisal (e.g. *nice, good, great, beautiful, pretty*; see Holmes 1986:490 on NZE, Manes & Wolfson 1981:117 on AmE). Among the verbs expressing the evaluative part of a compliment, *love* and *like* are used most frequently (Manes & Wolfson 1981:118), and this is usually done in the simple present or past tense (Manes & Wolfson 1981:122). In German (Golato 2005:77–78), Swedish (Nicolaysen 2007:92) and other languages, by contrast, the positive value of a compliment is not usually carried by the verb. Adverbs (e.g. *well*) and nouns (e.g. *genius*) are in general more rarely used to convey the positive evaluation. To boost the positive evaluation, many compliments contain intensifiers (e.g. *really good, so well*).

With respect to syntactic patterns, research has repeatedly found that most compliments correspond to a limited set of syntactic structures (e.g. Manes & Wolfson 1981). For Western native varieties of English, these syntactic patterns seem to occur in roughly similar frequencies. Holmes and Brown (1987) show that about 80% of both AmE and NZE compliments are constituted by the following three patterns, of which the first one is clearly dominant (amounting to about 50% in both varieties; see also Manes & Wolfson 1981: 120–121):

> Type 1: NP + VP$_{copula}$ + (Int) + Adj$_{pos}$ (e.g. *You look really good*)
> Type 2: Pro + VP$_{copula}$ + (Int) + (*a*) + Adj$_{pos}$ + NP (e.g. *That's really a nice coat*)
> Type 3: *I* + (Int) + VP$_{liking}$ + NP (e.g. *I simply love that shirt*)

From these three patterns, it becomes evident that the assessment segment is usually formed by an adjective (Types 1 and 2) and only occasionally by a verb (Type 3). Less common but still regular patterns are the following:

> Type 4: *You* + VP + (*a*) + (Int) + Adj$_{pos}$ + NP (e.g. *You did a really good job*)
> Type 5: *You* + VP + (NP) + (Int) + Adv$_{pos}$ (e.g. *You play the trumpet really well*)
> Type 6: *You* + *have* + (*a*) + (Int) + Adj$_{pos}$ + NP (e.g. *You have a very nice bag*)
> Type 7: *What* + (*a*) + Adj$_{pos}$ + NP (e.g. *What a nice bag*)
> Type 8: Adj$_{pos}$ + NP (e.g. *Nice bag*)
> Type 9: *Isn't* + NP + Adj$_{pos}$ (e.g. *Isn't this bag nice?*)
>
> [Abbreviations: Adj$_{pos}$/Adv$_{pos}$ = semantically positive adjective/adverb; Int = intensifier; NP = noun phrase; Pro = pronoun; VP = verb phrase; VP$_{copula/liking}$ = verb phrase headed by a copular verb/verb of liking]

Formulaicness is considered a universal characteristic of compliments by Chen (2010: 93). In all languages studied so far, compliments exhibit preferences for a limited range of syntactic structures. However, the degree to which this formulaicness holds may vary and for some European languages, it has been shown that compliments are less formulaic than in English (e.g. Herbert 1991: 391 and Jaworski 1995 on Polish; Sifianou 2001: 414 on Greek).

Although languages generally possess certain structures that are likely to surface in compliments, one also needs to take note of the heterogeneity of languages on the typological level. Even though the syntactic formulaicness of compliments manifests itself in predictable structures within a certain language, the cross-linguistic structural variability of compliments may be considerable. For European ELF, this means that despite the fact that "one language" (English) is spoken, the formulaicness of compliments may to some extent be less prominent due to the linguistic hybridity of ELF.

One study that points into this direction has been carried out by Ylänne-McEwen (1993), who studied complimenting behaviour in role play interactions of three groups: native speakers of BrE, native speakers of Finnish and Finnish non-native speakers of English. Although the compliments in all three groups exhibited a high degree of formulaicness (the three most frequent syntactic patterns accounted for at least 70% of all compliments), there were differences in the ranking of the top three patterns. The structure "NP + copular verb + (Int) + Adj" was the most frequent pattern in all three conditions (BrE speakers: 36%, Finnish speakers: 27%, Finnish English speakers: 39%). The pattern "*You have (a)* Adj NP" was not among the top three in the BrE group (7%), but ranked second with Finnish speakers of English (37%), which dovetails neatly with the fact that a similar Finnish structure ranked joint first in the Finnish group (27%) (Ylänne-McEwen 1993:502–503). In other words, there was a clear L1 transfer effect that caused the hybridity of the English compliments used by the Finnish speakers.

The nine common syntactic structures identified for English above can be considered typical of compliments and are therefore formal realisation types of direct compliments. Such compliments contain one semantically positive item (an adjective, verb or adverb) that carries most of the positive evaluative load. Utterances showing such structures are easily recognisable as compliments, even in isolation from any context. Compliments using other structures constitute indirect compliments because the complimentary intention has to be inferred from contextual evidence, which requires a higher cognitive effort (Boyle 2000:28; Jucker 2009:1612–1613; Maíz-Arévalo 2012).

Turning to function, compliments are widely recognised as an essential means of establishing and maintaining social relationships. They are generally considered as the classic example of a positive politeness strategy (Brown & Levinson 1987), because they pay attention to the addressee's positive face by highlighting characteristics of the addressee that are deemed valuable by both communicative parties. As compliments express a commonality of taste or interest with the addressee, they are powerful solidarity-creating devices (Manes & Wolfson 1981:124). According to Sifianou (2001:396), compliments can be linked to at least the following three positive politeness strategies as outlined by Brown and Levinson (1987): "Notice, attend to H[earer] (his interests, wants, needs, goods)", "Exaggerate (interest, approval, sympathy with H[earer]" and "Give gifts to H[earer]".

However, as noted by Holmes (1995:119ff), there is also a darker side to compliments, because they may not invariably create solidarity between complimenter and complimentee. The positive facework function generally attributed to compliments is in many contexts just one of several potential interpretations. Compliments may at the same time implicitly threaten the addressee's positive face (e.g. *I like that shirt. It makes you look so much thinner.*). Moreover, they can also be seen as a threat to the addressees' negative face, because they require some sort of compliment response through which complimentees have to position themselves vis-à-vis the compliment. This threat to the negative face may be particularly high in debt-sensitive cultures, where compliments on possessions are often understood as an expression of envy and may lead to the addressee offering the object to the complimenter in response, i.e. they trigger a perlocutionary effect typically associated with requests.

Furthermore, utterances may show the formal or semantic characteristics typically associated with compliments, but they may nevertheless have anything but a complimentary (or polite) function in a given context (compare, for example, ironic, teasing compliments or so-called "street remarks" [Cooke 1999; Kissling 1991], which are particularly likely to hurt the addressee's positive face). Finally, the speaker's and addressee's judgements of whether an utterance has a complimentary function may also diverge, which poses a serious challenge for the process of identifying compliments. All of these examples demonstrate that not every speech act that shows the typical formal features of a compliment also automatically functions as a compliment. As the form of utterances is not always helpful for the identification of compliments (see also Jucker, Schneider, Taavitsainen, Breustedt 2008 on the difficulties of extracting compliments from corpora), the latter have to be identified on a functional basis, taking local interactional norms into account.

Compliments have also been shown to be largely restricted to a limited set of topics such as appearance, possessions, personality or ability. Topics that occur frequently in compliments provide insights into the value system of a given society (Manes 1983) or, on a more local level, a particular community of practice. Compliments can be considered to pass on and stabilise the cultural norms expressed in their topics. For example, the fact that women are often complimented on their appearance in Western societies indicates that a good appearance is generally viewed to be more important for women than for men (Wolfson 1984). Such compliments are not just a mere reflection of a social fact but also further entrench this dominant discourse, because they are a driving force that causes many women to concentrate on their appearance. This seems particularly plausible because compliments, as positive politeness devices, are usually well received and may be taken as a form of positive evaluation of the success of the complimentee's identity performance.

6.3   The sociolinguistic dimension of compliments

Complimenting behaviour has also been studied from a range of sociolinguistic perspectives. For example, it has been found that compliments tend to be exchanged far more among status equals (in terms of power and age) than among people of unequal status (Holmes 1995: 134; Holmes & Brown 1987: 532; Knapp, Hopper & Bell 1984). Moreover, when compliments are in fact used between speakers of unequal status, they are more likely to be perceived in a negative light, namely as a form of power play that enables powerful speakers to praise the performances of less powerful people, or as an instance of flattery when a compliment is paid to a person of superior status. One is therefore safe to assume that the most prototypical kinds of compliments are those exchanged between status equals (colleagues, casual friends, acquaintances; Chen 2010:80), where they can more effectively fulfil their solidarity generating function.

Another dimension relevant to complimenting behaviour is the degree of familiarity in the relationship between complimenter and complimentee. Compliments are generally less frequently exchanged among intimates and strangers. It follows that they occur most often between people whose relationship can be described as somewhere in between these two poles, at a medium level of interpersonal familiarity (friends and acquaintances). A reason for this is that for intimates such as family members or romantic partners as well as for strangers there is less space for negotiating their relationships (Cordella, Large & Pardo 1995:246).

The social dimension that has been most extensively studied in relation to compliments is gender (e.g. Berlin 1997; Herbert 1990; Holmes 1988, 1995; Johnson & Roen 1992; Kharraki 2002; Matsuoka 2003; Parisi & Wogan 2006; Rees-Miller 2011; Ruhi 2002; Taavitsainen & Jucker 2008; Wolfson 1984). Studies on Western Anglophone cultures generally show that women are more often the givers and receivers of compliments, i.e. compliments among women form the most frequent category, whereas compliments among men represent the least frequent category (see Holmes 1995:122–123). Non-Anglophone European cultures tend to follow this pattern (see, for example, Sifianou 2001:401 on Greek). This has made some researchers speculate that women and men may possess a different understanding of compliments: whereas women are thought to view compliments as an affective means to establish solidarity, men are said to orient more to the referential or potentially face-threatening characteristics of compliments (Holmes 1995:123). However, such broad statements about female-male differences, not just in relation to complimenting behaviour, are increasingly met with reservation.

Compliment topics have also been found to vary with gender in a highly stereotypical way, i.e. appearance compliments are generally more common among women and compliments on possessions or ability among men (e.g. Holmes 1995:131 on New Zealand; Parisi & Wogan 2006, Rees-Miller 2011 on the US). Such patterns can be viewed as manifestations of heteronormative discourses (cf. Motschenbacher 2011). Ability or performance compliments, for example, are an integral part of performing hegemonic masculinities. Rees-Miller (2011:2686) found that especially in the realm of sports, such compliments are an important means of heterosexual male social bonding. Another finding that so far holds across all studies in which the influence of gender was tested is that male-male compliments are hardly ever appearance compliments (Holmes 1995:131–133). This marked status of appearance compliments among men can also be related to the heteronormativity at work in dominant discourses of masculinity (Rees-Miller 2011:2685). Showing a concern for grooming and appearance is traditionally associated with dominant discourses of femininity in Western cultures. This renders an appearance compliment between men a speech act that threatens the positive face of both complimenter and complimentee.

Male-female and female-male compliments are particularly likely to be interpreted along sexual lines as part of heterosexual courtship behaviour (as opposed
to male-male compliments; cf. Kiesling 2013). More specifically, women complimenting men on their possessions and/or abilities and men complimenting women
on their appearance are in accordance with normative heterosexuality discourses.
Male-male compliments, especially on appearance, are therefore normally avoided
by heterosexual men in order not to evoke any suspicion of homosexuality. Interestingly, the fact that compliments are generally most frequent among women
has not caused female-female compliments to be pereived as an index of lesbian
desire. Whereas the markedness associated with the low frequency of male-male
compliments seems to be compatible with gay male desire as a marginalised form
of sexuality, the fact that female-female compliments generally form a major part of
the compliment tokens observed cannot plausibly be linked to lesbian desire, which
is similarly marginalised.

A study by Doohan and Manusov (2004), in which participants were interviewed
and had to write a compliment diary, also sheds light on the role that compliments
play in romantic relationships. They found that the most frequent compliment topic
between partners in a heterosexual relationship was appearance. Both female and
male partners in the study reported that they gave and received appearance compliments most frequently (Doohan & Manusov 2004: 185). This indicates that intimate
heterosexual contexts are among the few in which it is also acceptable for men to
receive appearance compliments.

Another study by Parisi and Wogan (2006) on compliments collected on a US
university campus also explored their sexual dimension. The topic of appearance
dominated the male-female and the female-female compliments, whereas female-
male and male-male compliments were predominantly concerned with ability. It is
important to note that in this data the subjects were not couples in romantic relationships. Nevertheless follow-up interviews with the complimenters and complimentees
led the researchers to explain the results in terms of two prevailing mechanisms: firstly,
on the gender level, complimentary behaviour reflects social expectations about femininity and masculinity as tied to appearance and ability respectively. This explains
why women in general receive more appearance and men more ability compliments.
Secondly, on the sexual level, heterosexual courtship behaviour is tied to certain
normative scripts that have their repercussions in complimenting behaviour. As it is
traditionally men who are normatively expected to play an active role in heterosexual
courtship, women gave relatively few appearance compliments to men because they
did not want to be perceived as "coming on too strongly" with males or because they
did not want to send out flirtatious messages. It even turned out that the only male
person who had received several appearance compliments by women was in fact a
gay man, and the female complimenters reported that in his case they did not have to
worry about sending out the wrong message.

The sexual dimension of appearance compliments can furthermore be gauged by taking a look at the subject positions that they project on complimentees. As discussed by Kulick (2003), a similar mechanism pertains to the use of the word *no* in response to sexual advances. Whereas women are normatively supposed to say *no* in such contexts, hegemonic masculinity requires men to always consent to such advances (if not to initiate such advances themselves), and saying *no* would project a stereotypically female subject position on them. In a parallel interpretation, complimenting men on their appearance would also project a stereotypically female subject position on them, because they are confronted with beautification practices and made the object of the complimenter's gaze.

Finally, certain structural aspects of compliments also tend to show a gendered distribution. For example, among the positive adjectives that may be used, a certain set of adjectives, i.e. the "empty" adjectives of appraisal that Lakoff (1975) describes as an integral part of "women's language", are largely restricted to compliments by and to women. A similar trend pertains to adjectives of beauty (*beautiful, pretty*; Wolfson 1984: 239–240). Compliments in which the verb *love* expresses the positive evaluation are more rarely used by men, probably because of the high emotionality and emphasis connected to this verb (Herbert 1990: 206; see also Holmes 1995: 127–128). It may be suspected that the use of intensifiers, which are also stereotypically associated with "women's language" due to their high degree of emotionality, is also a feature that may be avoided by men. However, this feature has so far not been studied specifically in compliments.

When distinguishing types of personal focus in compliments (i.e. first person focus, second person focus or impersonal), Herbert (1990: 205) found that first person focus was most common among female speakers (*I like your hair that way*), especially when complimenting women, and that men clearly favoured impersonal constructions (*nice bike*), especially when complimenting men. Second person focus was found to be most frequent in female-female compliments and least frequent in male-male compliments. This distribution shows that compliments from and to women show a tendency to be more personal than compliments from and to men.

More recent research on complimenting behaviour and gender to some extent relativises the findings of earlier studies. Rees-Miller (2011), for example, conducted a study at a college in the US Midwest. She had her students collect compliments by means of the "notebook method" (the technique most frequently employed in linguistic research on compliments). Data were collected in 2008 and 2010. The 2008 data showed patterns reminiscent of earlier research: by far the highest number of compliments was used among women and compliments between women most often centered on appearance. Compliments on performance, on the other hand, were used particularly often (82.8%) among men. However, the 2010 data partly contrasted with earlier findings: here both types of same-sex compliments showed roughly the same frequencies (around 40%) and were consequently four times more frequent than female-male and male-female compliments. Moreover, all four giver-receiver combinations had performance as their most common topic. Male-male compliments were almost invariably on performance (95.5%) and appearance compliments were most common among women (but less common than performance compliments).

As a period of only two years seems unlikely to have led to such a great change, Rees-Miller (2011: 2679–2680) found on closer comparison of her two datasets that they differed in terms of setting. Whereas the compliments in the 2008 data mainly originated from unstructured settings (informal conversation), the 2010 data predominantly contained compliments that were voiced during goal-oriented activities. After re-classifying her data according to these two setting types, she found that in goal-oriented settings male-male compliments were more frequent (45%) than female-female compliments (36%). Moreover, it turned out that appearance compliments were most likely to occur in unstructured settings, while performance compliments clearly dominated in goal-oriented settings. The study as a whole suggests that gender is a less monolithic factor than has been claimed in earlier research. In other words, gendered usage patterns depend on the respective context. Other contexts in which men – against the general trend – have been found to use more compliments include voicemail messages (Hobbs 2003), Spanish literature (Duttlinger 1999: 385), German and Russian literature (Mironovschi 2009: 58–59) and US films (Rose 2001). However, what these contexts share is that they are not associated with naturally occurring speech data, which may be taken as an indicator that everyday speech patterns are still somewhat more traditional in this respect.

It is, of course, important to note that not all societies exhibit the same gender patterns in complimenting behaviour that have been identified for the majority of Western cultures. Ruhi (2002: 411), for example, shows that in Turkish society, men use more compliments and that most of their compliments are directed to women. Men are clearly more rarely the addressees of Turkish compliments, no matter whether the complimenter is female or male. Male-female and female-female compliments occur most frequently (40.4% and 35.2% respectively; Ruhi & Doğan 2001: 367–375). This clearly indicates a power dimension according to which women in Turkish society are generally complimentees whereas men are generally complimenters.

At the interface of sociolinguistics and pragmatics, compliments have traditionally been included in discussions of linguistic politeness phenomena. Earlier approaches to the study of politeness and, more specifically, compliments tended to adhere to a top-down model of politeness in which the notion of face was treated as universally valid (echoing Brown & Levinson's (1987) facework model). As a reaction to these earlier theorisations, more recent research on linguistic politeness or, more broadly construed, relational work is characterised by discursive or postmodern approaches (see Mills 2011 and Watts 2005 for overviews of such research) and commonly uses a bottom-up conceptualisation that focuses on how features such as compliments are in fact understood by the interactants in a given context (Watts 2003; Locher & Watts 2005). This shift was deemed necessary because the abstract facework model covers many phenomena that would not be considered polite by interlocutors themselves. Watts (2003) has therefore come up with a distinction between an interactant-based description of "first-order politeness" or "politeness1" and an analyst-based description of "second-order politeness" or "politeness2" (as found, for example, in Brown and Levinson's facework model). A research focus on politeness1 manages to cover all phenomena that are in a certain context actually perceived to be polite (or impolite) by the participants. Practices that would be perceived as normal in a given context are not described in terms of (im)politeness in such a framework but are rather treated as a matter of what Watts (2003) calls "politic behaviour" – a concept influenced by Bourdieu's notion of the habitus. As a result, facework and politeness are no longer seen as identical (Watts 2005: xxx), because the ritualised practices developed in a certain community of practice may constitute facework without being perceived as polite by participants. A similar point can be made about compliments, which often perform positive facework but are in many contexts not evaluated as polite behaviour. They rather form part of the normal interactional business.

As pointed out by Haugh (2010: 140), there is a lack of politeness-related research in intercultural settings. Addressing this lack of research, the following chapters study the complimenting behaviour of participants at ESC press conferences to yield insights into the patterns of politic behaviour that have evolved and are negotiated in this community of practice. Due to the Europeanness of the context, the relational work that is prevalent in this community also forms an important means of transnational European identity construction or is at least viewed as compatible with the notion of a pan-European affiliation.

6.4 Methodological preliminaries

Earlier research on compliments has been dominated by the ethnographically inspired notebook method, i.e. researchers observed complimenting behaviour in their environment and then noted down the compliments they were aware of (e.g. Wolfson & Manes 1981; Holmes 1995; Rees-Miller 2011). This method has even been claimed to be "the only reliable method for collecting data about the way compliments, or indeed, any other speech act functions in everyday interactions" (Manes & Wolfson 1981: 115). However, as Jucker (2009) points out, various methodologies may be fruitfully employed in compliment research, ranging from armchair methods (introspection or native-speaker interviews) to strictly empirical field methods (including the notebook method, the philological method, conversation analysis and corpus analysis) to laboratory methods (discourse completion tests and role-plays).

For the present analysis, a methodology was chosen that cuts across the notebook method and corpus analysis in order to overcome the weaknesses of the former. As Jucker (2009: 1621–1622) points out, with the notebook method researchers only note down those compliments they are aware of, i.e. usually the most prototypical kinds of compliments, whereas a number of less prototypical compliments may go unnoticed. Moreover, researchers do not have the chance to go back and listen to a stretch of talk again when they produce their transcript. Relying on human memory alone to transcribe spoken language data generally leads to unsatisfactory results that ignore central aspects of the local negotiation of compliments (such as hedges, discourse markers and other phenomena typical of spoken data). These problems are irrelevant in the present study, because there is video material on which the transcription of the dataset is based and that can be consulted repeatedly. A detailed manual inspection of the entire dataset ensures that all types of compliments are in fact extracted from the data, even less prototypical ones.

Another problem associated with the notebook method is that the resulting collection of tokens contains compliments from highly heterogeneous settings that are usually difficult to handle adequately in the analysis. Concentrating on complimenting behaviour in the context of ESC press conferences sheds light on the norms that have evolved in this particular community of practice. Participatory observation of the press conferences ensures that the analysis rests on an ethnographic basis, i.e. the observer is in an experience-based position to judge whether particular utterances are likely to be perceived as compliments by the press conference participants.

The notebook method has also been shown to be prone to gender bias. Female researchers, for example, tend to collect more compliments from female complimenters and may not have access to some male-dominated contexts. By contrast, a study conducted by a male researcher (Berlin 1997) found higher rates of male compliments including those directed at men, which have been found to be extremely rare in other studies. As an unobtrusive way of recording the data was chosen in the present study, there is no danger of researcher gender skewing the data.

The divergent methodologies, contexts and datasets used in earlier research make a (direct) comparison between the ESC-PC data and the data presented in other studies unfeasible, because a specific context (ESC press conferences) would be compared with data collected in a range of heterogeneous contexts. The research overviews presented in Chapters 6.2 and 6.3 therefore rather serve as a general point of orientation, documenting cross-contextually typical patterns of complimenting in native Western Anglophone cultures. Even though it can be expected that many of the aspects uncovered by these earlier studies bear some relevance to complimenting behaviour in general, it must be kept in mind that individual contexts may actually exhibit quite different patterns.

To obtain a working definition of the term "compliment" for the following analyses, the original definition by Holmes (once more provided below) is here taken as a starting point.

> A compliment is a speech act which explicitly or implicitly attributes credit to someone other than the speaker, usually the person addressed, for some 'good' (possession, characteristic, skill, etc.) which is positively valued by the speaker and the hearer.
>
> (Holmes 1986:485)

A decisive passage in this definition is "to someone other than the speaker, usually the person addressed", which implies that there are also compliments in which the receiver is not directly addressed (Duttlinger 1999:115; Lewandowska-Tomaszczyk 1989:74). This fact has to be highlighted here, because it turns out that compliments voiced in the third person are particularly frequent at ESC press conferences. What makes such comments about third parties compliments is the fact that the receivers, even though they are not directly addressed, are nevertheless likely to be present – either in the press conference hall or somewhere behind the scenes. The following two extracts illustrate this point (compliments underlined):

> (1)
> *FA1: oh yeah (.) over there is our red head darling pétur örn (.) strawberry blond we call him (.) he's a he's a backing uh singer on stage (.) and uh i mean (.) he's just i mean look at him <u>he's adorable</u> @@@@ (.) and he's but he's a bit boring though* [ISL1]

> (2)
> *MA1: oh i don't know we have been we have visited some some other countries and we met with uh the girl from georgia <u>she's a really good singer</u>* [...] [DAN1]

In the first extract, the Icelandic lead singer introduces one of her backing singers, who is sitting beside her, paying him a compliment on his looks (*he's just i mean look at him he's adorable*). That this compliment is made in jest is underlined by the laughter after the compliment and the following utterance (*but he's a bit boring though*), which clearly contrasts semantically with the preceding compliment. In the second extract, the Danish artist compliments the Georgian contestant, whom he had met before on a European promotional tour. In this case, the complimentee is not physically present in the press conference hall, but she (or other members of her delegation) may watch the press conference behind the scenes, where monitors are installed that televise the press conferences. The presence of journalists with the same national affiliation may also play a role in this context.

Compliment responses will not be discussed specifically in the present study. The reason for this is that the generic structure of press conferences does often not allow for more complex kinds of compliment responses. When compliments are made, they are usually accepted by the addressee through nodding or by a short thanking formula. This is due to speakers' stricter adherence to the rule that only one speaker should hold the floor at press conferences, unlike in other types of naturally occurring conversation. Moreover, the turns of the interviewed delegation members tend to be rather long and compliments in the middle of such turns do not allow for any compliment response. Another reason is that at ESC press conferences one frequently finds compliment types that do not necessarily call for a response (especially those that do not directly address the recipient). To sum up, the adjacency pair compliment – compliment response is in this context of only limited relevance and compliment responses do not exhibit the full structural and functional complexity that they have been shown to possess in other contexts. The context of the ESC may also contribute to this effect, because overt cases of non-acceptance or disagreement are generally avoided in this transnational context, as they may be perceived to stand in the way of a collaborative construction of transnational Europe as a harmonious space. Accepting a compliment, on the other hand, may also be problematic in this community of practice, because it would amount to an act of self-praise that is likely to carry nationalist undertones. This means that not responding to a compliment can also be seen as a ritualised practice that helps participants to avoid being caught in the ideological dilemmas that compliment responses impose on them. Despite the fact that compliment responses are not systematically studied in the present project, they still play a role in helping the analyst to decide whether an utterance has been interpreted as a compliment (at least where they occur).

Identifying compliments on a purely structural basis is impossible. Even though compliments have been shown to exhibit a high degree of structural formulaicness, research using automatic retrieval for the identification of compliments (and other pragmatic features) in language corpora is still in its infancy (see Jucker, Schneider, Taavitsainen & Breustedt 2008). It is doubtful whether automatic retrieval procedures will in the future be able to detect compliments with tolerable levels of precision and recall. Even if corpus linguistic queries may be used to search for those structural patterns that are typical of compliments, the problem remains that syntactic structure cannot be neatly mapped onto compliment function and that there is a substantial number of compliments that are not retrievable because they show less common syntactic patterns.

Purely semantic criteria are also insufficient for identifying compliments. Utterances that may in one context be understood as a compliment, and therefore fulfil the felicity condition that their attribution is viewed as desirable by the receiver, may have different functions in other contexts. For example, the speech act *you have put on weight* would in Western cultures generally be taken as an insult rather than as a compliment because gaining weight is not perceived to be compatible with normative body ideals. However, in a context where this utterance is said to a person who is underweight or who has been trying hard to gain weight, it can very well be interpreted as a compliment (Jucker 2009: 1619).

As syntactic and semantic criteria appear to be insufficient for the classification of an utterance as a compliment, the ESC press conference data were manually searched for compliments. In identifying compliments, the analyst has to face the problem that such speech acts represent a "fuzzy" concept and that a subjective element of interpretation can therefore not be entirely avoided (Jucker, Schneider, Taavitsainen & Breustedt 2008: 292). In the present study, compliments are identified on a pragmatic basis, i.e. the classification of an utterance as a compliment was in each case judged from the concrete interactional context and ritualised norms exhibited by the community of practice under study. Even though one has no direct access to the intention of the speaker or to the interpretation on the part of the recipient, contextual cues (such as intonation, gestures, the relationship between interlocutors, the conversational topic or response behaviour) enable the researcher to judge whether an utterance was particularly likely to be intended and/or perceived as a compliment. In addition to this, participatory observation of ESC press conferences has given the analyst background knowledge about which characteristics are generally perceived as positive in this community of practice. Many of the characteristics participants are complimented on are related to their work as professional artists, media officials or journalists.

The compliment selection procedure shall here be illustrated with the following extract:

> (3)
> *FP1: hello this is desiree from the netherlands uhm i know you uh played in the russian musical romeo and juliet (.) and when i saw your performance uh earlier today at the rehearsal i think it really reminded me of this musical (.) so could you tell me if your staging has to do anything with musical?*
> *FA1: uhm (.) no well uh it it it has the same uh uhm you know uh (.) uh choreographer and director and uh (.) that's it (.) nothing you know (.) i think that it very different from romeo and juliet but the experience does (.) nuh (.) doesn't work*
> *FA2: this is maybe the same spirit (.) that she has too (.) and the uh and the hand writing maybe of the song- singer hand writ- just the hand writing of the singer but nothing nothing in common*
> *FP1: it is it is meant as a compliment nothing more*
> *FA1: yeah yeah yeah sure thank you (.) [...] [GEO1]*

In this passage, a Dutch journalist (FP1) tells the Georgian delegation that she recognised certain similarities between the choreography of the Georgian ESC entry and the musical *Romeo and Juliet*, in which the Georgian singer had played the lead role. If one assumes that the journalist liked the musical, her utterance *when i saw your performance uh earlier today at the rehearsal i think it really reminded me of this musical* could well be taken as a compliment. However, it is clear from the reaction of the two Georgian delegation members (FA1 and FA2) that they did not perceive it as a compliment in the first place. Instead of showing a common compliment response type such as acceptance, they rather try to find explanations to legitimise the detected similarities between their ESC performance and the musical. Stating that there are such similarities is clearly seen as a criticism by them. It is only after the journalist has made it explicit that her utterance was meant as a compliment (*it is meant as a compliment nothing more*) that the Georgian singer accepts it as a compliment (*yeah yeah yeah sure thank you*). Even though the journalist explicitly classifies her own utterance as a compliment, it was not counted as a compliment in the present study. This decision was made, on the one hand, because it is evident from the data that it was not perceived as a compliment by the recipients. On the other hand, similarities between two musical pieces are generally not viewed as a positive aspect but rather as an accusation of plagiarism in this community of practice. In fact, it could be argued that the journalist realised from the delegates' reaction that her comment was not particularly well received and felt the need to declare it a compliment retrospectively.

The focus of the present study is on personal compliments, which include both compliments paid to individuals as well as to groups of people. It is decisive that the recipient of the compliment is also present at the venue. This is straightforward for individuals. Where groups of people are complimented, it is sufficient if at least one member of the group is present. Compliments at ESC press conferences are made to individual artists, delegation members or journalists, but they can also target the team of organisers, all ESC contestants, NOR as the host country or other European nations, with members of all these groups being present in the audience. For each compliment, the complimenter's and complimentee's gender was noted down for individuals. Most groups receiving compliments are of mixed gender.[2]

For the quantitative structural analyses, compliments were primarily identified by means of their central evaluative lexical item. Direct compliments possess one such lexical item, usually an adjective (Extract 4), sometimes a verb, noun or adverb (Extracts 5 to 7; evaluative lexical item underlined):

(4) *KS: you're a good salesman* [BLR1]
(5) *FA1: i love the guy's sound* [FIN1]
(6) *FA2: ⟨spel⟩ nrk ⟨/spel⟩ are magicians* [ARM1]
(7) *MA1: and you see so many people working so professionally* [LIT1]

Where possible, compliments were identified on a clausal basis to reflect the nine common syntactic formulas identified by Manes and Wolfson (1981:120–121) which are

---

2.   The following speech act types were not counted as compliments and therefore excluded from the data: positive evaluative comments about people who were not present (*I just love Beyoncé*), praise attributed to non-personal concepts (*Music is such a nice thing*) and self-praise (*Mum always told me "you're so cute"*).

represented generally as clauses. The following three extracts illustrate compliment formulas 1, 2 and 3, as outlined in Chapter 6.2 (compliments underlined):

(8) *MP1: uhm grea- great song congratulations on that and of course you're very charming and it's uh (.) [...] [SWE1]* → Type 1: NP + VP$_{copula}$ + (Int) + Adj$_{pos}$

(9) *FA1: yeah uh this is andrea (.) uh which is which i know for a long time she's also a great singer (.) [...] [ROM1]* → Type 2: Pro + VP$_{copula}$ + (Int) + (a) + Adj$_{pos}$ + NP

(10) **MP1*: hi guys alistair birch from australian radio (.) i love your song it's it's my favourite (.) [...] [CYP1]* → Type 3: I + (Int) + VP$_{liking}$ + NP

Extract 10 additionally contains a compliment with a structure that is not among the categories of Manes and Wolfson (1981): *it's my favourite*. Extract 8 also contains an example of a compliment that could not be grasped at a clausal level, as it represents an independent noun phrase (*great song*). In such cases, the phrasal level was used (see also type 8 in Wolfson and Mane's typology). This is also common for adjective phrases, which in the spoken language frequently occur in isolation:

(11) *MP5 [about the violin of one of the Finnish artists]: very beautiful [FIN2]*

In cases in which a compliment contained more than one evaluative lexical item, each of them was counted separately, even if these items occurred within the boundaries of one clause. For example, the following utterance contains two evaluative adjectives:

(12) *MA1: and they're so talented and so good-looking [LIT1]*

This utterance was counted as two compliments: one on the complimentees' ability (*talented*) and one on their appearance (*good-looking*). In terms of clausal structure, both compliments were treated as an instance of syntactic pattern 2.

For some compliments, more complex structures than a clause were noted down, namely in cases in which it is rather the combination of clauses that renders the utterance a positive evaluation:

(13) *MA2: [...] justin timberlake of course i think he's a great dancer (.) and i think milan is (.) also very very close to this [SER1]*

In Extract 13, the statement about *Justin Timberlake* (*he's a great dancer*) was not counted as a compliment because the person evaluated was not present at the venue. However, the following comment about the Serbian lead artist relates back to the preceding positive evaluation (*milan is (.) also very very close to that*) and only gains its complimentary function through this relation.

Indirect compliments, whose positive evaluation has to be inferred in the absence of a central evaluative lexical item, may also extend over structures larger than a clause.

In the following extract, a journalist compliments the Bulgarian artist on his photo that was printed on the promotional material handed out to the press:

(14) *MP2: when i first saw it i thought i was looking at david beckham* [BUL2]

In this example, no central evaluative lexical item is present. The complimentary meaning of the utterance has to be inferred. Cultural background knowledge makes European audience members interpret this as a compliment because *David Beckham* is widely known across Europe as a good-looking man epitomising the media image of the metrosexual. Likening the photo of the Bulgarian artist to a photo of *Beckham* can therefore be assumed to be perceived as a positive comment by speaker, complimentee and audience in this community of practice.

In total, 1,043 compliment tokens could be identified in the dataset. Each compliment token was annotated with information on the gender of complimenter and compimentee, syntactic structure, compliment topic (distinguishing ability, appearance, personality and possession) and whether the evaluative element was intensified.

6.5   Compliment frequency in ESC-PC

If one had to predict whether compliments are frequently used at ESC press conferences on the basis of the sociolinguistic evidence presented in Chapter 6.3, one would have to consider two aspects: the power dimension and the level of familiarity. The relationship between the participants of ESC press conferences (i.e. journalists, fans and delegation members) cannot be adequately described in terms of a power differential. Moreover, two salient factors of this context, namely popular culture and Europeanness, do not seem to be compatible with an overt display of power asymmetries. Viewed from this perspective, one would expect a substantial number of compliments to be exchanged at ESC press conferences, because participants are largely status equals. However, one would also need to acknowledge that the relationship between press representatives and national delegates is in most cases one of strangers rather than of personal acquaintances. This aspect would lead to the estimation that the number of compliments at ESC press conferences should be low.

If one calculates the compliment frequency per minute, one finds that it amounts to 0.67 compliments per minute (i.e. 1,043 compliments in a total of 1542 minutes of corpus data).[3] Even though there is no direct point of comparison for this finding

---

3.   If one subtracted the passages left untranscribed (i.e. musical performances and the Norwegian quiz), the frequency would be even higher.

because previous research has not quantified complimentary usage in the same way, it is apparent from this figure that compliments are particularly frequent at ESC press conferences. This can be seen as evidence for the fact that status equality outweighs social familiarity in this community of practice. The high frequency of compliments is even more remarkable if one reconsiders what has been outlined in Chapter 6.2, namely that most national cultures around Europe have been found to be less fond of compliments than Western Anglophone cultures. In other words, even though these national cultures tend to exhibit a lower usage of compliments, speakers nevertheless use many compliments in this transnational European ELF context. This indicates that compliments indeed function as an essential social lubricant in this community of practice.

In order to find out whether certain patterns in compliment usage can be discerned, compliment frequency per minute was calculated for the press conferences of all 39 national delegations (see Table 6.1).

Table 6.1. Country ranking according to compliment frequency in ESC-PC

Rank	Country	Press conference duration (mins)	Compliment frequency	Compliments per minute
1.	POR	43.5	7	0.161
2.	FRA	45	9	0.200
3.	RUS	43.5	9	0.207
4.	GRE	37.5	10	0.267
5.	MAC	31.5	9	0.286
6.	ISR	34.5	10	0.290
7.	SLK	48.5	15	0.309
8.	FIN	45.5	16	0.352
9.	ESP	41.5	15	0.361
10.	NOR	49.5	21	0.424
11.	BLR	44.5	19	0.427
12.	NED	22.5	10	0.444
13.	DAN	22	10	0.455
14.	LIT	37.5	18	0.480
15.	BEL	35	17	0.486
16.	SLO	31.5	16	0.508
17.	CRO	38.5	20	0.519
18.	SER	46.5	25	0.538
19.	MAL	36	20	0.556
20.	UKR	34	20	0.588

(Continued)

Table 6.1. (Continued)

Rank	Country	Press conference duration (mins)	Compliment frequency	Compliments per minute
21.	ARM	42	25	0.595
22.	MOL	40	25	0.625
23.	BOS	42.5	28	0.659
24.	LAT	43.5	30	0.690
25.	BUL	36	25	0.694
26.	EST	40	29	0.725
27.	SWE	26.5	20	0.755
28.	CYP	43.5	35	0.805
29.	GER	50	41	0.820
30.	SUI	36.5	31	0.849
31.	UK	39.5	38	0.962
32.	ISL	47	48	1.021
33.	POL	44.5	46	1.034
34.	TUR	32	34	1.063
35.	ROM	38.5	42	1.091
36.	AZE	38	46	1.211
37.	ALB	49.5	58	1.547
38.	GEO	41	64	1.561
39.	IRL	42	66	1.571

As can be seen in Table 6.1, the calculation of the index scores for compliments per minute results in a continuum of values, ranging from 0.161 compliments per minute (cpm) for POR up to 1.571 cpm for IRL. In other words, there is considerable variation in terms of compliment frequency, which points to the internal hybridity of European ELF communication on the pragmatic level. This hybridity is at least partly due to pragmatic variability across national cultures.

The ranking list opens up some interesting patterns. In accordance with a poststructuralist theorisation, it cannot be read as a ranking list that provides evidence for the degree of politeness of a given national culture. As in many other contexts, compliments are at ESC press conferences part of the unmarked verbal behaviour that has become ritualised in this community of practice. The list should therefore rather be seen as an index of how common relational work via complimenting behaviour is across the individual delegations, with two components playing a role: the way national delegates behave linguistically and (to a lesser extent) the way other participants talk to the national delegation.

If one separates the top ten and the bottom ten and contrasts them with the large middle part (ranks 11 to 29), one finds that EU membership has an effect on complimentary frequency. Among the top ten countries with the lowest compliment frequencies, four (40%) are non-EU countries: RUS, MAC, ISR and NOR. For the 19 countries ranking in the middle, the frequency of non-EU countries is similar (7 countries out of 19, i.e. 37%). Among the bottom ten countries with the highest compliment frequencies, six (60%) are non-EU countries: SUI, ISL, TUR, AZE, ALB, and GEO. In other words, there is a tendency for EU countries to cluster in the top and middle area (with lower compliment frequencies) and for non-EU countries to cluster in the bottom ten (with higher compliment frequencies). This, in turn, indicates that national delegates from non-EU countries and journalists talking to these delegates feel a higher need to employ compliments as a means of creating European solidarity than in the press conferences of EU countries,[4] whose European solidarity may be seen as more firmly established by their EU membership. In terms of cultural similarity, it is also interesting to see that SLO, CRO and SER rank very closely to each other, occupying positions 16, 17 and 18 (ranging from 0.508 to 0.538 cpm).

A closer look at the countries located in the top and bottom ten sheds light on two further aspects influencing complimenting behaviour. Power seems to play a role as well, with three of the "Big 5" countries (ESP, FRA, NOR) and RUS clustering in the top 10. This indicates that representatives of more powerful nations, and journalists talking to them, feel a somewhat lesser need for employing positive politeness strategies such as compliments to foster European solidarity. Considering Europe's history, it is not surprising that GER, another "Big 5" country, does not fit this pattern and shows a relatively high usage of compliments.

In the bottom ten, it is interesting to note that two of the four EU countries with the highest compliment rates are the two native English cultures (IRL and UK), with IRL showing the highest frequency of all countries. This confirms the finding that speakers from Western Anglophone cultures in general make greater use of compliments. In the case of the UK (a "Big 5" country), anglophonicity even seems to outweigh the power factor identified above for the top ten. ALB has the third highest compliment frequency and this can also be related to Anglophone cultures because the three background singers of the Albanian delegation, who came from the US, contributed significantly to the conversation at the press conferences. Another delegation in which native English speakers (from Wales) played a greater role was CYP, which also shows a relatively high usage of compliments (just missing out the bottom ten on rank 28).[5]

---

4.   Note that two of the four EU-candidate countries (ISL and TUR) are in the bottom ten.

5.   180 of the 1,043 compliments in the corpus (17.26%) were given by ENL or ESL speakers. The overwhelming majority of these are found at the press conferences of ALB, CYP, IRL, MAL and UK.

Viewed in total, the resulting continuum of compliment frequencies is an outcome of a combination of factors among which national culture, power, established European belonging and the felt need to create European solidarity figure most prominently. As these aspects vary across national delegations, compliment frequencies also vary substantially, causing the ELF talk at the press conferences to be (pragmatically) hybrid discourse.

6.6   Structural aspects of compliments in ESC-PC

For the structural analysis of the compliments in ESC-PC, the nine syntactic formulas identified for AmE by Manes and Wolfson (1981) had to be adapted. This was necessary because the original formulas evidently only cater for compliments directly addressing the recipient. As has been shown already, at ESC press conferences compliments voiced in the third person are common. Therefore the syntactic patterns identified by Manes and Wolfson had to be adjusted to include such compliments. Table 6.1a shows how the syntactic patterns were operationalised in the present study. Adaptations concern Types 2 to 7. The changes involve two aspects: (a) replacing specific subject pronouns by a more general category NP that also allows for third person subjects, and (b) replacing the form *a* with a general category "determiner" (Det).

Table 6.1a. Syntactic compliment formulas as operationalised in the present study

Type	Manes & Wolfson (1981: 120–121)	Present study
1	$NP + VP_{copula} + (Int) + Adj_{pos}$ (e.g. *You look really good*)	$NP + VP_{copula} + (Int) + Adj_{pos}$
2	$Pro + VP_{copula} + (Int) + (a) + Adj_{pos} + NP$ (e.g. *That's really a nice coat*)	$NP + VP_{copula} + (Int) + (Det) + Adj_{pos} + NP$
3	$I + (Int) + VP_{liking} + NP$ (e.g. *I simply love that shirt*)	$NP + (Int) + VP_{liking} + NP$
4	$You + VP + (a) + (Int) + Adj_{pos} + NP$ (e.g. *You did a really good job*)	$NP + VP + (Det) + (Int) + Adj_{pos} + NP$
5	$You + VP + (NP) + (Int) + Adv_{pos}$ (e.g. *You play the trumpet really well*)	$NP + VP + (NP) + (Int) + Adv$
6	$You + have + (a) + (Int) + Adj_{pos} + NP$ (e.g. *You have a very nice bag*)	$NP + have + (Det) + (Int) + Adj_{pos} + NP$
7	$What + (a) + Adj_{pos} + NP$ (e.g. *What a nice bag*)	$What + (a) + Adj_{pos} + NP$
8	$Adj_{pos} + NP$ (e.g. *Nice bag*)	$Adj_{pos} + NP$
9	$Isn't + NP + Adj_{pos}$ (e.g. *Isn't this bag nice?*)	$Isn't + NP + Adj_{pos}$

The structures in Table 6.1a allow for intermittent adverbials (typically prepositional or adverb phrases), which may occur in several slots within a clause, and for other intermittent items typically found in speech (hesitation markers, discourse markers etc.). Moreover, the order of determiner and intensifier in a clause may vary, which means that, for example, Type 2 can be realised as *That's really a nice coat* or *That's a really nice coat.*

During the analysis, it turned out that more than the nine syntactic patterns mentioned above were relevant for the press conference data. The following seven additional patterns could be identified, each of them occurring at least ten times in the dataset:[6]

Table 6.1b. Additional syntactic compliment formulas in ESC-PC

Type	Syntactic formula	Examples from the data
10	(Int) + AdjP$_{pos}$	*very nice* [IRL2]
11	NP + VP$_{copula}$ + (Int) + Adj$_{pos.emot.}$ + (PP/clause)	*we are very satisfied with the sound* [BOS1] *we're extremely proud to have niamh as our representative* [IRL2]
12	NP + VP$_{copula}$ + (Det) + (Adj$_{int}$) + NP$_{pos}$	⟨spel⟩ *nrk* ⟨/spel⟩ *are magicians* [ARM1] *she's a total pro* [IRL2]
13	Det + *favourite* + VP$_{copula}$ + NP	*my favourite is sweden* [LAT1]
14	NP + VP + (Det) + (Int) + (Adj$_{int}$) + NP$_{pos}$	*you got some really (.) huge fans over there* [ALB]
15	THANK/GRAT + *for/on* + (Det) + (Int) + Adj$_{pos}$ + NP	*thanks for this wonderful performance* [CYP2] *congratulation on very good song* [AZE1]
16	NP + VP + (NP) + Prep + (Det) + (Int) + Adj$_{pos}$ + NP	*olen has played with the most famous singers in italy* [ALB1] *i have to produce the track with lovely jonathan* [CYP1]

As has been outlined before, the prominence of Type 10 is a general phenomenon of language use in conversation, where turns may consist only of individual phrases instead of full clauses. As constructions involving positive emotional adjectives (e.g. *to be proud/inspired/satisfied/happy/honoured* etc.) appear regularly in compliments in the dataset, this structure was classified as Type 11. Patterns 13 and 15 are formulas that are typical of ESC press conferences, because they are used to talk about favoured

---

6. New abbreviations in Table 6.1b: Adj$_{pos.emot.}$ = adjective of positive emotion; PP = prepositional phrase; Adj$_{int}$ = intensifying adjective; NP$_{pos}$ = semantically positive noun phrase; THANK/GRAT = thanking/congratulation; Prep = preposition.

contestants (Type 13) or to express thanks or congratulations to artists (Type 15). Types 12 and 14 involve clauses in which the positive evaluation is mainly carried by a noun. Finally, Type 16 covers structures in which the positive adjective is embedded in an adverbial prepositional phrase.

Table 6.2 gives the frequencies of the 16 syntactic formulas in the press conference data:

Table 6.2. Frequencies of syntactic compliment formulas in ESC-PC

Type	Absolute frequency	Percentage
1	278	26.7%
2	122	11.7%
3	101	9.7%
4	27	2.6%
5	18	1.7%
6	69	6.6%
7	2	0.2%
8	44	4.2%
9	1	0.1%
10	66	6.3%
11	45	4.3%
12	27	2.6%
13	10	1.0%
14	15	1.4%
15	11	1.1%
16	19	1.8%
other	168	16.1%

The three most common patterns (Types 1, 2, 3) in the AmE/NZE data are also the most frequent patterns in ESC-PC. Among the nine patterns identified by Manes and Wolfson (1981), patterns 7 and 9, exclamative clauses (*What a…*) and negative polarity questions (*Isn't…?*), hardly occur at all in the ELF data. As these two types taken together account for only 3 out of 1043 compliment tokens, it can be concluded that the ELF speakers studied here almost exclusively voice compliments as declarative clauses or, less commonly, independent phrases. This may be an outcome of the form-follows-function principle, because non-declarative clause structures are often associated with other pragmatic functions (for example, asking for reassurance or expressing dislike). A concentration on declarative clauses and phrases can therefore be interpreted as a means of narrowing the gap between semantic and pragmatic meaning. Among the other, less frequent types, two more can be identified that are fairly common: Type 6 (a structure involving the verb *have*; 6.6%) and Type 10 (independent adjective phrases; 6.9%). All other types are marginal and have percentages of less than 5%. Patterns other than the 16 formulas identified in the data amount to 16.1% in total.

Even though the top three structures are identical to those identified for native varieties of English, the quantification shows that compliment structures in the ELF corpus are far more heterogeneous and that compliments in this community of practice are therefore less formulaic than in native English varieties in general. Table 6.3 contrasts the percentaged frequencies of earlier studies on American English data and New Zealand English data with ESC-PC:

Table 6.3. Frequencies of syntactic compliment formulas in AmE, NZE and ESC-PC

Type	AmE (Manes & Wolfson 1981: 120)	NZE (Holmes 1987: 529)	ESC-PC
1	53.6%	48.0%	26.7%
2	16.1%	12.0%	11.7%
3	14.9%	18.0%	9.7%
other	15.4%	22.0%	51.9%

In comparison to the two native datasets, the percentage of the most frequent pattern (Type 1) is much lower in ESC-PC (26.7% vs. around 50% in AmE and NZE). As a consequence, patterns other than the first three types amount to more than half of the compliment tokens in the ELF data (51.9%), while they only amount to 15.4% and 22.0% in the AmE and NZE data respectively.[7]

The higher heterogeneity is an outcome of three central aspects. Firstly, the ritualised practices of the community observed are responsible for the fact that some additional compliment formulas are more important than in everyday conversations (notably Types 13 and 15). Secondly, the higher degree of heterogeneity is also likely to be due to structural differences in the phrasing of compliments across European languages. For example, structural Type 3, which involves a verb of liking (*I love/like…*), is not equally common across European languages, and its frequency in the ELF corpus is accordingly somewhat lower than in the native corpora (AmE: 15.4%, NZE: 22.0% vs. ELF: 9.7%). Such effects document once more the hybridity of European ELF. Another factor that may have contributed to this difference is research design. As the

---

7.   Note that the European ELF data behave similarly to BrE in this respect, because Creese (1991) found a lower degree of formulaicness in her BrE data compared to AmE.

earlier studies have relied on the notebook method, it is possible that they have missed less prototypical kinds of compliments, whereas the research design of the present corpus-based study facilitated their inclusion.

Among the four word classes that may carry the positive evaluation in a compliment (adjective, verb, noun and adverb), adjectives are clearly most frequently used in the ELF data (just like in the native varieties). Out of 1,043 compliments, 809 (77.6%) incorporate a semantically positive adjective.[8] Table 6.4 lists the most frequent evaluative adjectives of compliments in AmE (Manes & Wolfson 1981: 117),[9] NZE (Holmes 1986: 490) and ESC-PC.[10]

Table 6.4. Most frequent evaluative adjectives in compliments in AmE, NZE and ESC-PC

Rank	AmE Manes and Wolfson (1981: 117)	NZE (Holmes 1986: 490)	ESC-PC
1	nice	nice (100)	good (135)
2	good	good (60)	great (100)
3	beautiful	lovely (42)	beautiful (87)
4	pretty	beautiful (34)	nice (49)
5	great	great (25)	amazing (41)

With respect to the choice of adjectives, the native data and the ELF data turn out to be relatively similar to each other. Of the five most frequent adjectives in AmE and NZE compliments, four are also found in the top five in the ELF data, even if in a different ranking order: *good*, *great*, *beautiful* and *nice* occupy the top four spots. The adjective *lovely*, which is only in the top five in the NZE data, ranks somewhat lower in the ELF data (rank 10). *Pretty* is in the top five in the AmE data but is used rarely in the ELF corpus. As far as the structural make-up in terms of syntax and lexis is concerned, one can conclude from these results that the compliments in ESC-PC are similar to native English compliments in the structure types they prefer. At the same time, it is evident that the ELF data, especially on the syntactic level, exhibit a higher degree of heterogeneity, which can be assumed to be partly caused by the specific requirements of the context and transfer of structures from speakers' L1 to English.

---

8.   Otherwise the positive evaluation is carried by verbs (118 tokens), nouns (64 tokens) or adverbs (22 tokens). In 30 compliments, no central positive lexical item could be located.

9.   Manes and Wolfson (1981) do not provide absolute frequencies for the adjectives in their data.

10.   For reasons of comparability, adjectives of positive emotion (see Type 11) were not included in this quantification, because these were evidently not incorporated in Holmes' (1986) study. Comparative and superlative forms are included under the positive forms listed.

6.7   Functional aspects of compliments in ESC-PC

As cross-national solidarity building is crucial to the European project, positive politeness strategies (Brown & Levinson 1987) such as complimenting play a central role in negotiating Europeanness. With compliments, Europeanness can be constructed through the positive evaluation of attributes of European fellow citizens, who often come from a national background other than that of the complimenter. Compared to the compliments studied in earlier research, the compliments paid at ESC press conferences therefore fulfil notably different functions. A decisive contextual aspect shaping their use is that they represent public compliments that are meant to be heard by the pan-European audience and not just by the complimentee as in more private conversations.

A central structural consequence of this function is the high occurrence of compliments voiced in the third person. Such compliments achieve two things at the same time: firstly, they compliment the receiver and, secondly, they praise him or her in front of the pan-European audience. This already indicates that complimenting is highly strategic in this context. Patterns of complimenting behaviour at the press conferences are likely to be in tune with the behaviour that is normatively expected in a pan-European media context (in the sense of Watt's (2003) politic behaviour). In other words, it can be assumed that the way participants use compliments in this community of practice tells us something about ritualised strategies of creating pan-European solidarity.

The frequency of compliment topics sheds light on which concepts are generally valued in the community of practice at hand. Out of 1,043 compliments, 505 are on ability (48.4%), 107 on appearance (10.3%), 238 on personality (22.8%), and 193 on possessions (18.5%). The high frequency of ability compliments contrasts with other studies on Anglophone cultures such as the US, in which appearance was generally found to be the most prominent topic, whereas at ESC press conferences it is the least frequent one. However, given the task-orientedness of the present context it is anything but surprising that ability compliments occur most often, simply because participants commonly discuss the musical performances of the preceding rehearsals. Moreover, the fact that this is a public media context may also be responsible for the relative rarity of appearance compliments compared to more private contexts. The frequency of possession compliments (18.5%) may seem rather high for a context like press conferences. The kinds of complimented possessions in this context again differ drastically from more private contexts. In the latter, people often compliment each other on material possessions that could in principle be handed over to the complimenter, and this is why such compliments are sometimes perceived as expressing envy and therefore as face-threatening. At ESC press conferences, by contrast, the possessions complimented can in most cases not be handed over to the complimentee.

For example, cases in which lead artists received compliments on their songs were counted as possession compliments.[11] Similarly compliments on any aspect of the host city Oslo were counted as compliments on possessions of NOR. Since it is obvious that such possessions cannot easily be given to the complimentee, the respective compliments appear less potentially face-threatening than more prototypical types of possession compliments.

Five major patterns of paying compliments can be identified. The first one concerns compliments from journalists to artists. Such compliments are often employed strategically by press representatives, namely before they voice their actual questions. In general, asking people a question constitutes a threat to the addressee's negative face. In the present context, this face threat is relatively high because interviewers and interviewees are strangers, which in other contexts prohibits similarly investigative behaviour. Compliments seem to be employed here in order to pave the way for a following journalistic question. This is illustrated by Extracts 15 and 16:

> (15)
> MP1: *hello i'm sören from german radio good morning (.) uh <u>what a great song to start a semi-final</u> and uh <u>this has to be the most enjoyable press conference so far</u>*
> KS: *@@@*
> MA1: *⟨screaming⟩ yea::h ⟨/screaming⟩*
> MP1: *so now i have a question about the video that you made uh was it shot in a flat or uh do you do you went into the studio to shoot it because it looked like it was filmed in one flat* [LIT1]

In this passage, a German journalist (MP1) talks to the Lithuanian delegation. After introducing himself, he pays the delegation members two compliments, one on their ESC entry (*what a great song to start a semi-final*) and one on their press conference (*this has to be the most enjoyable press conference so far*). It is only after these two compliments that the journalist turns to asking his actual question about the shooting of the videoclip. Note that the question whether the clip was shot in a flat (and not in a studio) may also be read as a criticism, namely that of having invested only a small budget to promote one's national representative. As criticism typically represents a threat to the addressee's positive face, the face-saving mechanisms commonly associated with compliments are here used to create a background in front of which criticism can be voiced.

Extract 16 is taken from the Belarusian press conference. It shows how a journalist first congratulates and compliments the artists on their song, before he strikes a more critical note in his question about the selection procedure in BLR.

---

11.   Note that compliments on songs that were directed to composers or lyricists were counted as ability rather than possession compliments.

(16)

MP1: hello uhm <u>congratulations on a great song</u> uhm but that initially you had selected another song for belarus in a completely different register it was in a more uptempo number were you not satisfied with that song that you decided to change it to a ballad? [BLR1]

Again the compliment paves the way for further investigative behaviour. The journalist orients to the contrast between saving the artists' positive face through a compliment and the following critical question, which clearly threatens the artists' positive face, by means of the conjunction *but*. He confronts the artists with the fact that the group had originally selected another song that they decided to replace relatively shortly before the nomination deadline (without letting the Belarusian public have its say).

Somewhat less frequent but still fairly common are compliments in the opposite direction, from artists to journalists. These are just as strategic as their counterparts. Complimenting journalists functions as a solidarity-creating device that is supposed to make journalists more well-disposed towards the artists. After having received a compliment, it is usually harder for a journalist to ask a critical question. In the following extract, for instance, the Irish lead artist (*FA1*) compliments a Luxembourgish journalist (MP5) on his t-shirt before he has even started to ask a question:

(17)

MP5: hello niamh
FA1: ⟨about MP5's t-shirt⟩ <u>i'm loving yellow very ⟨6⟩ nice</u> @@@ ⟨/6⟩
MP5: ⟨6⟩ oh thank you @@ ⟨/6⟩ the flash is on again [...] [IRL2]

As the following extract shows, once a critical question has in fact been asked, the artists may feel an even greater need to resort to complimenting as a means of creating solidarity:

(18)

MP1: [...] (.) there are a lot of people in the audience who write on weblogs and forums bloggers (.) you once made a very controversial comment about forums on the web (.) uhm would you can you repeat that comment and explain what you meant
MA1: [...] i didn't know you know (.) no that uh congratulation <u>you're a very nice reporter good reporter</u> [BOS1]

In this passage, a journalist (*MP1*) confronts the Bosnian lead artist (MA1) with a negative statement the latter had made about bloggers in the past. This direct way of confrontation is relatively unusual for ESC press conferences, where participants generally collaborate to avoid conflicts. The confrontation is intensified by the presence of numerous ESC bloggers in the audience. This induces the artist (after a long stretch of talk which has been left out here and in which he tries to qualify his earlier statement) to give a compliment to the journalist, praising his skills as a reporter (*congratulation you're a very nice reporter good reporter*). This may be taken as a (successful) attempt to prevent any further conflictual interaction.

The third pattern concerns delegation members paying compliments to the team of the Norwegian broadcaster *NRK* (the organiser of the ESC) or to NOR as the host country. It is interesting to note that such compliments hardly ever occur at the press conferences of the Norwegian delegation. This points to the fact that complimenting the organiser is a clearly transnational business that is supposed to create solidarity between the host country and the various national delegations. The following two extracts illustrate this practice.

> (19)
> *MA1:* [...] *uh every city is different and uh (.) i uh <u>i like it very much here</u> i just arrived today but i uh have uh other experience in norway <u>i like the country very much</u> and uh i'm happy to be here again* [GER1]

> (20)
> *MA1: the rehearsal went very well the wind machines work perfect and uh <u>i'm impressed by the uhm professional attitude of everyone organising the rehearsals process</u> because everything is done on time everything is very disciplined and i admire that* [UKR2]

In Extract 19, a German delegation member (MA1) repeatedly asserts that he likes NOR, whereas in Extract 20, a Ukrainian delegation member compliments the team of the Norwegian broadcaster on its professionality. The strategicness with which such compliments may be employed at ESC press conferences is furthermore illustrated by the following extract from the Bulgarian press conference:

> (21)
> *KS: tell us about the rehearsal how did that go*
> *MA1: uh guys first of all i want thank to all of the crew of eurovision <u>amazing job</u> (.) <u>amazing job</u> (.) the stage is so sweet so beautiful uh (.) with your permission (.) i prefer to speak in my mother language*
> *KS: of course*
> *MA1: can i?*
> *KS: yeah*
> *MA1: yeah thank you ⟨Norwegian⟩ takk ⟨/Norwegian⟩*
> {*MA1 speaks Bulgarian (11)*} [BUL1]

In this exchange, the Bulgarian lead artist (MA1) first compliments the organising team on its work and then asks in the same turn for the permission to use his mother tongue instead of English. The reasoning behind this strategy seems to be that complimenting the host broadcaster paves the way for using one's L1 for the rest of the press conference, which may well be interpreted as an act of privileging national over transnational European affiliations. The importance that is attributed to these compliments by the speaker can also be gauged from the fact that he is so absorbed with complimenting that he does not answer the moderator's initial question about the rehearsal. After the moderator has granted that the artist may speak Bulgarian, the latter thanks the audience both in English and in Norwegian, which again represents a tokenistic attempt to tone down the national indexical potential of using one's mother tongue in front of a pan-European audience.

Another main pattern involves delegation members complimenting other nations or artists representing other nations. Such practices help the contestants to construct themselves as not exclusively nationally focused. Keeping in mind that it is first and foremost the purpose of these press conferences to promote one's own entry, such compliments can be understood as a form of national crossing that carries European prestige in this context. When the respective compliment targets other artists, it enables delegation members to demonstrate awareness of their European fellow contestants and to signal that they appreciate good music, independently of the national background of the performing artist. A very common complimenting phenomenon at ESC press conferences is therefore the mentioning of personal favourites, as illustrated by the following excerpt:

> (22)
> FA4: *my favourite is the* (.) *uh girl from ukraine* (.) *i think she has a beautiful voice and the song is also with a pretty deep meaning* (.) *and uhm my second fa- uh actually they're both* (.) *my first favourites is the ukrainian girl and the lithuanians* [LAT1]

In Extract 22, a Latvian artist (FA4) compliments the Ukrainian contestant as being her favourite together with the group from LIT. The Ukrainian artist is complimented more specifically, namely on her voice and the lyrics of her song (*she has a beautiful voice and the song is also with a pretty deep meaning*). Note that in these acts of complimenting the complimentees are invariably constructed along national lines (as *girl from ukraine* and as *lithuanians*), even though a strictly personal (and therefore denationalised) reference by the artists' names would have been equally possible. This indicates that it is particularly important to explicate that one pays compliments to highlight positive aspects connected to (participants from) other nations, not one's own.

Compliments directed at countries other than one's own also have an important denationalising effect. The cross-European solidarity-enhancing potential of such compliments is particularly evident in the following exchange that took place during the Danish press conference:

> (23)
> FA2: [...] (.) *danish people i just love them*
> MA1: *ooh*
> FA1: *we love YOU*
> MA1: *thank you* (.) [...] [DAN1]

FA2 is a backing singer of the Danish lead artists but originally comes from SWE. To dissolve any thoughts of cross-national animosities, she states that she loves the Danish (*danish people i just love them*), and this is immediately reciprocated by one of the Danish lead artists (*we love YOU*).

The final common complimentary pattern concerns national delegates paying compliments to their fellow delegation members. This is a rather sensitive business, which is caused by an ideological dilemma that, on the one hand, forbids artists to praise themselves and, on the other hand, urges them to promote their national delegation in the contest. Paying compliments to members of one's own national delegation can be viewed as an outcome of this dilemma, because it helps delegates to say something positive about their national team without saying something positive about themselves. It is apparent that compliments to members of one's own national delegation (as opposed to those directed to other competing teams) are not usually framed in terms of nationality, i.e. complimentees are constructed as artists with great abilities, personality or appearance and not as national representatives. This means that the national function that such compliments fulfil, namely that of promoting one's own national team in front of the (potentially voting) European audience, is concealed. The following passage taken from the Azerbaijani press conference illustrates these mechanisms:

> (24)
> FA2: *i'm* ⟨pvc⟩ *accompinated* ⟨/pvc⟩ <u>*by four talented and beautiful back-up vocalists*</u> samantha powell marlene strand anna bergenholtz and johanna eriksson and <u>*it's really amazing to work with such talented beautiful girls*</u>
> KS: maybe you all girls can introduce yourself and tell us uh a little bit about what you have been doing before you met uh safura
> FA3: oh wow @ uh my name is anna bergenholtz i'm from sweden uh well i've been working as a singer as a dancer and as a performer before i met safura and <u>*i'm very very happy to work with her*</u> <u>*she's such a talented uh singer*</u> and a woman (.) it's so much fun
> *FA4*: i'm samantha powell i'm from the ⟨spel⟩ uk ⟨/spel⟩ based in los angeles uhm i'm actually a record producer and songwriter (.) uhm but <u>*love the song*</u> wanted to back up safura have some fun uhm but yeah normally i'm in the studio (.) pressing buttons writing songs that's me
> FA5: and i'm marlene strand from sweden and i've been uh working in a lot of studios and as samantha been songs and uh i've had a band and made a lot of live performances and so and <u>*safura is such a great singer*</u> so <u>*it's a pleasure ⟨3⟩ to be ⟨/3⟩ with her*</u>
> FA1: ⟨3⟩ thank you ⟨/3⟩ [AZE2]

In this extract, we see that FA2 (translating the lead artist's [FA1] utterances into English) initiates this sequence by complimenting the group of backing singers, describing them as *four talented and beautiful back-up vocalists* and stating that *it's really amazing to work with such talented beautiful girls*. This is a common pattern found at ESC press conferences, where one delegation member may introduce the rest of the delegation to the audience. After this initial series of compliments, the moderator (KS) asks the backing singers (FA3, *FA4*, FA5) to introduce themselves. Here it becomes evident that when the backing singers talk about themselves, they never praise their own positive qualities but give a rather neutral account of their professional lives. The compliments in their utterances are invariably directed at the lead singer (identified as *Safura*). The entire sequence of introductions and compliments is free of explicit national Azerbaijani construction (even though all delegates are in fact complimented). The denationalisation effect is in this extract further supported by team member crossing because the backing singers are originally from SWE and the UK, not from AZE.

It is remarkable that instances of miscommunication in connection with compliments occur very rarely in this community of practice, despite the fact that one would expect complimenting norms to vary across European national cultures. One potential instance of such a misunderstanding was already discussed above (Extract 3). Apart from that episode, there is only one more extract in the entire dataset that would allow for a similar reading:

> (25)
> *FP1: kristina from russian delegation uhm <u>you have an interesting t-shirt</u> who is uh on your t-shirt and does it mean something?*
> *MA1: no it doesn't mean anything for me (4) bob marley but uh it doesn't mean anything for me because i i think i'm the opposite of him (.) why do you like it? it's bob marley (.) do you like it? (.) i can give it to you if you want [ISR2]*

In this extract, a Russian journalist (FP1) tells the Israeli lead singer (MA1) that he is wearing an *interesting t-shirt*. The evading reaction of the artist may be taken as evidence that he has interpreted this utterance as a compliment, but it also suggests that the compliment is interpreted by him as face-threatening rather than face-saving. First he outright denies that the t-shirt carries any deeper meaning for him, without responding to the journalist's question about who is pictured on the t-shirt. The fact that the journalist seems to be more interested in the person on the t-shirt than in her interviewee clearly threatens the positive face of the artist. After a four-second break, he finally answers this question, but he clearly distances himself from the depicted person (*bob marley but uh it doesn't mean anything for me because i i think i'm the opposite of him*). In the end, the artist even offers to give the t-shirt to the journalist, which may be taken as an indication that the complimentee has taken the journalist's utterance to express a desire to possess the object complimented on.

With the exception of the two occurrences discussed above (Extracts 3 and 25), there is no evidence that participants at ESC press conferences have difficulty with the employment and negotiation of compliments. As has already been shown in Extract 24 above, these ELF speakers also demonstrate a sense of avoiding self-praise, which is additionally illustrated in the following extract:

> (26)
> *KS: what do you do*
> *MA2: uh well i'm from italy i was raised and born in albania so i grow up in (.) in albania so i'm coming directly from rome cause ardit asked me (.) to take care of this incredible thing* i'm so happy to be here in norway *(.)* it's really cool i like it *i like the family i like the (.) the whole thing (.) i played violin actually that's why that's the best thing i can do probably*
> *MA1: maybe maybe he doesn't want to to talk about of himself because it's a little bit difficult but* olen has played with the most famous singers in italy *(.) he has played now (.) from uh in the first of may which is in italy it's a very big event and he he was performing there which was televising live (.) uh and it's an an audience more than ten million viewers (.) so and uh* he's one of the best violinists *[…] [ALB1]*

In response to the moderator's question, the Albanian artist (MA2) provides a neutral description of his regional origins and profession (playing the violin). Furthermore, he compliments NOR and the ESC in general. This induces another delegation member (MA1) to take over the floor and praise MA1's achievements as a violinist, explaining that *maybe he doesn't want to to talk about of himself because it's a little bit difficult*. In other words, MA2 delivers the compliments that MA1 is socially prohibited to pay.

On the other hand, *when* self-praise is indeed voiced, this is normally done by quoting a third party who is said to have given the compliment in the first place (see Speer 2011 on third party compliments):

> (27)
> *MA1: […] uhm dana international uh uh uh she told me that she's very proud and she uh wishes me success and* she's think that the song is uh very beautiful *[…] [ISR2]*

> (28)
> *MA1: well uh we've had a very good feedback uh there are* a lot of people saying wow great song we love portugal congratulations *[…] uh and uh okay you know we have been with some fans in europe uh and we have uh (.)* they all say way well great voice filipa great song *so i some of them are being kind i guess but uh uhm there's more than words and you f- you you can feel the atmosphere […] [POR2]*

In these two extracts, the Israeli and Portuguese artists state that other people they have talked to (former ESC winner *Dana International*; *a lot of people*; *some fans in europe*) have complimented them on their performances. Reproducing such compliments second-hand seems to be the only way in which (national) self-praise can legitimately be voiced in this community of practice.

Furthermore, the ELF speakers at the press conferences demonstrate an understanding that compliments may in fact be insincere and politically motivated. This is already expressed in Extract 28 above, in which the Portuguese delegate says about the complimenters that *some of them are being kind*, meaning that people may pay insincere compliments in order to be friendly. This indicates that the phatic dimension of compliments is at times deemed to be more important than sincerity (Ruhi & Doğan 2001: 381). Similar attitudes are expressed in the following two extracts:

(29)
MA1: well after first rehearsal i don't know if i'm allowed to say this but uh the man that's working uh the stage manager he said sound depart- sound department's got a new favourite so if he's not made to say that we're good [BOS2]

Again we see here a form of self-praise that is expressed as a third-party compliment (*he said*). At the same time the Bosnian artist is aware that such compliments may in fact not be genuine but rather belong to the routine behaviours of good hosts (*if he's not made to say that*). In Extract 30, one member of the Turkish delegation compliments the Turkish band and stresses that this is not an empty compliment (*i'm not saying that cause they are on my right right now looking at me*), which in turn implies that many other compliments indeed are somewhat less than sincere:

(30)
FA2: well uhm it's very interesting cause uhm (.) to work with a rock band is already a challenge […] and i guess (.) we were really blessed and extremely lucky (.) and i'm not saying that cause they are on my right right now looking at me but we really really were blessed to meet amazing human beings and amazing performers […] [TUR2]

The analysis of the functions of compliments at ESC press conferences demonstrates that these European ELF speakers are anything but pragmatically deficient language users, despite the fact that most of them are non-native speakers of English and pragmatic conventions are likely to differ across European national cultures. What emanates from the compliment data above is that the members of this community of practice are able to successfully negotiate such cultural differences and that they employ compliments strategically as a pertinent solidarity-creating device across national boundaries, which in turn allows speakers to downplay their national affiliations in front of the pan-European audience. In sum, the press conference participants document an understanding of the use of compliments as a solidarity-creating device in transnational communication. Beyond this, they are aware of the difficulties associated with (national) self-praise and the strategicness and potential insincerity with which compliments may be employed.

6.8   Compliments, gender and sexuality in ESC-PC

The way in which compliments are used at ESC press conferences also sheds light on the construction of gender, sexual desire and sexual identities via ELF in this transnational community of practice. As has been outlined in Chapter 6.3, previous sociolinguistic research on complimenting behaviour in Western Anglophone cultures detected several patterns associated with gender and sexuality. The present chapter provides similar analyses, taking note of complimenter and complimentee sex, complimentary topics, and intensification in compliments.

With respect to sex of complimenter and complimentee, earlier research found that compliments generally are most frequently used among women and least frequently among men, with mixed-sex combinations falling in between. In other words, women were found to both pay and receive more compliments than men in Western Anglophone cultures.

Table 6.5. Complimenter sex in ESC-PC

Compliments by female speakers	Compliments by male speakers
female delegates: 388	male delegates: 380
female journalists: 13	male journalists: 150
	male moderator: 76
total: 401 compliments	total: 606 compliments

As can be seen in Table 6.5, men pay considerably more compliments in ESC-PC than women.[12] However, these absolute frequencies do not tell us much. There are two main reasons why men use more compliments. The first is that, among the journalists in the audience, there are clearly fewer female than male press representatives. In this respect, the audience resembles ESC fan communities, which have been found to consist mainly of (gay) male fan members. The second reason is that the moderator, who frequently gives compliments to the national delegations, is male. As far as delegation members are concerned, the distribution between female and male members is more balanced and this is also reflected in similar absolute compliment frequencies. Judging from these figures, one cannot conclude that men use more compliments than women. But still it needs to be pointed out that ESC press conferences are a context in which men seem to be less inhibited by normative restrictions associated with complimenting behaviour: men give compliments very frequently in this community of practice.

---

12.   Note that 36 compliments given by female speakers translating male speakers or vice versa have been excluded from this quantification.

Table 6.6 provides a similar quantification for sex of complimentee:

Table 6.6. Complimentee sex in ESC-PC

Female complimentees	Mixed-gender complimentees	Male complimentees
female delegates: 308	delegates: 112	male delegates: 287
female journalists: 1	journalists: 3	male journalists: 35
female organisers: 2	organisers: 142	male moderator: 5
	Norway: 83	
	other nation(s): 65	
total: 311	total: 405	total: 327

We can see that female and male participants are complimented in roughly equal frequencies (311 and 327 compliments respectively). The somewhat higher absolute frequency of male complimentees is again due to the fact that the audience comprises few female journalists and therefore compliments directed at male journalists (35 tokens) are more frequent than those targeting female journalists (only one token). It is also apparent that most compliments are received by delegation members (in total 707), which is not surprising for press conferences as an interactional genre. A substantial amount of compliments is also paid to the organisers (149 tokens in total, including the moderator), the host country (83 tokens) and other nations (65), whereas compliments paid to journalists are more exceptional (39 tokens). Again it can be said that ESC press conferences turn out to be a context in which male participants frequently receive compliments – just like female participants.

For the exploration of sexual construction via compliments, one needs to look at the relationship between complimenter and complimentee. The respective quantification is given in Table 6.7.

Table 6.7. Complimenter-complimentee dyads in ESC-PC

Compliments by women: 401	Compliments by men: 606
→ to women: 108 (26.9%)	→ to women: 197 (32.5%)
→ to men: 137 (34.2%)	→ to men: 185 (30.5%)

Table 6.7 shows how many compliments women and men in the data gave to female and male complimentees (mixed-sex groups of complimentees ignored). The percentaged frequencies are relatively similar to each other, ranging from 26.9% for female-female compliments to 34.2% for female-male compliments. When testing for statistical significance (here and in the following by means of the chi^2-test), one finds that there are no significant differences between female and male complimenters: women and

men pay roughly equal amounts of compliments to women and men. The evidence therefore suggests that if complimenting behaviour is to be viewed as gendered or sexualised, the message conveyed is rather one of gender similarity than of gender difference. Both women and men can easily pay compliments to women and men in this context and cross-sex compliments are equally common as same-sex compliments. This finding contrasts with earlier research, in which female-female compliments were generally found to be most frequent and male-male compliments least frequent. In fact, it is in this context the female-female compliments that show the lowest percentaged frequency.

To test whether female and male complimenters used different syntactic formulas for their compliments, only those formulas that occurred in higher frequencies (more than 40 tokens in the data) were analysed. For the structures with lower frequencies, statistical significance cannot be tested (**indicates statistically significant differences).

Table 6.8. Complimenter sex and compliment syntax in ESC-PC

Female complimenters	Male complimenters
Type 1: 106 (26.4%)	Type 1: 161 (26.6%)
Type 2: 51 (12.7%)	Type 2: 66 (16.5%)
Type 3: 54 (13.5%)**($p = 0.001$)	Type 3: 44 (7.3%)
Type 6: 26 (6.5%)	Type 6: 42 (6.9%)
Type 8: 11 (2.7%)	Type 8: 33 (5.4%)
Type 10: 19 (4.7%)	Type 10: 46 (7.6%)
Type 11: 20 (5.0%)	Type 11: 23 (3.8%)
[all compliments: 401]	[all compliments: 606]

As is shown in Table 6.8, women and men overall do not use different compliment structures. Of the seven structures tested, six show no significant difference between the sexes. Only pattern 3 is used significantly more often by women ($p = 0.001$). In this type, the positive evaluation is expressed by a verb of liking. Most common among these verbs are the forms *like* (47 tokens) and *love* (44 tokens). Even though compliments with the verb *love* can be considered to possess a higher emotional intensity and are therefore compatible with female speech stereotypes, women and men use such compliments in roughly equal frequencies (22 vs. 21 tokens) in ESC-PC.

Compliments may also be gendered because they frequently contain intensifiers that cause them to be perceived as highly affective speech acts (Ruhi & Doğan 2001: 371). Studies on intensifier use have figured prominently in research on typically female speech features. This research area includes studies making observations on stereotypes of "women's language" (Lakoff 1975; Kramer 1977;

Giles, Scholes & Young 1983; Gottburgsen 2000: 174; Motschenbacher 2006, 2007) as well as a range of sociolinguistic studies which generally find that women use more intensifiers than men (e.g. Bradac, Mulac & Thompson 1995; Grimm 2008; Lapadat & Seesahai 1977: 7; McMillan et al. 1977; Mulac, Seibold & Farris 2000; Stenström 1999; Thomson & Murachver 2001; Xiao & Tao 2007: 248, and summarising, Mulac 1999: 90–91). Men did not use significantly more intensifiers than women in any of these studies. Such findings have often been explained, rather stereotypically, in terms of women being more likely to use hyperbole and emotionalised speech.

To study the use of intensifiers in compliments given at ESC press conferences, only those compliments were analysed that contained an adjective that was intensifiable. Thus, all comparative and superlative adjectival forms were not included in the calculation because they do not normally allow for intensification. The following three extracts illustrate cases of compliments in ESC-PC that incorporate a plain adjective (Extract 31), an intensified adjective (Extract 32) or a multiply intensified adjective (Extract 33). The degree of affectiveness is generally perceived to increase across these three types:

> (31) *FA1: the sound was <u>perfect</u>* [MAC2]
> (32) **MP1*: the butterfly dresses are uh <u>completely fabulous</u>* [BLR2]
> (33) *FA1: and both of them have <u>very very beautiful</u> voices* [CYP1]

Table 6.9 shows how often female and male complimenters intensified adjectives in their compliments:

Table 6.9. Sex and adjective intensification in compliments in ESC-PC

Compliments by women	Compliments by men
with plain adjective: 166 (57.6%)	with plain adjective: 239 (53.3%)
with intensified adjective: 122 (42.4%)	with intensified adjective: 209 (46.7%)
multiple intensification: 12 (4.2%)	multiple intensification: 20 (4.5%)

There are no statistically significant differences between women's and men's compliments with respect to adjective intensification. Men use intensifiers just as frequently as women do and can therefore be said to be equally affective in their speech behaviour.

The next aspect to be explored is compliment topics in relation to gender. Table 6.10 gives the frequencies with which female and male complimenters used a certain compliment topic:

Table 6.10. Complimenter sex and compliment topics in ESC-PC

Female complimenters' topics	Male complimenters' topics
ability: 165 (41.1%)	ability: 323 (53.3%)**
appearance: 41 (10.2%)	appearance: 62 (10.2%)
personality: 120 (29.9%)**	personality: 110 (18.2%)
possession: 75 (18.7%)	possession: 111 (18.3%)
[total: 401]	[total: 606]

Earlier research found that appearance compliments were more frequent among women whereas compliments on ability and possessions were more frequent among men. In ESC-PC, by contrast, both women and men compliment most frequently on ability (41.1% and 53.3% respectively) and least frequently on appearance (both 10.2%). For appearance and possession, the percentaged frequencies are very similar for women and men. Still there are two statistically significant differences: men compliment more often on ability ($p < 0.001$), while women compliment more often on personality ($p < 0.001$).

Table 6.11 relates compliment topics to sex of complimentee:

Table 6.11. Complimentee sex and compliment topics in ESC-PC

Topics women are complimented on	Topics men are complimented on
ability: 164 (52.7%)	ability: 161 (49.2%)
appearance: 51 (16.4%)	appearance: 38 (11.6%)
personality: 74 (23.8%)	personality: 82 (25.1%)
possession: 22 (7.1%)	possession: 46 (14.1%)**
[total: 311]	[total: 327]

Again more similarity than difference can be detected. Both women and men are most often complimented on their abilities (52.7% and 49.2%). Personality ranks second for both sexes. Appearance and possession rank third and fourth among the female-targeted compliments and show the opposite ranking order among male-targeted compliments. However, the only statistically significant difference is that men are more often complimented on possessions than women ($p = 0.004$). Viewed in total, the findings for compliment topics in relation to gender do not reflect the findings from earlier research. Over wide stretches, no gender differences can be detected at all. Those that can be identified are not particularly clear-cut either (with one of the two percentage figures being around 10% higher). This can be taken as evidence that traditional gender and sexuality norms are less effective in this community of practice.

As the sexual dimension of compliments is most obvious for appearance compliments, it is worthwhile to take a closer look at them.

Table 6.12. Gender and appearance compliments in ESC-PC

Appearance compliments by women (41 tokens)	Appearance compliments by men (62 tokens)
female-to-male: 17 (41.5%)	male-to-male: 20 (32.2%)
female-to-female: 13 (31.7%)	male-to-female: 36 (58.1%)**
female-to-mixed-gender: 11 (26.8%)**	male-to-mixed-gender: 6 (9.7%)

The distribution of appearance compliments along gendered lines given in Table 6.12 provides evidence that such compliments are indeed a gendered and sexualised business. The majority of appearance compliments are given to individuals (and more rarely groups) that are specifically gendered. Mixed-gender groups receive appearance compliments more rarely. Women give most appearance compliments (41.5%) to men and men give most of them (58.1%) to women. However, the same-sex combinations are anything but infrequent, amounting to about one third of the compliments given by women and men. Compared to earlier research, the rate of female-female compliments seems relatively low, whereas that of male-male compliments is surprisingly high. Women and men compliment men equally often (the difference between 41.5% and 32.2% is not statistically significant). On the other hand, men compliment women on their appearance more than women do ($p = 0.009$) and women pay more appearance compliments to mixed-gender groups than men do ($p = 0.022$). The ESC press conference data again departs from the patterns identified by earlier studies: neither are female-female appearance compliments most frequent nor are male-male appearance compliments least frequent.

The substantial number of male-male appearance compliments in ESC-PC can be explained by the fact that ESC press conferences are a context in which heteronormative discourses are clearly less prevalent than in other contexts. One reason for this is that many members of the audience and at least some of the national delegates involved in the press conferences are gay men. Another aspect that may play a role is that the Europeanness of the context is felt to be less compatible with traditional gender and sexuality discourses.

To conclude, the use of compliments at ESC press conferences appears to be unaffected by the traditional gender and sexuality norms commonly found to be operative in other contexts. It can therefore be argued that the high transnational European prominence of the context has an influence on the linguistic behaviour of the participants. Complimenting is practiced in a similar fashion by women and men in this community of practice, which indicates that the participants can easily violate the dominant discourses typically found on the national level without having to fear social sanctions. Especially men seem to face fewer (if any) inhibitions at ESC press conferences compared to (mainstream) Western Anglophone contexts, where compliments by and to men were found to underlie severe social restrictions. Furthermore, the consistency of gender similarity patterns across the aspects studied in the data suggests that gender similarity rather than difference has become ritualised in this community of practice.

6.9   Conclusions: Pragmatic negotiation and identity construction via ELF

The preceding chapters have provided an in-depth study of complimenting behaviour at ESC press conferences, identifying patterns of compliment frequency, structure, function and gendered and sexualised usage. With respect to frequency, it could be shown that ESC press conferences represent a community of practice in which compliments are highly common. At the same time, the hybridity of ELF was apparent in the distribution of compliment frequencies across national delegations. The press conferences of native English, less powerful and non-EU countries showed a tendency to contain more compliments than those of non-Anglophone, powerful and EU nations. On the structural level, this hybridity was also documented, namely in the shape of a greater heterogeneity in the syntactic formulas used in the European ELF data, which is likely due to the influence of speakers' L1s.

On the functional level, complimenting behaviour at ESC press conferences largely conforms to native English contexts in the sense that compliments are generally used as solidarity-creating devices. What makes the complimenting practices in this community different from those in other contexts is their publicness and transnational strategicness. European ELF communication prototypically involves transnational facework, and compliments are a prototypical means of performing this facework. Earlier research on ELF discourse has sometimes described ELF speakers as pragmatically deficient (see House 2008b: 358 on politeness in ELF talk). House (2008b: 360), for example, describes ELF speakers' communicative behaviour in relation to the discourse marker *you know* as largely "self-oriented" (despite the fact that this form is in native talk generally used as an addressee-oriented device). This finding cannot be replicated in the present study. Even though the participants at ESC press conferences come from a wide range of European national cultures, they nevertheless behave linguistically in all but a self-oriented way. Moreover, they exhibit an understanding of the importance of compliments for the context at hand, of the kinds of compliments that are deemed adequate, and of contextually appropriate compliment responses (where they occur). Viewed from an interactional perspective, these European ELF speakers engage successfully in complimentary negotiation behaviour and can therefore not be characterised as pragmatically deficient. The data documents participants' need for creating solidarity across national boundaries in this transnational European context, which is not surprising if one considers that Europe is historically the cradle of nationalism.

Another issue that the analyses of complimenting behaviour at ESC press conferences have touched upon is the role of ELF as a medium of identity construction, and more specifically of identities that go beyond Anglo-American assimilation or L2 learner status. As shown above, it is easy to draw a link between complimenting, the downtoning of national affiliations and the construction of a European orientation. They involve, for example, complimenting across European nation states and the use of more complex mechanisms to compliment members of one's own national delegation (individualisation and denationalisation, avoiding self-praise).

On the sociolinguistic level, the press conference data differs markedly from Western Anglophone contexts through the notable absence of traditional gendered and sexualised usage patterns and the prevalence of gender similarity. This effect cannot be explained in terms of the hybridity of European ELF, simply because these equality discourses have so far not been documented for complimenting behaviour in individual European national cultures. It can therefore be assumed that the transnationality of the context contributes significantly to this outcome. In the past, it has indeed been shown that traditional gender and sexuality discourses are often an integral part of the homogenisation practices pertinent to the discursive construction of the nation (Berlant & Warner 1998; Peterson 1999). This indicates that the transnational level may leave more space for alternative gender and sexuality discourses. In the community of practice of ESC press conferences, the construction of extensive gender similarity via ELF seems to have become ritualised, probably in part due to the predominance of participants that do not adhere to heteronormative imperatives.

Chapter 7

Relativisation patterns in European ELF talk

7.1   Introduction

After tackling the levels of code choice, metaliguistic comments and pragmatics in Chapters 4 to 6, the present chapter sets out to explore the structural dimension of European ELF. Whereas in the previous chapter on compliments qualitative and quantitative methods were used side by side, the current chapter uses a largely quantitative approach to look at the structural feature of relativisation and its variability in ESC-PC.

Structural linguistic categories usually lend themselves easily to quantification and corpus-based studies have yielded intriguing insights into the structural make-up of ENL and ESL varities. It can therefore be concluded that quantitative methods are indeed a useful tool for analysing linguistic structures and their variability. Quantitative methods also do not per se contradict a postmodernist approach to language and linguistic variability, especially not if they are used as just one component in triangulation with other methods (as in the present book). However, there is a crucial aspect in which the structural analyses carried out here differ from more traditional ones, namely the main purpose behind structural description and quantification. Whereas quantification of structures within corpus data has traditionally been used to find evidence for the internal structural homogeneity of English varieties and their structural divergence from other ENL and ESL varieties, the present study sets out to do exactly the opposite. The main purpose is to find evidence for the internal structural hybridity of European ELF – a hybridity that contradicts the notion of a description as a "variety" in the classic sense. Moreover, another important point is to document the fundamental overlap between ENL and ELF usage, which contests the notion of systematic differences between European ELF and native Englishes.

Chapter 7.2 presents a short overview of the areas covered by structure-oriented ELF research to date. The focus is then placed more specifically on relativisation as a feature that is stereotypically said to show idiosyncrasies in ELF usage (Chapter 7.3). The methodological underpinnings of the VARBRUL analysis to be conducted in the empirical chapters are outlined in Chapter 7.4. Based on typological considerations, relativisation practices at ESC press conferences are then related to various potentially relevant factors, namely syntactic function (Chapter 7.5), humanness of antecedent

(Chapter 7.6), the speaker's L1 background (Chapter 7.7), active speaker participation (Chapter 7.8), European region (Chapter 7.9), and EU status (Chapter 7.10). A multivariate analysis identifying the relative strengths of these individual factors is carried out in Chapter 7.11.

7.2   The structural description of ELF

As has been outlined in Chapter 2.3, (purely) structural descriptions of features are no longer viewed as primary in current ELF research, which rather sees the structural make-up of ELF as an outcome of the "form follows function" principle and therefore prioritises functional descriptions. This development is concomitant with a shift in the motivations underlying ELF research. In earlier, structure-oriented ELF research, structural features used to be described to establish ELF as a "legitimate" variety or as the potential basis of an alternative curriculum in ELT. However, now that the study of ELF has matured and forms a more coherent field with an established research agenda that departs from that of the more traditional World Englishes framework, issues such as establishing variety status and attempts at neostandardisation have been shifted to the background. Accordingly, these aspects do also not play a role in the present book and, more specifically, in the current chapter.

Still, this does not mean that structural analyses of ELF are considered dispensable or uninteresting. Structural features – however interesting they may be in themselves – are in current ELF research generally related to their functional or pragmatic value as linguistic devices that ensure communicative efficiency in ELF interactions. Additionally, structural analyses are still relevant in ELF research because they enable researchers to document the internal hybridity of ELF. This variability is more subtle than can be grasped by the traditional variety concept.

With the advent of such large ELF corpora as *VOICE* and *ELFA*, empirical studies on ELF talk have recently gained momentum. Such studies differ from earlier research on non-native speakers' linguistic practices in that they do not adopt a prescriptive stance that would relegate typical ELF features to the status of learners' errors. This strand of research rather treats the idiosyncrasy, creativity and negotiability of ELF as legitimate phenomena and highlights the fact that not all EFL speakers wish to emulate native speakers or aim at Anglo-American assimilation. A range of ELF features has been studied to date, including phatic communication and agreement tokens (Kordon 2006), repetition (Lichtkoppler 2007), formulaic language (Kecskes 2007), idiomaticity (Prodromou 2008; Seidlhofer 2009c), code switching (Klimpfinger 2007), pragmatic particles (Prodromou 2008), lexical cognates (Hülmbauer 2011) or the third person singular marker -*s* (Breiteneder 2009) (for an overview of earlier research, see Seidlhofer 2004). One of the most comprehensive studies to date is provided by

Dröschel (2011), who analysed a range of features in a corpus of intranational ELF communication between German, French and Italian L1 speakers in SUI. Features investigated in this study include the use of articles, pluralisation, tense, aspect, *if-*clauses, non-finite complements, the placement of adverbials and word order in questions. Another recent comprehensive treatment of ELF can be found in Cogo and Dewey (2012), who present the structural make-up of ELF in the light of pragmatic mechanisms discussing, for example, lexicogrammar, adaptive processes, meaning negotiation, backchannels or simultaneous talk.

Many of the studies mentioned above provide evidence for the form-follows-function nature of ELF talk. However, this principle surfaces in different ways depending on the feature studied. As Kecskes (2007) shows in a study on formulaic language use, ELF speakers will usually rely less on idioms or other features that are semantically less transparent (and therefore a potential danger to communicative success). It is often the literal meaning of linguistic items that stands in the foreground. This in turn results in a minimisation of pragmatic mechanisms of meaning generation, which are more likely to vary across cultures. In other words, ELF speakers tend to reduce the pragmatic gap between what is said and what is meant in order to ensure communicative efficiency.

Not surprisingly, language use at ESC press conferences exhibits many of the characteristics that have been documented as typical of European ELF in the research literature. For example, the data contains some instances of pluralisation of nouns that are in standard grammar considered non-count nouns (e.g. *advices*; Extract 1), instances in which the prescriptively required adverb is replaced by an adjective (Extract 2), or double marking of comparative forms, i.e. synthetic and analytic marking at the same time (Extract 3):

(1)
FA2: [...] (.) we didn't have so much <u>advices</u> for them that something that he already didn't know [...] [BOS1][1]

(2)
MA1: [...] so what our chances here i think our chances is are good (.) uh because uh because our song is good (.) because we (.) sing we are singing <u>good</u> @@ yes (.) that is why i think that the the press and audience and jury will uh treat us <u>good</u> [RUS1]

(3)
MA1: [...] demands uh to ourselves is much <u>more higher</u> from ourselves much <u>more higher</u> and we we know that we have to do our music perfectly [...] [RUS1]

---

1.   The form *advices* occurs in seven out of 78 press conferences: EST1, FIN1, BOS1, ISL2, ARM2, SUI2, NOR2.

A common characteristic of ELF is the use of language material in innovative ways compared to traditional native norms. Such language use may involve the regularisation of certain grammatical patterns or creative use of English language material. ELF speakers in ESC-PC, for example, show practices such as the regularisation of irregular verbs in the past tense (Extract 4), transfer of the third person singular present tense ending to the past tense form (Extract 5), or extension of the morphological productivity of native word-formation patterns (for example, derivation and conversion as in Extracts 6 and 7).

> (4)
> *MA1: uhm well (.) i also went to to to school but but only one year and then then then i ⟨pvc⟩ quitted ⟨/pvc⟩ [...] [BEL2]*

> (5)
> *FA1: uh the changes yeah were uh ⟨pvc⟩ cames ⟨/pvc⟩ from the camera in fact uh i was uh able to be (.) focused (.) [...] [ALB2]*

> (6)
> *FA1: the exam uhm the exams in germany are not uh ⟨pvc⟩ unmakeable ⟨/pvc⟩ it's uhm you CAN do you CAN do it [GER2]*

> (7)
> *FA1: we're also ⟨pvc⟩ rehearsaling ⟨/pvc⟩ a lot [...] [BLR2]*

What such linguistic practices have in common is a high semantic transparency value that in many cases exceeds that of native-like or grammatically correct English usage. Forms used in ELF talk may show explicit morphological marking of the past tense (*quitted*) or the third person singular (*cames*), where native English would not offer such explicitness. Or they may be an outcome of transparent word-formation processes (e.g. *rehearsal > rehearsaling*, a denominal verb formed through conversion), at times influenced by the speaker's L1 (compare *unmakeable* with the parallel German formation *unmachbar*).

In ESC-PC, there is abundant evidence of the hybridity typically found in ELF. Even though speakers use English surface forms, the structures of their L1s are likely to shine through (as in Extracts 8 and 9), which leads to a de-anglicised use of ELF as a medium of communication.

> (8)
> *FA1: i will celebrate my birthday with many many party hats (.) everyone becomes a party hat is isn't that nice? [GER1]*

> (9)
> *KS: tell me about th- the way till oslo like (.) how was you (.) th- the contes- the competition in in finland how was it (.) you you won with forty percent right? [FIN1]*

In these extracts, it is obvious that structures of the underlying L1 have been transferred to English. The German ELF speaker in Extract 8 uses the English verb *become*
in the sense of "to obtain", i.e. in the meaning of the German "false friend" verb *bekom-
men*. The Norwegian moderator in Extract 9, on the other hand, uses the English
preposition *till* in a prepositional phrase denoting the direction of a movement (*till
Oslo* in the sense of "to Oslo"), which represents a transfer of the usage conditions of
the Norwegian preposition *til*.

Despite the fact that these features are clearly non-native, the participants at
ESC press conferences never discern this non-nativeness as problematic. This is
part of the well-known normalisation strategy that has been found to operate in
ELF talk. ELF speakers do not usually construct themselves as imperfect users of
English or "L2 learners". Rather they aim at drawing attention away from this status (Firth 1996). In some cases such non-native aspects play a role in the local
linguistic negotiation, i.e. ELF speakers may adopt the non-native features of their
conversational partners and use them in a normalised fashion, thereby creating
idiosyncratic local norms. One example of this can be found in the following
excerpt:

> (10)
> *KS: but you will you see anything around* <u>*the norway*</u> *while you're here? will you go uh*
> *MA1: well we we just came uh yesterday and uh (.) i saw this uh shopping mall and it
> like oh come on @@*
> *MA2: no we have a we have a plan we have a master plan and (.) and that is to to like
> tour the throughout* <u>*the oslo*</u> *with bikes (.) that's it*
> *MA1: yeah we we we're gonna ride bike all across* <u>*the norway*</u> *yeah* [BOS1]

In this passage, the utterance of the Norwegian moderator (KS) contains an instance
of the place name *Norway* premodified by the definite article *the*, with which it would
not normally occur in native varieties of English (*the norway*). Interestingly, the two
Bosnian speakers (MA1 and MA2) appropriate this pattern in their following utterances, using the phrases *the oslo* and *the norway*. That this is an instance of local
accommodative negotiation can be judged from the fact that before this passage a
range of other country names are used without any article by the very same participants: *Belarus, Bosnia, Denmark, Finland, Luxembourg*, and *Norway*. Even the form
Netherlands, for which the use of the definite article would normally be required, is
used without article (*first we have a question from netherlands*; BOS1). Such negotiation
practices can be seen as a powerful means of local in-group bonding (see Seidlhofer
2009c on the negotiation of idioms in ELF). They constitute processes of convergence
for which the goal is not nativeness (i.e. an out-group referee design; Bell 1999) but the
non-native conversational partner.

In other cases, ELF speakers may repeat passages uttered by the previous speaker, often as a means of reassurance, and thereby adopt their idiosyncrasies (for instance, double past tense marking as in Extract 11):

> (11)
> *MP4: uh i would like to ask you to tell me some things about uh your uh real surname and how did you came up with the the idea of using another name*
> *MA1: how did i came up uh with the idea?*
> *MP4: of changing your uh real surname* [BEL2]

The ELF-typical features illustrated above correspond to the form-follows-function principle of ELF talk because they are unlikely to result in miscommunication or communication breakdown and can therefore be considered legitimate indexes of cooperative non-native European speaker identities.

Recapitulating earlier structure-oriented ELF research, there is some concern as to the way structural properties are related to ELF. Mortensen (2013) notes that, when structural features of ELF are analysed, care has to be taken not to "reify" ELF as a language system or variety. He opposes the frequently found claims that certain features are typical of ELF, because they contribute to the effect of hypostatising ELF as a clearly bounded linguistic entity, despite the fact that it contests such a notion as hardly any other form of language use. Mortensen uses the third person zero inflection to illustrate this point. Studies exploring this feature in ELF talk have come up with vastly different findings concerning the commonness of this feature. While Cogo and Dewey (2012: 49–52), for example, attest a relatively high usage of zero-inflection, Breiteneder (2009) finds that the presence of the inflection -s clearly dominates the picture (ranging around 90% and higher). In other words, the frequency of zero-inflection seems to be heavily context-dependent and often so low that it is awkward to claim that it constitutes a "typical feature of ELF". Moreover, as discussed in Cogo and Dewey (2012: 82–84), the third person zero inflection is clearly not restricted to ELF usage and can also be found in many (non-standard) native varieties of English (for example, in East Anglian dialects or African-American Vernacular English) or ESL varieties (Jenkins 2012: 488). It has long been noted that features occurring in ELF interactions bear some similarity to those typically found in ESL varieties. This indicates that more general processes of language change in contexts of language contact are at work and that these mechanisms are not specific to ELF at all (Ferguson 2012: 178).

When talking about the structural make-up of ELF, one has to make clear from the start that what one is going to describe is not stable or system-like but rather a manifestation of heterogeneous linguistic practices, which in turn disqualifies terms like "language system" or "variety" as descriptors. In the present study, the focus is on one particular set of ELF structures (namely relativisation) and how it is shaped by the context (ESC press conferences). Generalising across different kinds of ELF communities of practice in this respect represents a difficult or even impossible undertaking. Instead of focussing on the commonalities and regularities of ELF usage in general, a practice-oriented approach to ELF as adopted in the current book concentrates on the inherent structural variability of ELF in a particular community of practice.

7.3   Relativisation in English: Usage patterns, processing, language typology

Relativisation is among the features that are often cited in connection with non-native ELF speakers' linguistic behaviour (e.g. Jenkins 2011: 929; Seidlhofer 2005b: 68). More specifically, non-native speakers are said to use the relative pronouns *who* and *which* interchangeably, thereby neutralising the contrast between personal and non-personal reference as evident in standard English grammar. However, such a description is too simplistic, even though it may have some significance. It is certainly not the case that all (non-native) ELF speakers use the two forms interchangeably. Moreover, relativisation in English involves a greater set of competing forms than the two mentioned, with *that* and ZERO representing other frequently occurring alternatives. It is important to look at the overall distribution of relativisation strategies when judging the use of relativisers by European ELF speakers. Within the framework of the current project, it is worthwhile to examine relativisation because it represents a linguistic aspect that can be linked to Europeanness from a language typological perspective (see, for example, Haspelmath 2001; Kurzová 1981; Zifonun 2001).

In the following section, the usage of relative pronouns by the European ELF speakers at ESC press conferences will be studied in detail. The description of relativisation in grammars of English is an important starting point for this analysis. However, these grammatical descriptions are here not taken as an evaluative yardstick distinguishing correct from incorrect language use. In accordance with ELF theorisation, the relativisation practices of the participants at ESC press conferences are seen as a phenomenon in its own right for which native English standards are only of secondary importance (namely as a source of linguistic input in formal language education). The form-follows-function principle of ELF allows for a high degree of variation in the choice of relativisers. For example, using *who* in contexts where *which* is prescribed by normative grammar and vice versa is unlikely to cause communication difficulties or breakdown. Viewed from this perspective, such divergences from the normative native pattern represent legitimate indexes of non-native speaker identities.

Most English relative clauses are introduced by a relativiser. Within the clause, the latter can fulfil different syntactic functions such as subject, object, complement or adverbial. Relative pronouns normally refer back to, and formally agree with, an antecedent in the preceding main clause. Restrictive relative clauses are closely connected to their antecedents and – as the name suggests – restrict their reference (e.g. *We read about the Greeks who fought at Marathon,* i.e. only those Greeks who participated in that battle). This is different for nonrestrictive relative clauses, which constitute parenthetic comments that merely describe the antecedent (e.g. *We read about the Greeks, who fought at Marathon,* i.e. an additional comment about the Greeks as an entire people involved in a conflict).

Table 7.1. English relativisers and their functions (adapted from Quirk et al. 2003 [1985]: 366)

	restrictive		nonrestrictive	
syntactic function	human	non-human	human	non-human
subject	*who* *that*	*which* *that*	*who*	*which*
object (incl. object of stranded prep.)	*who(m)* *that* *ZERO*	*which* *that* *ZERO*	*whom*	
object of fronted prep. (pied piping)	*whom*	*which*		
complement	*which*			
genitive	*whose*			

Usage patterns of English relative pronouns are subject to a complex set of factors. The following description is based on the relevant chapters in one of the most widely used reference grammars, the *Comprehensive Grammar of the English Language* (CGEL; Quirk, Greenbaum, Leech & Svartvik 2003 [1985]: ch. 6.32–6.35 and 17.9–17.25). Central factors that normatively influence relativiser choice are represented in Table 7.1. These normative patterns along the lines of restrictiveness, syntactic function and humanness of antecedent are also relevant for the present study because they represent the primary input for ELF users around Europe, most of whom have acquired English in formal education. Non-standard native English varieties may show other relativisers such as *what* or *as*. Such forms are unlikely to occur in the press conference data because non-native ELF speakers tend to have little (if any) exposure to such forms and the native speakers involved in the press conferences do not use such dialectal variants.

From Table 7.1, the following normative usage patterns can be deduced:

a. case is only distinguished in the forms *who – whom – whose* (not for *that, which* and ZERO),

b. humanness is only distinguished in the forms *who(m)* and *which* (not in *that,* ZERO and *whose*),

c.   *that* and ZERO are only used in restrictive relative clauses (as opposed to *who(m)*,
     which and *whose*, which can also be used in nonrestrictive relative clauses),
d.   ZERO only occurs in restrictive object relative clauses,
e.   *which* is the only option when the relativiser functions as a complement, even for
     personal reference (e.g. *She is the perfect accountant which her predecessor was not.*
     Quirk et al. 2003 [1985]: 1248),
f.   *whose* is the possessive relativiser in all contexts,
g.   nonrestrictive relative clauses require *wh*-forms as relativisers,
h.   objects of fronted prepositions (pied piping: *the chair on which she is sitting*)
     require *wh*-forms as relativisers, whereas objects of stranded prepositions pattern
     with plain objects (*the chair which/that/ø she is sitting on*).

In this normative description only a restricted set of grammatical contexts allows for
various formal realisations, namely restricted relative clauses in which the relativiser
functions as subject, object or complement of a stranded preposition. These will also
be the contexts studied in terms of variance in the present data. In all other contexts,
relativiser choice is categorical and does not allow variance from a normative point of
view. The fact that normative grammar does not allow for variance in these contexts
does of course not per se rule out such variance for ELF talk. However, an examination
of the press conference data shows that these other contexts occur rarely and that ELF
speakers show no variable linguistic behaviour in them.

   However – a point also acknowledged in the CGEL – many of the rules deduced
from Table 7.1 are not absolute. They rather represent dominant usage patterns. For
example, the case distinction between *who* and *whom* is not always followed systematically. In the objective case, both *who* and *whom* are regularly found, the latter option
being rather formal and therefore generally avoided in informal speech (Quirk et al.
2003 [1985]: 367). Another example is the use of *whose*, which according to Table 7.1
is unrestricted. Despite this many speakers show a reluctance to use this form with
non-personal antecedents and may therefore replace it by *of which* (Quirk et al. 2003
[1985]: 1249), i.e. they tend to generalise the usage conditions of *who* and *whom*
(humanness) to the formally related pronoun *whose*. Similarly, *that* is often felt to be
inadequate for personal reference (e.g. *The ladies that were present*; Tottie 1997a: 87)
even though standard grammar would, in principle, allow it.

   Among relative clauses, one can distinguish adnominal relative clauses (i.e. those
referring to an antecedent noun phrase; see examples given so far), nominal relative
clauses (i.e. those which already contain their antecedent; e.g. *What surprises me is
that they came to the party.*) and sentential relative clauses (whose antecedent is an
entire sentence rather than a noun phrase; e.g. *They came to the party, which surprised
me*; Quirk et al. 2003 [1985]: 1244). Common usage patterns show that restrictive
relative clauses are clearly more frequent than their nonrestrictive counterparts; and

adnominal relative clauses are more frequent than nominal and sentential relative clauses (Quirk et al. 2003 [1985]: 1245). The analysis of the press conference data will concentrate on adnominal restrictive relative clauses as the most frequent type.

Relativisation in English is a well documented research object and has been studied in major national English varieties (e.g. Aarts 1993, 1994; Fox & Thompson 2007; Geisler & Johansson 2002; Guy & Bayley 1995; Schmied 1993; Sigley 1997; Tottie 1995, 1997a/b; Yamashita 1994), English dialects (e.g. Bayley 1999; D'Arcy & Tagliamonte 2010; Herrmann 2005; Levey 2006; Tagliamonte, Smith & Lawrence 2005, and contributions in Poussa 2002) and with diachronic data (e.g. Ball 1996; Nevalainen 2012; Peters 1992; Suárez-Gómez 2008).

Tottie (1997a: 88ff), for example, compared American English (AmE) and British English (BrE) usage patterns for subject relativisers. For newspaper texts, Tottie found that both AmE and BrE show a preponderance of *who* for human antecedents (95%). For nun-human antecedents, AmE shows an equally strong dominance of *that* (95%), whereas in BrE both *that* and *which* are commonly used (55% and 45% respectively). Furthermore, Tottie compared samples from the following three corpora of spoken English: the *Santa Barbara Corpus* (SBC; for AmE), the *London-Lund Corpus* (LLC; for BrE, mainly academic speakers) and the spoken component of the *British National Corpus* (BNC; for BrE). She found that for human antecedents, all three corpora favour *who*, but the academic speakers in LLC (91%) more so than the internally more heterogeneous other two corpora (SBC: 64%; BNC: 67%). For non-human antecedents, the two latter corpora favour *that*. The AmE data show an almost categorical (96%) use of and BNC a strong preference for *that* (74%). In the LLC, usage rates of *that* and *which* were roughly equal (with 49% and 51% respectively). To summarise, *who* remains the most common choice for human antecedents in both varieties. For non-human antecedents, *that* is the most common strategy, but it competes in formal and written BrE usage with *which*. For object relative clauses, Fox and Thompson (2007) found a preponderance of ZERO (60%) in spoken AmE, whereas Tagliamonte, Smith and Lawrence (2005) found that ZERO amounts to 45% and *that* to 52% in three BrE vernaculars.

Historical studies (Ball 1996; Peters 1992; Suárez-Gómez 2008) have shown that *that* and ZERO are the older variants, whereas the *wh*-forms entered the language during the Middle English period, probably due to intensive influence from French and Latin, i.e. languages in which interrogative pronouns are also used as relativisers. The form *who* was the latest relativiser to develop in Late Middle English and has spread, whereas *which* seems to be on the decrease due to competition from *that* for non-human antecedents. Moreover, there is mounting evidence that the introduction and spread of *wh*-forms represents a change from above and has mainly been promoted by normative language education. As a consequence, *wh*-forms have in many regions not entered the spoken vernacular to a significant extent (see, for example, Tagliamonte, Smith & Lawrence 2005, who found a frequency of 64% for *that* followed by ZERO with 28% in BrE vernaculars). Leech, Hundt, Mair and Smith (2009: 233–234) identify a decline of *wh*-forms for written language use and a concomitant rise of *that* and ZERO, which they explain in terms of an on-going trend of colloquialisation. As will become more transparent in the discussion of relativisation from a typological perspective later in this chapter, this development equals a divergence from prototypically European relativisation patterns. This, in turn, may indicate that this trend is less likely to occur in European uses of English.

As previous research demonstrates, relativisation represents a particularly interesting feature, as it has been found to be influenced by a whole array of linguistic and social factors (i.e. besides syntactic function, humanness of antecedent and restrictiveness). For example, written and/or formal language use generally favour *wh*-forms, whereas *that* and ZERO are more frequent in spoken and/or informal language use (see Guy & Bayley 1995; Sigley 1997). Adjacency of antecedent and relativiser generally favours ZERO (see Fox & Thompson 2007; Guy & Bayley 1995). The realisation of the subject in object relative clauses is also influential: personal pronouns (especially *I*; e.g. *the car I saw*) favour ZERO in object relative clauses (see Fox & Thompson 2007; Tottie 1995). The length of the relative clause may also play a role, i.e. shorter relative clauses favour ZERO (see Fox & Thompson 2007; Tagliamonte, Smith & Lawrence 2005). Finally, the effect of social class has been documented, according to which middle-class speakers use higher rates of *wh*-forms than working-class speakers (see Bayley 1999; Tottie 1997c). Other social factors that have been found to influence relativiser choice are, for example, age, education and occupation (see D'Arcy & Tagliamonte 2010: 397).[2] It must be noted that not all of these factors are equally relevant across English varieties and future research will have to test in how far ELF users show similar usage patterns.

Studies of relativisation in non-native speakers' language use are rarer (examples include Durham 2007; Flanigan & Inal 1996; Hadic Zabala 2004; Olofsson 2009a/b and Kiss-Gulyás 2004). They tend to focus on the written work of "learners" and are therefore deeply rooted in the ELT research tradition, which describes learners' linguistic output (rather negatively) as "interlanguage". Similar studies that are based on an ELF theorisation are missing. Nevertheless earlier studies on relativiser use by non-native speakers provide an important point of orientation for the present study. The results of three such studies (Flanigan & Inal 1996; Olofsson 2009a and Durham 2007) shall be outlined in the following.

In Flanigan and Inal (1996), subjects were give a written production task in which they had to combine sentences through relativisation. They found that out of the three options for object relativisers (*wh*-, *that* and ZERO), native AmE speakers preferred

---

2. This is not an exhaustive list. An overview of factors that have been shown to influence relativisation is given by Durham (2007: 162). See also Fox and Thompson (2007).

ZERO (53.1%), whereas non-native speakers who had resided less than two years in the US preferred *wh*-forms (69.8%). Non-native speakers whose period of residence was longer than two years showed a tendency to approach native speaker patterns, i.e. they still showed a preference for *wh*- in their production (48.1%) but also a relatively high frequency of ZERO (31.1%). Additionally, subjects' use of relativisers in speech was studied in a preference test. Here it turned out that non-native speakers used *wh*-, *that* and ZERO to a roughly similar extent, whereas native speakers showed a preference for ZERO and disfavoured *wh*-. For the written language, native speakers overwhelmingly reported use of *that*, while non-native speakers reported using *wh*- the most. Interestingly, the native speakers stated in the preference task that they preferred *that* (60.2%) in writing, but produced ZERO in the majority of the cases in the production task (53.1%). Non-native speakers said they preferred *wh*- in writing in the preference task and accordingly also produced more *wh*-forms in the written production task. The mismatch shown between the claimed preference and the production of the native speakers is not surprising if one considers that these speakers are less likely to be exposed to an explicit teaching of the grammatical rules connected to relativiser use, whereas non-native speakers are much more likely to have been taught these rules explicitly in ELT classes, where greater emphasis is usually placed on the *who-which* distinction.

Olofsson (2009a) studied the use of relativisers in the *International Corpus of Learner English* (ICLE), which contains argumentative texts written by advanced learners. He found that Swedish and Dutch learners of English did not differ significantly in the frequencies with which they chose ZERO as a relativiser (55% and 58% respectively). This is remarkable because Swedish allows for ZERO relativisers in a similar way as English, but Dutch does not. An L1 transfer effect can therefore be ruled out for these data.[3] However, there was a difference when these results were compared to those retrieved from American and British students. Both native groups favoured overt realisation types over ZERO in their writing (53% and 71% respectively).

Durham (2007) carried out a study in which she analysed Swiss speakers' use of English as an intranational lingua franca (between the French-, German- and Italian-speaking population) in comparison to native English data. Relativisation is one of the features analysed in this study. The patterns of relativisation detected by Durham do not yield any evidence of focussing – the process that would lead to a distinctly Swiss variety of English. For human subject relatives, all four speaker groups studied (French, German, Italian and English L1 speakers) used *who* more often than *that*. For non-human subject relatives, three of the groups used *that* more frequently than

---

3.   L1 transfer was more plausible for preposition stranding in relative clauses, which is not possible in Dutch but in Swedish. Accordingly, Swedish learners used a higher percentage of stranding (70%) compared to Dutch students (46%; Olofsson 2009a: 342).

which; only the German speakers showed the opposite pattern. For object relatives, all four groups favoured ZERO, mostly followed by *that* and then *which*, with again only the German speakers showing more cases of *which* than *that* (Durham 2007: 171–172). In other words, the native English speakers showed similar patterns as the French and Italian Swiss speakers of English, whereas the three Swiss speaker groups did not exhibit such similarities. Both of these mechanisms – distance from native English and similarity between French, German and Italian groups – would have been necessary for declaring Swiss English as a variety. Durham concludes that non-native and native speakers in her data use relativisation in much the same fashion. She takes this as evidence that the variation documented in the data is due to a successful acquisition of the native variable rules governing relativiser choice, with L1 transfer being minimal (Durham 2007: 181–183).

For reasons of communicative efficiency, it can be expected that overt relativisers are used more often in ELF than in interactions between native speakers of English, because they help to avoid ambiguity and in doing so facilitate processing. One would therefore expect that ZERO, the least explicit form (see Temperley 2003: 471–472), occurs less frequently in ELF communication. Among the group of overt relativisers, *who* and *which* are semantically more specific (and less ambiguous) than *that*, because they carry the additional feature [± human]. Moreover, the form *that* is more ambiguous with respect to its word-class status. It can function as relative pronoun, demonstrative pronoun, demonstrative adjective or subordinating conjunction, whereas *who* and *which* can only function as relative or interrogative pronouns. It can therefore be expected that ELF talk contains higher frequencies of *wh*-forms than (informal) interactions among native speakers, i.e. clarity and explicitness is prioritised over the lower encoding effort associated with the invariable relativiser *that* (Seidlhofer 2011: 107). However, it should be noted that a previous study on written material from the ICLE conducted by Olofsson (2009b) came up with quite different results: German, Italian and Swedish learners were shown to use more instances of ZERO in their writing than American and British students (Olofsson 2009b: 238). ESC-PC differs in two important aspects from the ICLE data: on the one hand, the former corpus documents spoken ELF use and, on the other hand, the community of practice studied here does not consist of people who can be considered as "learners" of English in the first place.

The processing-governed principles outlined above are further supported from the perspective of European language typology (e.g. Cristofaro & Giacalone Ramat 2007; Fiorentino 2007; Haspelmath 2001). Such research demonstrates that there are connections between relativisation and typological Europeanness. When speakers across Europe communicate, they are particularly likely to use ELF. However, on the structural level, English departs in many respects from the typological concept of Standard Average European and is therefore a less prototypical representative of this category (Haspelmath 2001: 1493). If one assumes a certain degree of structural transfer from speakers' L1s to their use of ELF, it may be expected that European ELF will depart from native English in those features that English does not share with Standard Average European. Such a structural make-up would also be compatible with recent findings of research on English varieties from a typological point of view. Szmrecsanyi and Kortmann (2011), for example, have found that European EFL varieties show significantly different typological profiles from ENL and ESL varieties, with the former exhibiting a higher degree of analyticity.

In terms of relativisation, English is among the few languages in Europe that allow gapping in relative clauses (i.e. the use of ZERO in object relative clauses). Outside Europe, gapping is a frequent strategy (Nikolaeva 2006: 504). The use of an overt relative pronoun is the dominant pattern across European languages. Interestingly, this seems to be an areal phenomenon pertaining to Europe in a geographical sense, because (a) it is mainly the Indo-European languages spoken in Europe (as opposed to those spoken in Asia) that show this pattern, and (b) this pattern is, in general, rarely found in languages outside Europe (Comrie 1998; Comrie & Kuteva 2005: 496).[4] On the other hand, non-Indo-European languages spoken in Europe such as Finnish, Hungarian or Georgian also possess this overt realisation type, probably as a result of intra-European language contact (Comrie 1998: 61). Overt postnominal relativisation, in which a relative pronoun introduces the relative clause, can therefore be considered a linguistic Europeanism (Fiorentino 2007). Accordingly, it can be expected that European EFL speakers use ZERO less frequently than ENL/ESL speakers and that this may also have repercussions in European ELF, at least in contexts in which non-native speakers predominate.

The concrete realisation of an overt relativiser may either be a relative pronoun, i.e. a relativiser that is variable and shows agreement with its antecedent, or a relative particle, i.e. an invariable relativiser. That relative pronouns show more nominal properties than relative particles can be deduced from the fact that only the former may be preceded by a preposition (e.g. English *of which*/*of that*), whereas relative particles require preposition stranding (Comrie 1999: 81–82; Tagliamonte, Smith & Lawrence 2005: 95). In most European languages, both types exist side by side. In English, for example, the *wh*-relativisers constitute relative pronouns (Andrews 2007: 218), whereas *that* represents a relative particle. However, some European languages show a preference for relative particles even though both strategies are feasible. This is true for

---

4. The European pattern is rather exceptional on a global scale. Comrie and Kuteva (2005: 494) find that for subject relatives out of a total of 166 languages investigated only 12 (7.2%) show a preponderance of this strategy, most of which are European languages. Gapping is in fact the most common strategy, found in 125 out of 166 languages (75.3%). Two further relativisation strategies that are uncommon in Europe are nonreduction (14.5%) and pronoun retention (3.0%). For relativisation on obliques, gapping is found in 55 (49.1%) and the relative pronoun strategy in 13 out of 112 languages (11.6%; Comrie & Kuteva 2005: 496).

the North Germanic languages (Danish, Norwegian, Swedish), the Semitic languages (Hebrew, Maltese) and Modern Greek. The Romance languages show a development of relative pronouns turning into relative particles (Zifonun 2001: 28). Relative particles are also commonly found outside Europe. The relative pronoun strategy, by contrast, is largely restricted to European languages and some languages in contact with the former (Comrie 2006: 136; Haspelmath 2001: 1495).[5]

With respect to the connection between relativisation and Europeanness, it is also noteworthy that the *wh*-forms were not originally used as relativisers in Old English. They adopted this function in the course of the Middle English period as a result of intensive language contact with Romance sources (D'Arcy & Tagliamonte 2010: 386–387). It could therefore be argued that this change has led to the introduction of a feature into English that is common across European languages, namely interrogative pronouns used as relativisers (see Haspelmath 2001: 1494).[6] It is interesting to note that this feature may now play a role in European uses of English as a lingua franca.

Based on the typological considerations above and because of the fact that EFL speakers form the dominant part in European ELF, it can be expected that European ELF shows higher frequencies of *wh*-forms than native English discourse. This seems even more likely if one considers that *wh*-forms have been shown to be marginal in spoken native English varieties (Fiorentino 2007: 269).

> Hypothesis 1:
> European ELF communication will show
>   a)   lower frequencies of ZERO, and
>   b)   higher frequencies of *wh*-forms than native English usage.

7.4   Methodological preliminaries

In order to arrive at a sophisticated picture of the internal structural hybridity of European ELF, relativisation patterns in the press conference data are in the following chapters first related to a range of individual factors. In the end, a VARBRUL (variable

---

5.   As Comrie (2006: 134–136) points out, there are three criteria characterising the relative pronoun strategy: 1. it is an externally headed construction, 2. the relative pronoun indicates the syntactic or semantic role of the antecedent in the relative clause through agreement, 3. the relative pronoun (or the phrase containing it) introduces the relative clause.

6.   Interrogative pronouns are a source for relativisers in all Romance languages, all Slavic languages, some Germanic languages, and some other European languages such as Georgian, Greek and Hungarian. Two exceptions are constituted by German and Finnish (Haspelmath 2001: 1494).

rule) analysis is conducted (see discussions of this methodology in Tagliamonte 2006 and J.A. Walker 2010). This kind of analysis is useful in the present context, because it provides more precise information of the relative weight of the factors influencing relativiser choice. Moreover, such an analysis can easily incorporate the factor groups that go beyond the three criteria incorporated in Table 7.1. VARBRUL analysis has for a long time been central to sociolinguistic research on native English varieties. Its usefulness for the study of non-native speakers' linguistic output has also been demonstrated, even though such research is not based on an ELF theorisation (see Flanigan & Inal 1996; Young & Bayley 1996; Zabor 1998).

A VARBRUL analysis only makes sense for those contexts in which the linguistic variable at hand shows variation. In other words, categorical contexts in which a certain variant is chosen in all instances must be ruled out in advance. Consequently, the analysis is at this point confined to restrictive relative clauses whose relativisers either function as subject, direct object or complement of a stranded preposition. Nonrestrictive relative clauses, which are clearly less frequent than their restrictive counterparts, are excluded. As discussed by Tagliamonte, Smith and Lawrence (2005:85), they differ from restrictive relative clauses formally (they allow only *wh-*), semantically (they provide supplementary information rather than restricting the reference of the antecedent) and prosodically (they are often marked off by pauses and prosody), and can therefore not be grouped together with restrictive relative clauses. In the present study, nonrestrictive relative clauses were identified on a semantic basis, i.e. all relative clauses were excluded that (a) did not restrict the reference of the antecedent but rather conveyed extra information, (b) relativised an entire clause rather than an antecedent noun phrase (sentential relative clauses), or (c) relativised a proper noun, whose reference de facto cannot be restricted (see Tagliamonte, Smith & Lawrence 2005:85–86). Occasionally, relative clauses allow for both a restrictive and a nonrestrictive reading. In such cases, the video recording was consulted in order to see whether there are any prosodic cues that point to one of the two readings. If the ambiguity could not be resolved, the relative clause in question was included in the analysis.

Even with restrictive relative clauses, not all allow for multiple variants (see Table 7.1). This led to the exclusion of restrictive relative clauses in which the relativiser functions as complement of a fronted preposition (pied piping constructions) or as a genitive.[7] Adverbial relative clauses use a more heterogeneous set of relativisers (e.g. *the time when; the place where; the reason why; the same as*) and were therefore also excluded.

---

7.   The genitive relativiser *whose* occurs only once in the entire corpus (in UKR1). There is no relative clause in which the relativiser functions as an indirect object, subject complement or object complement in the data.

The entire press conference corpus was manually searched to identify the relevant relative clauses. A manual search was necessary to also retrieve instances of ZERO, which would otherwise not have been identifiable in an untagged corpus (see Lehmann 1997). Overall, 701 relevant relative clauses were identified in the dataset. Some tokens had to be excluded because they could not be definitely assigned to one of the values in the factor group. This is true for instances of false starts or self-corrections in which two alternative variants are used consecutively, as in the following extract:

> (12)
> *MA1: we have made a a nice album <u>who</u> is <u>which</u> is uh released on the twenty-first or twenty-third here in may* [DAN1]

If one and the same variant is immediately repeated by the same speaker (see Extract 13), only one of these instances was counted as a token.

> (13)
> *FA1: [...] everything is uh (.) yeah everything <u>that</u> you asked <u>that</u> we asked for just came and (.) so we're really happy* [ISL2]

The remaining tokens were incorporated in the programme *Goldvarb X* and coded for a range of factor groups in order to submit the data to a VARBRUL analysis. As has been noted in Chapter 7.3 above, a whole range of factors are potential candidates that may affect relativiser choice. From the pool of options, six factor groups were chosen whose relevance for the ELF data at hand seemed particularly plausible. Chapters 7.5 to 7.10 discuss the individual factor groups tested: syntactic function, humanness of antecedent, the speaker's L1 background, active speaker participation, European region and EU status.[8]

The dependent variable is relativiser choice. It consists of the following factor values (*Goldvarb* codings in parentheses):

> *who* (o),
> *which* (i),
> *that* (a),
> ZERO (z),
> *what* (x).[9]

The form *whom* occurs only once in the entire corpus, namely in a pied piping construction (*voting for whom you'd like*; IRL1), i.e. a context that has been ruled out for

---

8.   I would like to thank James A. Walker for his comments on the coding scheme employed in this study. All insufficiencies remain my own, of course.

9.   This category was originally called "other", but it turned out in the analysis that apart from the common relativisers there are only four instances in which *what* is used as a relativiser.

the VARBRUL analysis. Despite the fact that the data document ELF talk, relativisers other than the ones mentioned above do not occur.

The following samples from the corpus illustrate the use of the four major relativiser types found in the data for the three non-categorical contexts in which variation may occur:[10]

>   (a) Relativiser as subject
>
>   (14) *MA3: and the girl (.) WHO sang it was (.) she was really free* [EST1]
>   (15) *MA2: making the final arrangements of the of the song WHICH is already here* [ALB1]
>   (16) *FA2: this is the kind of song THAT (.) can have many things going on in it* [LAT1]
>   (17) *KS: do we have ⟨pvc⟩ anyones ⟨/pvc⟩ (.) Ø wanna know something?* [SLK1]
>
>   (b) Relativiser as direct object
>
>   (18) **FA1*: she's (.) the person WHO i believe apart from god obviously* [MAL2][11]
>   (19) *MA1: i can sing it on a on a language WHICH i can't sp- speak* [RUS2]
>   (20) *MP1: can you tell us a bit (.) about the video THAT you made* [ALB1]
>   (21) *MA2: a selection committee uh checking on all the: the artists Ø you have in belgium* [BEL1]
>
>   (c) Relativiser as complement of stranded preposition
>
>   (22) *FA1: the uh (.) ideal planet WHICH we're all dreaming of* [UKR1]
>   (23) *MA1: since it's uh (.) two countries THAT i'm dealing with* [ROM1]
>   (24) *KS: is it possible to hear f- you sing something from the artist Ø you are influenced by?* [BEL2]

Relative *who* does not occur as complement of a stranded preposition in the corpus.

Of the four instances of relative *what* in the corpus, three are object relativisers (as in Extract 25) and one is a subject relativiser (Extract 26):

>   (25) *FA1: everything WHAT you're doing should represent yourself* [BUL2]
>
>   (26) *FA2: there was one group (.) WHAT was like everybody was thinking okay they will win* [FIN1]

As the low frequency of relativiser *what* is not sufficient to perform statistically meaningful analyses, this form is excluded from the quantification in the following chapters. This leaves us with 697 restrictive relative clauses to be studied.[12]

---

10.   Note that in the data extracts of the present chapter relativisers are capitalised. This does not mean that they carry stress.

11.   Note that the only time *who* is used as an object relativiser in the entire corpus, it is not used by an EFL speaker but by an ESL speaker from MAL.

12.   Note that factor groups 2 and 3 show a smaller total amount of relative clauses studied (690 and 694) because for some tokens the value "not applicable" had to be assigned.

7.5 Relativisers and syntactic function

Factor groups 2 and 3 deal with two structural aspects that are central to any discussion of relativiser choice: syntactic function of relativiser and humanness of antecedent. As these two criteria also figure prominently in foreign language teaching, it can safely be assumed that they will also play a role in ELF relativisation strategies.

Factor group 2 describes the syntactic function of the relativiser within the relative clause and consists of the following factor values:

> subject (s),
> direct object (o), and
> complement of stranded preposition (p).[13]

With respect to this factor group, English behaves in a similar way as the majority of European languages. All European languages show subject and object relative clauses. A decisive difference, however, can be found for the clauses in which the relativiser is a prepositional complement. In these, English allows for pied piping (*the car of which I dreamt*) or preposition stranding (*the car which/that/Ø I dreamt of*; see Hoffmann 2007). The latter strategy is uncommon across European languages, but in English it represents the dominant pattern in informal conversation, because pied piping constructions are perceived as highly formal.

Table 7.2 provides the overall frequencies of relativisers across the three syntactic functions in ESC-PC:

Table 7.2. Relativisers and syntactic function in ESC-PC

Syntactic function	who	which	Σ wh-	that	ZERO	total	%
subject	176 [51.0%]	26 [7.5%]	202 [58.5%]	139 [40.3%]	4 [1.2%]	345	50.0%
object	1 [0.3%]	15 [4.9%]	16 [5.2%]	145 [47.1%]	147 [47.7%]	308	44.6%
prep. object	–	2 [5.4%]	2 [5.4%]	14 [37.8%]	21 [56.8%]	37	5.4%
total	177 [25.7%]	43 [6.2%]	220 [31.9%]	298 [43.2%]	172 [24.9%]	690	

---

13. The two structural factor groups 2 and 3 additionally contain the category "not applicable" (/), to which tokens were assigned if the value within the respective factor group could not be assigned. This may occur when utterances involving relativisers constitute incomplete sentences or when passages surrounding the relativiser are inaudible.

The most common relativiser in ESC-PC is *that* (43.2%), followed by *wh*-forms (31.9%; mainly *who* with 25.7%) and ZERO (24.9%). *Which* is relatively infrequent (6.2%). It can also be seen that individual syntactic functions favour different relativisers. In subject function, *wh*-forms account for 58.5% of the relativisers used, followed by *that* with 40.3%. ZERO hardly ever occurs in subject function (1.2%), which may be taken as an indicator that normative grammar is generally adhered to in this context.

In object function, *wh*-forms are marginal (5.2% altogether), whereas *that* and ZERO dominate the picture with roughly equal frequencies (47.1% and 47.7% respectively). The form *who* is virtually restricted to subject function and occurs only once in object function. Cases in which the relativiser is the object of a stranded preposition are relatively rare and amount to only 5.4%. ZERO (56.8%) is the most common relativiser in this function, followed by *that* with 37.8%. To sum up, *wh*-forms and ZERO show an almost complementary distribution, whereas *that* is common in all syntactic functions.

The overall distribution of relativisers found in this ELF data corresponds neatly to common patterns identified in earlier research on native spoken English (Tottie 1997c: 471; Weinert 2004: 12) and therefore cannot be said to be per se different. The data shows that predominantly the first two functions in the Noun Phrase Accessibility Hierarchy (Keenan & Comrie 1977) occur: subject and direct object relativisers. Complements of stranded prepositions are marginal, but more frequent than pied piping constructions.[14] However, there is one aspect in which the ELF data show a higher divergence from native spoken English. Many studies found that spoken English shows *that* and ZERO as the most frequent relativisers (e.g. Tagliamonte, Smith & Lawrence 2005; Weinert 2004: 19). Even though these two relativisers are also common in the ELF data, amounting to 43.2% and 24.9% respectively, *wh*-forms prove to be more frequent (31.9%) than ZERO. It is especially the use of *who* in subject function that accounts for this relatively high frequency. This may be a consequence of L1 transfer or of formal language education, in which great emphasis is normally placed on teaching the distinction between *who* and *which* along humanness lines. Therefore it seems that Hypothesis 1 may be confirmed by the data. A more detailed comparison of ESC-PC and native English corpora is presented at the end of the next chapter.

7.6 Relativisers and humanness of antecedent

Factor group 3 represents a semantic classification of the antecedent in terms of humanness:

---

14. The entire corpus contains only three restrictive relative clauses with a pied piping construction. Constructions with preposition stranding are more than ten times more frequent (37 instances).

human common noun (h; examples: *person, artist*),
human collective noun (c; examples: *delegation, family*),
the noun *people* (p),[15]
human pronoun (x; examples: *everybody, someone*),
non-human common noun (n; examples: *rehearsal, microphone*), and
non-human pronoun (y; examples: *something, everything*).[16]

The humanness distinction in relative pronouns (*who* vs. *which*) is an aspect in which English departs from other European languages on the typological level. Although quite a few European languages possess relative pronouns that are gender-inflected (e.g. German *der, die, das*; Croatian *koji, koja, koje*), these usually cut across the humanness distinction because they are applicable to human as well as non-human nouns of the respective grammatical gender. Therefore it can be hypothesised that European ELF speakers may not necessarily make this distinction and may to a certain extent use *who* with non-human antecedents and *which* with human antecedents.

> Hypothesis 2:
> European ELF speakers will show instances of relativiser *who* referring to non-human antecedents and of relativiser *which* referring to human antecedents.

Table 7.3 shows the distribution of the various relativisers across the different antecedent types. Human referents are predominantly relativised by means of *who* (63.3%) and to some extent by *that* (24.4%) in ESC-PC. For non-human antecedents, *that* is used in 55.1% of the cases, followed by ZERO (35.1%). Apart from *which* (the least frequent relativiser), all other relativisers show large frequency differences across the human/non-human distinction. This is hardly surprising for *who*, but even *that* and ZERO, which in principle can easily be used for both human and non-human reference, are clearly more frequent with non-human reference. The frequencies of *who, that* and ZERO across the six subcategories show a strong humanness effect without any overlap between the frequencies for human and non-human. Only *which* behaves unusually in this respect, because its frequency for non-human pronominal antecedents is slightly lower than that of all types of human antecedents.

---

15.   The noun *people* was treated separately because, as opposed to other human collective nouns, it does not allow for the use of either *who* or *which* but only goes with the former.

16.   The category animacy could not be tested with this data because nearly all relativisers referring to animate entities refer to human beings. There is only one instance in the data in which an animal noun is relativised (*bird – that* in MAL1).

Table 7.3. Relativisers and humanness of antecedent in ESC-PC

Antecedent	who	which	Σ wh-	that	ZERO	total	%
human pronoun	63 [81.8%]	–	63 [81.8%]	8 [10.4%]	6 [7.8%]	77	11.1%
people	34 [61.8%]	2 [3.6%]	36 [65.4%]	14 [25.5%]	5 [9.1%]	55	7.9%
human collective noun	17 [58.6%]	1 [3.4%]	18 [62.0%]	9 [31.0%]	2 [6.9%]	29	4.2%
human common noun	60 [52.6%]	6 [5.3%]	66 [57.9%]	36 [31.6%]	12 [10.5%]	114	16.4%
non-human common noun	6 [1.8%]	33 [10.1%]	39 [11.9%]	181 [55.5%]	106 [32.5%]	326	47.0%
non-human pronoun	0	2 [2.2%]	2 [2.2%]	50 [53.8%]	41 [44.1%]	93	13.4%
total	180 [25.9%]	44 [6.3%]	224 [32.2%]	298 [42.9%]	172 [24.8%]	694	
Σ human	174 [63.3%]	9 [3.3%]	183 [66.5%]	67 [24.4%]	25 [9.1%]	275	39.6%
Σ non-human	6 [1.4%]	35 [8.4%]	41 [9.8%]	231 [55.1%]	147 [35.1%]	419	60.4%

Within the categories human and non-human, one finds a certain degree of variance. In the group of human antecedent types, *who*-usage ranges from 52.6% for common human nouns up to 81.8% for human pronominal heads with collective human nouns and the noun *people* clustering in between. This increase is inversely related to a decrease in the use of *that* across these categories of human reference. ZERO, on the other hand, shows a relatively stable pattern across human reference types, hovering between 6.9% and 10.5%. For non-human reference types, *that* is most common (55.5%) with both common nouns and pronouns (53.8%). ZERO is also common with non-human antecedents, but more so for pronouns (44.1%) than for common nouns (32.5%). Even though *which* is normatively restricted to non-human antecedents, it plays only a marginal role here. It has the highest frequency with non-human common nouns (10.1%).

With respect to Hypothesis 2, Table 7.3 shows that *which* is in these ELF data not restricted to non-human antecedents.[17] Its usage seems to be more constrained

---

17. According to Herrmann (2005:42) *which* is not restricted to non-human antecedents in BrE dialects either.

by pronominal antecedents, with which it hardly ever occurs (only two such occurrences vs. 42 non-pronominal occurrences), than by humanness (9 instances for
human vs. 35 for non-human). Conversely, *who* is not restricted to human reference
either. In cases of non-human reference, it occurs exclusively with common nouns
(6 times) and never with pronouns. This confirms Hypothesis 2. As *who-which*
confusion does not cause comprehension problems in the data (and does therefore
qualify as a non-core feature of ELF), this variance can be considered a legitimate
index of second language identities (Block 2007). The following two extracts from the
corpus illustrate such occurrences:

> (27) *FA1: yesterday we was in in this (.) great restaurant (.) WHO WHO is v- th- the
> view is* [LAT2]

> (28) *MA1: we see a lot of singers all over the world WHICH are speculating with art*
> [ALB1]

However, the use of *who* for non-human reference and *which* for human reference
is clearly marginal in the data. That this feature has been described as typical of ELF
talk must therefore be met with some reservation in the light of these European data.
Out of the 701 restrictive relative clauses studied, only 14 (2.1%) showed instances of
who-which confusion. Among the *wh*-forms used, this amounts to merely 6.25%.[18]
12 out of these 14 cases involve *who-which* confusion with common nouns. In the
two remaining cases, the noun *people* is the antecedent. The data also show that the
humanness distinction between *who* and *which* seems to be strictly applied only with
pronominal antecedents, which never show *who-which* confusion. The single case
in which a collective human noun is pronominalised with *which* does not constitute
an instance of *who-which* confusion because these nouns normally also allow both
options in standard grammar. As it can safely be assumed that the vast majority of the
speakers did not use *who* and *which* interchangeably, it is not legitimate to consider
this a feature frequently found in European ELF.

Considering the use of *wh*-forms in ESC-PC, one finds that, even though these are
relatively frequently used, they do not seem to exhibit the features typically associated
with relative pronouns as opposed to relative particles. In the restrictive relative clauses
in ESC-PC, the inflected case forms *whose* and *whom* do not occur. Furthermore, we
have seen that the humanness distinction between *who* and *which* is to some extent
blurred. In other words, there is a tendency in the ELF data to use relative pronouns
in a manner similar to relative particles. This formal levelling and functional extension may be seen as a typical consequence of language contact between ELF speakers'

---

18.   Rosenberger (2009:196) and Durham (2007) find similarly low frequencies of *who-which*
confusion in their Swiss ELF data.

L1s and English. However, judging from the low frequency of *who-which* confusion, this process can maximally be said to be in its initial stages. Moreover, this process is unlikely to gain momentum in European ELF, as it would lead to a de-Europeanisation from a typological point of view, because relative particles (as opposed to relative pronouns) are also common in languages outside Europe.

Tables 7.4 and 7.5 compare the distribution of relativisers in ESC-PC to spoken data from two major native English corpora documenting AmE and BrE usage: the *Santa Barbara Corpus* (SBC) and the *British National Corpus* (BNC; data taken from Tottie 1997c).

Table 7.4. Subject relativisers in spoken AmE/BrE (Tottie 1997c: 472) and ESC-PC

	AmE (SBC)		BrE (BNC)		ESC-PC	
	human	non-human	human	non-human	human	non-human
who	(49) 64%	(1) 2%	(47) 67%	–	(170) 72.6%	(6) 5.4%
which	–	–	–	(23) 20%	(9) 3.8%	(17) 15.2%
Σ wh-	(49) 64% [p = 0.039]	(1) 2% [p = 0.003]	(47) 67%	(23) 20%	(179) 76.5%	(23) 20.5%
that	(25) 33% [p = 0.041]	(46) 96% [p = 0.009]	(18) 26%	(84) 74%	(50) 21.4%	(89) 79.5%
ZERO	(2) 3%	(1) 2%	(3) 4%	(6) 5%	(4) 1.7%	–
total	76	48	70	113	234	112

As Table 7.4 shows, the three corpora exhibit a similar distribution for subject relativisers. Error likelihood levels are specified only for those usages in which ESC-PC differs significantly from AmE or BrE.[19] The evidence suggests that relativisation in ESC-PC is less inclined to follow AmE usage. For the more common forms, BNC shows a trend to pattern between SBC and ESC-PC. For example, ESC-PC has the highest frequency of *wh*-forms in general (76.5%), whereas SBC shows the lowest frequency of these (64%). Only *which* with non-human reference occurs slightly more often in BNC than in ESC-PC. *Who* with human reference also occurs most frequently in ESC-PC (72.6%) and least frequently in SBC (64%). The figures for *who* with non-human reference and *which* with human reference are generally low, but

---

19.   Statistical significance was established by means of chi-square tests. Differences are declared statistically significant if the likelihood of error is below 5% (p < 0.05).

such instances are largely limited to ESC-PC (there is only one such case in SBC, none in BNC). *That* with human reference is most common in SBC (33%) but least common in ESC-PC (21.4%). Only for *that* in non-human function, the frequency in ESC-PC lies in between SBC (96%) and BNC (74%). But also in this case, the percentage in ESC-PC (79.5%) is closer to the one in BNC than to the one in SBC. The frequencies of ZERO are low and stable across corpora and humanness. Another aspect pointing to a closer similarity of ESC-PC and BNC is that SBC does not show any instances of *which*, whereas BNC and ESC-PC do.

There are no significant differences between BNC and ESC-PC. By contrast, the use of *wh*-forms is significantly higher in ESC-PC compared to SBC, whereas the frequencies of *that* are significantly lower in ESC-PC than in SBC. As a consequence, both BNC and ESC-PC show a more European pattern from a typological point of view. This pattern is somewhat more pronounced in ESC-PC because of its higher frequency of *wh*-forms. AmE usage can therefore not be said to be a model for European ELF users.

Table 7.5. Object relativisers in spoken AmE/BrE (Tottie 1997c: 472) and ESC-PC

	AmE (SBC)		BrE (BNC)		ESC-PC	
	human	non-human	human	non-human	human	non-human
who	–	–	(1) 7%	–	(1) 3.3%	–
which	–	–	–	(11) 5%	–	(15) 5.4%
Σ wh-	–	–	(1) 7%	(11) 5%	(1) 3.3%	(15) 5.4%
that	(3) 60%	(35) 48%	(3) 21%	(72) 32% [p = 0.001]	(13) 43.3%	(129) 46.4%
ZERO	(2) 40%	(38) 52%	(10) 71%	(142) 63% [p < 0.001]	(16) 53.3%	(131) 47.1%
total	5	73	14	225	30	278

Table 7.5 compares the distribution of object relativisers in the three corpora. In this function, *wh*-forms are rarely used in all three corpora. For *that* and ZERO in object function, the outcome is different from that found for subject relativisers: ESC-PC patterns in between the two native corpora for *that* with human and non-human reference and for ZERO with human reference. For ZERO with non-human reference, the frequencies of ESC-PC lie below those of the two native corpora. Calculating the statistical significance reveals that there are no significant differences between SBC and ESC-PC and only two significant differences between ESC-PC and BNC which both

concern non-human reference: ESC-PC shows a significantly higher frequency of *that* and a significantly lower frequency of ZERO than BNC (which is in tune with typological Europeanness). For object relativisers, it can therefore be said that European ELF behaves relatively similar to both AmE and BrE usage and regularly clusters in between the two native corpora.[20] However, as far as the patterning of *wh*-forms is concerned, ESC-PC is again closer to BNC because SBC does not show any instances of *wh*-forms whereas the former two corpora do.

Hypothesis 1 is only partly confirmed. ESC-PC indeed shows higher frequencies of *wh*-forms and lower frequencies of ZERO than the native English corpora, but these differences are only significant in comparison to one of the two contrastive corpora (SBC and BNC) and associated with specific uses of the respective relativisers: higher use of *wh*-forms is only significantly different from SBC and restricted to subject relativisers; lower use of ZERO is only significantly different from BNC and restricted to object relativisers with non-human antecedents. The difference in usage patterns between ESC-PC and the native corpora is more salient for relativisers in subject function, because for these ESC-PC is mostly located at the extreme points, whereas for object relativisers ESC-PC generally patterns in between the two native corpora:

> Subject relativisers: AmE – BrE – ESC-PC
> Object relativisers: AmE – ESC-PC – BrE

Table 7.6. Syntactic function of relativiser for ENL/ESL and EFL speakers in ESC-PC

	ENL/ESL speakers			EFL speakers		
	subject	object	stranded	subject	object	stranded
who	29 [55.8%]	1 [1.8%]	–	147 [50.2%]	–	–
which	2 [3.8%]	3 [5.3%]	–	24 [8.2%]	12 [4.8%]	2 [8.0%]
Σ wh-	31 [59.6%]	4 [7.0%]	–	171 [58.4%]	12. [4.8%]	2 [8.0%]
that	21 [40.4%]	31. [54.4%]	4 [33.3%]	118 [40.3%]	114 [45.4%]	10 [40.0%]
ZERO	–	22 [38.6%]	8 [66.7%]	4 [1.4%]	125 [49.8%]	13 [52.0%]
total	52	57	12	293	251	25

---

20.   Tottie (1997c) points out that there are no significant differences between SBC and BNC for object relatives, which indicates that these may be a less useful candidate for distinguishing English varieties in general.

It may be suspected that a reason for the fact that many differences between the native corpora and ESC-PC were not significant is that ESC press conferences involve both native and non-native speakers of English. Therefore, it was also tested whether ENL/ESL speakers in ESC-PC use relativisers differently from EFL speakers in the corpus. For this purpose, speaker identity has been cross-tabulated with the factor groups "syntactic function" and "humanness of antecedent". With respect to syntactic function, no statistically significant differences between ENL/ESL and EFL speakers in ESC-PC can be identified (see Table 7.6).

Table 7.7. Relativisers and humanness of antecedent for ENL/ESL and EFL speakers in ESC-PC

	ENL/ESL speakers		EFL speakers	
	human	non-human	human	non-human
who	30 [60.0%]	–	144 [64.0%]	6 [2.7%]
which	–	5 [7.1%]	9 [4.0%]	30 [8.6%]
Σ wh-	30 [60.0%]	5 [7.1%]	153 [68.0%]	36 [10.3%]
that	9 [18.0%]	46 [65.7%]	58 [25.8%]	185 [53.0%]
ZERO	11 [22.0%] [p < 0.001]	19 [27.1%]	14 [6.2%]	128 [36.7%]
total	50	70	225	349

The cross-tabulation for speaker identity and humanness of antecedent (Table 7.7) shows only one significant difference between ENL/ESL and EFL speakers: the former use significantly more instances of ZERO for human reference (a finding that supports the idea that native English is a less prototypical representative of Standard Average European). There is no significant difference in the use of *wh*-forms between the two speaker groups in ESC-PC.

The overall picture one gets from these comparisons is one of extensive similarity between ENL/ESL and EFL speakers in ESC-PC. Whereas Hypothesis 1 was partly confirmed for a comparison between ESC-PC and major corpora of AmE and BrE, the ESC-PC-internal comparison yielded only minimal evidence for differences. As the data in ESC-PC come from one and the same community of practice, this indicates that convergence processes between ENL/ESL and EFL speakers may have taken place in this data.

7.7   Relativisers and L1 background

Factor group 4 classifies speakers according to their L1 background. Again language typological considerations were used to divide up the larger group of EFL speakers. This results in the following values:[21]

> ENL/ESL speaker (n; speakers from IRL, UK, MAL, rarely from Australia or the US),
> EFL speaker with North Germanic L1 (g; speakers from DAN, NOR, SWE),
> EFL speaker with another Indo-European L1 (i; the majority of speakers),
> EFL speaker with non-Indo-European L1 (x; speakers from AZE, EST, FIN, GEO, ISR, TUR).

ENL/ESL speakers constitute the minority of speakers in the dataset. However, there are some press conferences at which the majority of the delegation members have an ENL or ESL background, namely those of CYP, IRL, MAL and the UK. ENL/ESL speakers may also be actively involved in other press conferences that are otherwise dominated by EFL speakers, but in these cases they contribute a smaller amount of discourse. Due to their exceptionality in the data at large, ENL and ESL speakers are for the quantitative analysis grouped together. This is legitimated by the fact that they generally have experienced a higher exposure to English than EFL speakers. Assigning Maltese speakers to the same category as speakers from IRL and the UK in this context is also motivated by the fact that this distinction is in greater accordance with the perceptual realities across Europe as they have evolved historically in the ESC. IRL, MAL and the UK were countries that could use English in the contest even during the years in which the national language rule was in place. Regular ESC viewers are therefore likely to contrast the use of English in the contest along these national lines rather than in accordance with a native vs. non-native distinction. However, as speakers from MAL constitute only a small percentage of the group of ENL/ESL speakers in the data,[22] the comparison is also likely to provide findings that pertain in a similar fashion to a distinction between native and non-native speakers of English in Europe.

---

21.   The automatic division of speakers along national lines may be viewed critically. Even though speakers come from a certain country, their L1 need not necessarily be the national language of that particular country. However, such cases are often explicitly addressed at the press conferences because they represent instances of national crossing that possess transnational European prestige. Accordingly, the national language was assumed as a default value if speakers did not claim a different linguacultural background.

22.   Apart from the Maltese press conferences, there is only one more press conference (UKR2) in the data at which a Maltese journalist asks a question (see the list of press conferences in the Appendix: Chapter 9.2).

Among the EFL speakers, the classification is motivated by the degree of structural divergence from English to be assumed for the respective L1. The North Germanic languages Danish, Norwegian and Swedish behave as English with respect to gapping as a relativisation strategy (Olofsson 2009a; Platzack 2002: 83).[23] Similarly, they allow preposition stranding, which is uncommon in other European languages (Kurzová 1981: 101; Zifonun 2001: 52).[24] For this reason, L1 speakers of these languages are categorised separately from L1 speakers of other Indo-European languages, in which ZERO is uncommon. The remaining EFL speakers were categorised as speakers with a non-Indo-European L1. The separation of this latter group is motivated by the fact that in these languages the structural differences from English are generally larger. For example in Turkish (a Turkic language), the relative clause generally precedes the head noun as opposed to the Indo-European languages spoken in Europe, in which the relative clause is generally postnominal (Comrie & Kuteva 2005: 496; Dryer 2005: 368; Lehmann 1986: 671; Zifonun 2001: 26). Moreover, Turkish behaves differently from other European languages, because its relative structures are generally non-finite whereas most other European languages have finite relative clauses (Zifonun 2001: 19). In Hebrew, a Semitic language, pronoun retention in the relative clause is a common relativisation strategy that is only rarely found in other European languages (Comrie 2006: 143). Even though the gapping strategy is also common in Hebrew, the contexts in which it is used are markedly different from English. Whereas standard English allows for gapping in object relative clauses, Hebrew requires the omission of the relativiser in subject relative clauses (Andrews 2007: 222).

Most European speakers will not be used to the ZERO strategy from their L1 and can be expected to use this variant in lower frequencies compared to ENL speakers. Overt relativisers represent a safe default strategy for EFL speakers. Apart from stylistic considerations in terms of formality level (ZERO is associated with more informal contexts), the normatively correct application of ZERO in English (i.e. exclusively in restrictive object relative clauses) requires EFL speakers to internalise relatively complex usage conditions that necessitate distinguishing restrictive from non-restrictive relative clauses as well as object relative clauses from those with other syntactic functions (Olofsson 2009a: 334).

---

23. This is only true for the mainland Scandinavian languages, but not for the insular Scandinavian languages Faroese and Icelandic (see also Platzack 2002; Smits 1989: 70–71). Consequently, L1 speakers from ISL were not included in this group of speakers.

24. This structural similarity is probably due to the close historical relatedness of Old English and Old Norse.

According to the typological observations made above, the following hypothesis can be formulated:

> Hypothesis 3:
> (a) Among the EFL speakers in ESC-PC, those with a Danish, Norwegian or Swedish L1 background will show the highest frequency of ZERO (i.e. typologically the least European pattern).
> (b) The other two groups of EFL speakers will show lower frequencies of ZERO than ENL/ESL speakers (i.e. typologically the most European pattern).

Table 7.8 compares relativiser use of ENL/ESL and EFL speakers in ESC-PC. The majority of 82.6% of the relativiser tokens in the data originates from EFL speakers. When comparing the frequencies of *wh*-forms, *that* and ZERO, one finds that ENL/ESL and EFL speakers show remarkably similar patterns overall. Both groups favour *that* followed by *wh*- and ZERO, all with roughly similar percentages.

Table 7.8. Relativiser use of ENL/ESL and EFL speakers in ESC-PC

Speaker	who	which	Σ wh-	that	ZERO	total	%
ENL/ESL speakers	30 [24.8%]	5 [4.1%]	35 [28.9%]	56 [46.3%]	30 [24.8%]	121	17.4%
Σ EFL speakers	150 [26.0%]	39 [6.8%]	189 [32.8%]	245 [42.5%]	142 [24.7%]	576	82.6%
total	180 [25.8%]	44 [6.3%]	224 [32.1%]	301 [43.2%]	172 [24.7%]	697	

The picture changes somewhat when EFL speakers are differentiated into the three sub-groups of factor group 4 (see Table 7.9):

Table 7.9. Relativiser use of ENL/ESL speakers and three EFL speaker groups in ESC-PC

Speaker group	who	which	Σ wh-	that	ZERO	total	%
ENL/ESL	30 [24.8%]	5 [4.1%]	35 [28.9%]	56 [46.3%]	30 [24.8%]	121	17.4%
EFL: North Germanic L1	46 [31.9%]	–	46 [31.9%]	36 [25.0%]	62 [43.1%]	144	20.7%
EFL: other Indo-European L1	94 [24.5%]	38 [9.9%]	132 [34.4%]	179 [46.6%]	73 [19.0%]	384	55.1%
EFL: non-Indo-European L1	10 [20.8%]	1 [2.1%]	11 [22.9%]	30 [62.5%]	7 [14.6%]	48	6.9%
total	180 [25.8%]	44 [6.3%]	224 [32.1%]	301 [43.2%]	172 [24.7%]	697	

Table 7.9 shows that all speaker groups favour *that* except EFL speakers with Danish, Norwegian or Swedish as L1 (henceforth DNS-L1 speakers). This latter group favours ZERO (43.1%), i.e. the variant that is only in third position for all the other groups and the least European from a typological point of view. *That* in fact only ranks in third position (25.0%) for DNS-L1 speakers. ENL/ESL speakers and EFL speakers with an Indo-European L1 except DNS show similar frequencies of *that* (46.3% and 46.6% respectively). EFL speakers with a non-Indo-European L1, by contrast, show a significantly higher tendency to use *that* (62.5%; p = 0.038). This may be a reflection of the fact that invariable relative particles (like *that*) are generally more frequent outside Indo-European languages than inflected relative pronouns. The exceptional status of DNS-L1 speakers also shows in the group of *wh*-forms, where they show higher frequencies of *who* than the other speaker groups. Moreover, they form the only group that never uses *which*.

These findings confirm Hypothesis 3a, because DNS-L1 speakers use ZERO most frequently of all speaker groups (43.1%). However, these speakers clearly exceed ENL/ESL speakers in their use of ZERO (24.8%), which means that their usage pattern does not approximate native usage. This difference is statistically significant (p = 0.002). The high frequency of ZERO may be due to the fact that this strategy is even more common in North Germanic languages than in English. The idiosyncratic pattern of the North Germanic speakers would have been covered up by a mere distinction between ENL/ESL and EFL speakers (as in Table 7.8). EFL speakers with an Indo-European L1 except DNS and ENL/ESL speakers exhibit similar usage patterns overall. This dovetails neatly with the fact that English and Indo-European languages like Albanian, Dutch, French, German, Greek, Italian, Portuguese, Romanian, Spanish are more prototypical representatives of Standard Average European than the North Germanic languages and the non-Indo-European European languages (see Haspelmath 2001:1505).

Hypothesis 3b is only weakly confirmed: ELF speakers with an Indo-European L1 except DNS or a non-Indo-European L1 use lower frequencies of ZERO than ENL/ESL speakers (19.0% and 14.6% vs. 24.8%). However, this difference is not statistically significant. On the other hand, DNS-L1-speakers and other Indo-European L1 speakers use *wh*-forms more frequently than ENL/ESL speakers, but again this difference is not significant. That non-Indo-European L1 speakers show the lowest frequency of *wh*-forms and the strongest preference for *that* is in tune with the fact that these languages are generally less prototypical representatives of Standard Average European.

7.8   Relativisers and active speaker participation

Factor group 5, active speaker participation, examines whether processes of accommodation are at work in the relativisation practices of the participants at ESC press conferences. It classifies relativiser tokens depending on what kinds of speakers have been involved in the respective press conference. The following types are distinguished: press conferences involving

> EFL speakers exclusively (f),
> mainly EFL speakers and exactly one ENL/ESL speaker (1),
> mainly EFL speakers and two or more ENL/ESL speakers (2), and
> mainly ENL/ESL speakers (n; i.e. the press conferences of the delegations of CYP, IRL, MAL, UK).[25]

None of the press conferences includes ENL/ESL speakers exclusively, because all were conducted by a non-native moderator. As ELF has been characterised as a negotiable enterprise in which processes of accommodation play a critical role, it may be expected that the greatest difference in the usage patterns will be between press conferences involving mainly ENL/ESL speakers and those involving exclusively EFL speakers. If convergence has taken place in the usage of relativisers, the other two categories should pattern in between these extreme points.

> Hypothesis 4:
> Relativiser use will exhibit a continuum of usage patterns ranging from ENL/ESL-speaker dominated press conferences down to those in which EFL speakers are involved exclusively.

Table 7.10 contrasts relativiser choice at press conferences dominated by EFL speakers with those dominated by ENL/ESL speakers. There are no significant differences as far as the three major variants *wh-*, *that* and ZERO are concerned. Only *which* is used more frequently at EFL-speaker dominated press conferences.

Table 7.10. Relativiser use in relation to speaker participation in ESC-PC: Part I

Speaker participation	who	which	Σ wh-	that	ZERO	total	%
EFL-speaker dominated	154 [26.3%]	42 [7.2%]	196 [33.5%]	251 [42.9%]	138 [23.6%]	585	83.9%
ENL/ESL-speaker dominated	26 [23.2%]	2 [1.8%] [p = 0.032]	28 [25.0%]	50 [44.6%]	34 [30.4%]	112	16.1%
total	180 [25.8%]	44 [6.3%]	224 [32.1%]	301 [43.2%]	172 [24.7%]	697	

---

25.   The press conference list in the Appendix (Chapter 9.2) specifies which of the four values has been assigned to each press conference. The Cypriot press conferences were assigned to the ENL/ESL-dominated category because CYP was represented by a group of mainly British artists.

Table 7.11 splits up the EFL-speaker dominated press conferences into the groups identified as factor values of factor group 5:

Table 7.11. Relativiser use in relation to speaker participation in ESC-PC: Part II

Speaker participation	who	which	Σ wh-	that	ZERO	total	%
exclusively EFL speakers	21 [20.6%]	7 [6.9%]	28 [27.5%]	38 [37.3%]	36 [35.3%]	102	14.6%
EFL speakers + 1 ENL speaker	93 [27.4%]	19 [5.6%]	112 [33.0%]	151 [44.4%]	77 [22.6%]	340	48.8%
EFL speakers + 2 or more ENL sp.	40 [28.0%]	16 [11.2%]	56 [39.2%]	62 [43.4%]	25 [17.5%]	143	20.5%
mainly ENL/ESL speakers	26 [23.2%]	2 [1.8%]	28 [25.0%]	50 [44.6%]	34 [30.4%]	112	16.1%
total	180 [25.8%]	44 [6.3%]	224 [32.1%]	301 [43.2%]	172 [24.7%]	697	

First it needs to be noted that the types of press conferences that were deemed to be located at the two extreme points, i.e. those in which exclusively EFL speakers and mainly ENL/ESL speakers participated actively, show no significant differences whatsoever in relativiser choice. All press conference types have in common that they favour *that* as the most frequent variant. Table 7.11 documents that convergence processes cannot be verified. Hypothesis 4 is therefore not confirmed. This means that, although accommodation may be at work for other linguistic features, it is not verifiable in a systematic fashion for relativisation in this community of practice.

The two kinds of press conferences that were hypothesised to pattern between the two extreme points only do so for *that*. For *wh-* and ZERO, these press conferences rather show a process of divergence, exhibiting higher rates of *wh-* (33.0% and 39.1% compared to 27.5% and 25.0%) and lower rates of ZERO than in the other two contexts (22.6% and 17.5% versus 35.3% and 30.4%). From a typological point of view, these shifts represent a move towards higher European prototypicality. In other words, the active participation of ENL/ESL speakers at press conferences that are otherwise dominated by EFL speakers make the latter choose relativisation patterns that diverge from ENL/ESL usage patterns and are more typically European. In principle, one could also assume that the ENL/ESL speakers at these press conferences accommodate to a more European pattern, but this interpretation is less plausible because the share of the conversational contribution of ENL/ESL speakers is small. Another reason for this divergence may be that in the presence of ENL/ESL speakers, EFL speakers may feel a higher need to use forms that they have been taught to use in formal education contexts. In doing so, they depart both from talk among EFL speakers exclusively, whose interaction may be said to be less restricted by normative standards, and from interactions between mainly ENL/ESL speakers, whose vernacular has been shown to be less affected by *wh*-forms. It is intriguing to see that it is the active participation of ENL/ESL speakers at EFL-dominated press conferences that seems to trigger this divergence (for similar findings, see also Ehrenreich 2011:16; Jenkins 2011:929). It must be noted that even though only EFL speakers may speak at a press conference, there are still ENL/ESL speakers in the audience as passive participants. However, this mere presence does not seem to cause such divergence in EFL speakers.

7.9   Relativisers and European region

The remaining two factor groups test Europeanness in the geographical and political sense. Factor group 6 "European region" divides the press conferences up into seven regions of the Eurovision territory:

> north west, NW (n) [BEL, DAN, FIN, ISL, NED, NOR, SWE],
> south west, SW (s) [ESP, FRA, POR],
> central (c) [GER, POL, SLK, SLO, SUI],
> north east, NE (o) [BLR, EST, LAT, LIT, MOL, RUS, UKR],
> south east, SE (b) [ALB, BOS, BUL, CRO, GRE, MAC, ROM, SER],
> far south east (f) [ARM, AZE, CYP, GEO, ISR, MAL, TUR], and
> British Isles (i) [IRL, UK].

With this classification, it can be tested whether relativiser choice shows certain regional trends within Europe. This may seem plausible in the light of research that documents that English proficiency levels are generally higher (a) in the north compared to the south of Europe, and (b) in the west compared to the east of Europe (see European Commission 2006). Following this line of argumentation, one would expect the press conferences of countries in the north western region to approximate EFL teaching standards the most whereas those of countries from the far south eastern region would be expected to depart from these to the highest extent. However, the conceptualisation of proficiency on which these considerations are based is a highly traditional and questionable one. It equates proficiency with native-likeness and/or standard conformity and is therefore less relevant for ELF communication, where speakers' proficiency levels would rather be judged in relation to communicative efficiency and the ability to negotiate meaning in cross-cultural interaction. It is unconvincing to relate proficiency in the ELF sense to Europeanness. Therefore, Europeanness is here not conceptualised in terms of proficiency levels but in a strictly areal sense. From a strictly geographical perspective, one would expect a prototype effect, with regions lying in the centre of Europe showing more typically European patterns than peripheral regions.

Hypothesis 5:
Prototypically European relativisation patterns (i.e. high frequencies of *wh*-forms and low frequencies of ZERO) are more prevalent in central European regions.

Table 7.12. Relativisers and European region in ESC-PC

European region	who	which	Σ wh-	that	ZERO	total	%
British Isles	14 [20.6%]	1 [1.5%]	15 [22.1%]	34 [50.0%]	19 [27.9%]	68	9.8%
NW	19 [22.9%]	2 [2.4%]	21 [25.3%]	30 [36.1%]	32 [38.6%]	83	11.9%
SW	10 [27.0%]	1 [2.7%]	11 [29.7%]	18 [48.6%]	8 [21.6%]	37	5.3%
Central	25 [35.2%]	7 [9.9%]	32 [45.1%]	25 [35.2%]	14 [19.7%]	71	10.2%
NE	40 [30.2%]	13 [11.1%]	53 [41.3%]	40 [34.2%]	24 [20.5%]	117	16.8%
SE	34 [17.8%]	17 [8.9%]	51 [26.7%]	100 [52.4%]	40 [20.9%]	191	27.4%
Far SE	38 [29.2%]	3 [2.3%]	41 [31.5%]	54 [41.5%]	35 [26.9%]	130	18.7%
total	180 [25.8%]	44 [6.3%]	224 [32.1%]	301 [43.2%]	172 [24.7%]	697	

The distribution of relativisers across European regions (Table 7.12) reveals that different regions favour different forms. *That* is favoured on the British Isles and across Southern Europe (i.e. the regions SW, SE and Far SE). Central and North Eastern Europe, on the other hand, favour *wh*-forms. The difference between these two and the other regions is statistically significant.[26] In the NW area, relativiser use is most balanced between the three variants. The most common strategy in this area is ZERO, which is not surprising if one considers that this region includes the three groups of Danish, Norwegian and Swedish speakers, who have already been shown to produce higher frequencies of ZERO. ZERO is in fact the variant used least in most of the areas studied (except NW, where it is favoured, and the British Isles, where *wh*-occurs less frequently). With five out of seven regions using ZERO least frequently, it seems that low frequencies of ZERO are a candidate for a typically European usage pattern, which is also in accordance with typological Europeanness. Not surprisingly,

---

26. Comparison of the NE value (41.3%) and the Far SE value (31.5%): p = 0.026.

the British Isles and the NW show the highest percentages of ZERO (27.9% and 38.6% respectively). Four of the five other regions (SW, Central, NE and SE) hover around 20% in their usage of ZERO. The Far SE region approximates the British Isles and the NW with 26.9%. It can therefore be seen that ZERO is the least frequent variant in a large central European area, whereas those regions in which this is not or less the case can be found on the northwestern and far southeastern fringes of the ESC territory. One also needs to note that *wh*-forms show the lowest ranking and percentage (22.1%) on the British Isles and in the NW (25.3%). All other regions show higher percentages, culminating in 45.1% for Central Europe. This suggests that European ELF talk at ESC press conferences departs from native English usage patterns in its higher use of *wh*-forms and its lower use of ZERO. *That*, by contrast, is common in all regions (ranging from 34.2% in NE to 52.4% in SE) and is nowhere the least favoured variant.

The following continuum can be set up for the use of ZERO across European regions:

Central (19.7%) < NE (20.5%) < SE (20.9%) < SW (21.6%) < Far SE (26.9%) < Brit. Isl. (27.9%) < NW (38.6%)

For the use of *wh*-forms, a similar continuum evolves:

Central (45.1%) > NE (41.3%) > Far SE (31.5%) > SW (29.7%) > SE (26.7%) > NW (25.3%) > Brit. Isl. (22.1%)

In these continua, the two extrema are invariably formed by central/NE on the one side and NW/British Isles on the other side. The southern regions (SE, SW, Far SE) cluster between these two extrema, even if in varying orders. The most prototypical European patterns (i.e. lower frequencies of ZERO and higher frequencies of *wh*-) are found in central and NE Europe, while the British Isles and the NW region exhibit the least prototypically European patterns (see also Table 7.13). Hypothesis 5 is therefore largely confirmed.

Table 7.13. Ranking of relativiser types across European regions in ESC-PC

	1.	2.	3.
British Isles	*that*	ZERO	*wh-*
NW	ZERO	*that*	*wh-*
SW	*that*	*wh-*	ZERO
Central	*wh-*	*that*	ZERO
NE	*wh-*	*that*	ZERO
SE	*that*	*wh-*	ZERO
Far SE	*that*	*wh-*	ZERO

7.10   Relativisers and EU status

Factor group 7, EU status, tests whether the patterns of relativiser choice in the data correspond to political realities in contemporary Europe. For this purpose, the press conferences are divided up into those of

> Anglophone EU member states (a) [IRL, MAL, UK],
> other EU member states (e) [BEL, BUL, CYP, DAN, ESP, EST, FIN, FRA, GER, GRE, LAT, LIT, NED, POL, POR, ROM, SLK, SLO, SWE],
> official EU membership candidates (c) [CRO, ISL, MAC, TUR], and
> non-EU countries (n) [ALB, ARM, AZE, BLR, BOS, GEO, ISR, MOL, NOR, RUS, SER, SUI, UKR].

If one accepts the EU as the central political institution of Europe, one would expect that the usage patterns found for EU countries are approximated more by the four EU membership candidate countries than by the other non-EU countries.

> Hypothesis 6:
> EU candidate countries will pattern in between EU and non-EU countries.

Table 7.14. Relativisers and EU-status in ESC-PC

EU status	who	which	Σ wh-	that	ZERO	total	%
Anglophone EU	25 [26.0%]	1 [1.0%]	26 [27.1%]	44 [45.8%]	26 [27.1%]	96	13.8%
Other EU	71 [24.0%]	25 [8.4%]	96 [32.4%]	118 [39.9%]	82 [27.7%]	296	42.5%
EU candidates	16 [23.2%]	2 [2.9%]	18 [26.1%]	31 [44.9%]	20 [29.0%]	69	9.9%
Non-EU	68 [28.8%]	16 [6.8%]	84 [35.6%]	108 [45.8%]	44 [18.6%]	236	33.9%
Total	180 [25.8%]	44 [6.3%]	224 [32.1%]	301 [43.2%]	172 [24.7%]	697	

When looking at the relationship between relativiser use and the political affiliation of the respective countries (Table 7.14), one finds that there is much less variance associated with this factor group compared to the geographical division in the preceding chapter. At the press conferences of all status groups (EU members, non-EU countries and candidate countries), *that* is used most frequently (with frequencies ranging from 39.9% to 45.8%). The frequencies for *wh-* and *that* do not show any significant differences between the four groups of countries. Still, one can detect certain mechanisms at work for the use of ZERO. The Anglophone and other EU countries show frequencies around 27% for ZERO. The non-EU countries show a lower percentage of this variant (18.6%). The four candidate countries do not pattern between the non-EU and the EU countries (Hypothesis 6 is, therefore, not confirmed). They do not just approximate ZERO usage in the EU member countries but even slightly exceed the latter, having the highest frequency of 29.0%. This finding is reminiscent of the common pattern found in numerous sociolinguistic studies where lower middle class speakers outperform the higher middle class speakers as a consequence of their motivation to climb up the social ladder (a phenomenon known under the name "hypercorrection"). If one takes a closer look at the frequencies of the *wh*-forms, one finds a similar pattern. The candidate countries (26.1%) exceed the EU countries (27.0% and 32.4%) in having the lowest frequency of *wh*-forms. The non-EU countries, in turn, show the highest frequency of *wh*-forms (35.6%). In other words, it is the non-EU countries and the candidate countries that form the extreme poles:

> *wh*-forms: non-EU > other EU > Anglo EU > candidates
> ZERO: non-EU < Anglo EU < other EU < candidates

The non-EU countries clearly form the group that departs most from the other three: they show the lowest frequency of ZERO and the highest frequency of *wh*-. If one relates this to language typology, it is interesting to note that the non-EU countries show the most typically European pattern, together with the non-Anglophone EU countries. In this sense, the EU candidate countries show the least prototypical European pattern, having higher rates of ZERO than *wh*-. This may indicate that the prestige target for these countries is not so much European ELF but normative English teaching standards. In other words, aspiring to EU status goes with a greater desire to speak "native-like English".

7.11   Multivariate analysis

To find out the relative weight of the six independent factor groups, the data were submitted to a VARBRUL analysis. A VARBRUL analysis automatically corrects for associations between certain factor groups, identifying the model that describes the data best. All three major variants were tested selecting the option "binomial step-up/step-down" in *Goldvarb X*.

For the use of *that*, the programme identifies four out of six independent variables that are found to have a significant impact on relativiser choice (log likelihood = −412.019; p = 0.047):

1. syntactic function: subject favours *that*; direct object and complement of stranded preposition disfavour it,
2. humanness of antecedent: human antecedents disfavour *that*; nonhuman antecedents favour it,
3. L1 background of speaker: DNS-L1 speakers strongly disfavour *that*; non-Indo-European L1 speakers strongly favour it,
4. European region: a continuum of factor weights, with the NE region disfavouring *that* the most and the SE region favouring it the most.

The variables active press conference participation and EU status do not lead to significant effects for *that*.

For the use of *wh-*, the programme identifies three variables that are found to have a significant impact (log likelihood = −251.568; p = 0.018):

1. syntactic function: subject favours *wh-*; direct object and complement of stranded preposition disfavour it,
2. humanness of antecedent: human antecedents favour *wh-*; nonhuman antecedents disfavour it,
3. European region: NE and central regions favour *wh-*, the other regions slightly disfavour it.

The variables L1 background of speaker, active press conference participation and EU status do not lead to significant effects for *wh-*.

For the use of ZERO, the programme identifies three variables that are found to have a significant impact (log likelihood = −238.702; p = 0.038):

1. syntactic function: subject strongly disfavours ZERO; direct object and complement of stranded preposition strongly favour it,
2. L1 background of speaker: DNS-L1 speakers strongly favour ZERO; non-Indo-European L1 speakers strongly disfavour it,
3. EU status: EU candidate countries favour ZERO, non-EU countries disfavour it.

The variables humanness of antecedent, active press conference participation and European region do not lead to significant effects for ZERO.

Table 7.15 gives the factor weights for the five variables out of the six tested that show significant effects. Factor weights larger than 0.5 favour the variant; factor weights below 0.5 disfavour the variant ("ns" stands for "not significant"). The range of the factor values indicates the strength of the effect. From these range values, one can see that the structural factor groups (syntactic function and humanness of antecedent) in general have a stronger effect than the other factor groups. Moreover, there is no factor group for which *that* has the strongest effect, which again points to the higher diagnostic value of *wh-* and ZERO.

Table 7.15. Factor weights of factors significantly influencing relativiser choice in ESC-PC

Factor groups	wh-	that	ZERO	Tokens
Syntactic function				
– subject	0.763	0.610	0.085	345
– object	0.247	0.392	0.912	308
– stranded prep. object	0.176	0.384	0.923	37
	range: 0.587	range: 0.226	range: 0.838	
Humanness of antecedent				
– human pronoun	0.894	0.106	ns	94
– *people*	0.772	0.242	ns	55
– human common noun	0.767	0.325	ns	114
– human collective noun	0.718	0.384	ns	30
– nonhuman pronoun	0.075	0.679	ns	77
– nonhuman common noun	0.381	0.685	ns	328
	range: 0.819	range: 0.579		
L1 background of speaker				
– ENL/ESL speaker	ns	0.536	0.396	144
– DNS-L1 speaker	ns	0.341	0.794	121
– other Indo-European L1	ns	0.518	0.435	386
– non-Indo-European L1	ns	0.731	0.298	50
		range: 0.390	range: 0.496	
European region				
– British Isles	0.425	0.572	ns	68
– Northwest	0.439	0.485	ns	84
– Central	0.560	0.448	ns	71
– Northeast	0.716	0.390	ns	118
– Southwest	0.407	0.526	ns	37
– Southeast	0.433	0.600	ns	192
– Far Southeast	0.462	0.445	ns	131
	range: 0.309	range: 0.210		
EU status				
– Anglophone EU	ns	ns	0.577	96
– other EU	ns	ns	0.548	299
– EU candidates	ns	ns	0.594	69
– non-EU	ns	ns	0.383	237
			range: 0.211	

Not significant: active speaker participation

It turns out that the three major relativisers are influenced by different factor group combinations. Syntactic function is the only variable that has a significant impact on the use of all three variants. This is the least surprising for ZERO, which shows a nearly categorical distribution and is virtually confined to non-subject functions. In addition, the other two variants show clear preferences despite the fact that they could easily be used in all three syntactic functions: both *wh-* and *that* favour subject function and disfavour the other two functions.

Humanness of antecedent is also a variable that has proven to be relevant in many previous studies. Undoubtedly, it has a powerful impact on the choice of *who* vs. *which*, also in the ELF data at hand. But the VARBRUL analysis conducted here has tested *wh-* forms in general. Theoretically, all three major variants, *wh-*, *that* and ZERO, could be used for human and non-human antecedents. In spite of this, humanness of antecedent exerts a powerful influence on two of these variants: *wh-* and *that*, the former favouring human antecedents and the latter favouring non-human antecedents.

The remaining four factor groups have tested the influence of variables that have so far received less, if any, attention in studies on relativiser choice. The factor group "active speaker participation" yielded interesting results when considered in isolation. However, the VARBRUL analysis showed that its actual impact on the data is relatively low compared to the other factors. The remaining three factor groups indeed showed significant effects.

The L1 background of the speaker influences the usage patterns for *that* and ZERO. More specifically, non-Indo-European L1 speakers disfavour ZERO and favour *that*, while it is the other way round for DNS-L1 speakers.

The factor European region has a significant impact on the use of *wh-* and *that* in the ELF data. The factor weights for *that* show a relatively narrow range (from 0.390 to 0.600) and no clear center-periphery effects, maybe because *that* functions over wide stretches as a default relativiser and relative particles cannot be linked to Europeanness in terms of language typology. Although ZERO was found to be associated with a center-periphery continuum of frequencies when viewed in isolation, the influence of European region was observed to be low in the VARBRUL analysis. *Wh-* showed a similar continuum of percentages and was identified as significantly influenced by European region. The NE and the central region favour *wh-* and therefore show the typologically most European pattern.

Finally, Europeanness in the political sense (EU status) is identified in the VARBRUL analysis to have a significant effect on the use of ZERO, which is strongly disfavoured by speakers from non-EU countries (0.383) and generally favoured by EU countries, with EU candidate countries favouring it the most (0.594). The fact that political circumstances may influence language is not remarkable as such. One needs only to consider that national politics have in the past frequently been adduced to account for the separation of "languages" from what would linguistically be more adequately described as a dialect continuum (see, for example, Wright 2011). However, such nationalist language policies and the Ausbau processes promoted by them are invariably a matter of con-scious intervention. The usage patterns of ZERO along EU lines at ESC press confer-ences, by contrast, can be considered a more subconscious mechanism.

7.12   Conclusions: The formal hybridity of European ELF

Relativiser use at ESC press conferences provides strong evidence for the internal structural hybridity of European ELF. The relativisers used by these European ELF speakers are mostly in accordance with normative grammar and only rarely diverge from it (few instances of relativiser *what* or *who-which* confusion). It is, therefore, not justified to consider non-standard relativisation a typical feature of European ELF. The repertoire of forms used in this community of practice does not usually cause commu-nication problems and is therefore in tune with the form-follows-function principle of ELF talk. A clear orientation towards BrE or AmE as the two major reference varieties used in European ELT could not be verified. Moreover, a range of factors was shown to have an impact on which forms are used – a finding that contradicts a characterisation of European ELF as a stable variety. Among these are structural factors that speakers are likely to have learnt about in formal foreign language education (syntactic function of relativiser and humanness of antecedent) as well as the speakers' L1 backgrounds and Europeanness in the regional and political sense. The importance of the three lat-ter factors indicates that linguistic variability in transnational communication may not necessarily be adequately described using explanatory factors that have been found to be at work for native variation.

It is furthermore interesting that language typology may prove to be an explana-tory tool for the variation exhibited by structural features in transnational commu-nication via ELF. The usage of *wh*-forms and ZERO showed the highest degree of variation, whereas *that* produced more stable patterns and so appears to be the default relativiser (common across syntactic functions and contexts). Higher frequencies of *wh*-relativisers and lower frequencies of ZERO render ELF usage typologically more European, whereas the use of the relative particle *that* is not connected to such an effect. Research on the connection between language typology and sociolinguistics is still in its infancy (see Trudgill 1997), but may become more important when linguists need to explain patterns of language use in transnational contexts.

Still, one also needs to take note of the limitations of the analysis of relativisation carried out here. A more detailed description of European ELF would need to look at a whole range of typologically relevant features and their manifestation in Euro-pean ELF. Moreover, the quantitative methodology adopted here would have to be supplemented by qualitative procedures in order to shed light on the local negotiation processes (such as accommodation) that may also affect the use of structural features.

The finding that accommodation as a factor seems to be of relatively little import for relativisation practices in ELF may be considered surprising. Accommodative linguistic behaviour has been highlighted as a (if not *the*) central process at work in ELF talk (see, for example, Dewey 2011). Furthermore, common motivations attested for convergence such as a desire for social acceptance or greater intelligibility would certainly be compatible with the transnational European salience of ESC press conferences as an interactional context. Accommodation is, of course, a general socio-linguistic phenomenon that is not restricted to ELF communication. The fact that its influence on relativisation practices is smaller than that of other factors indicates that it may not possess the ubiquitous quality in ELF talk that has widely been assumed.

One reason for this may be that accommodation assumes that speakers adapt their speech behaviour to the linguistic behaviour of their interlocutors or to the communicative needs of the latter. However, ESC press conferences represent a relatively large and culturally diverse community of practice, and it can therefore be difficult to judge which linguistic behaviour or communicative needs a certain interlocutor may have. This means that the point of orientation for accommodative behaviour is in many cases vague or left to conjecture. Another reason may be that convergence does not take place systematically in ELF talk but at a strictly local level. Interlocutors may, for example, only converge temporarily when they anticipate that communicative difficulty is arising (compare Extract 10). Such instances of selective convergence cannot be captured using quantitative techniques and need to be studied at the qualitative level, where they have also been amply illustrated in previous ELF research (e.g. Cogo & Dewey 2012: ch. 4.5; Dewey 2011: 210).

Chapter 8

Synthesis: The discursive formation of European ELF

8.1 Introduction

In the preceding empirical chapters, we have looked at various levels of the discursive formation of European ELF at ESC press conferences. Although communities of practice that contribute to this discursive formation are numerous, the context studied here can be considered as central in this respect. There are two reasons for this. First, ESC press conferences constitute a pan-European media context whose potential reach extends well beyond the participants present in the press conference hall. This means that the way European ELF is performed in this community of practice is received by a much larger pan-European audience than is the case for most other institutional ELF contexts, which are not normally broadcast on television or published on the internet. Second, the ELF interactions carried out at ESC press conferences involve speakers from 39 different national backgrounds to roughly equal proportions, who engage in transnational intra-European communication. This fact, together with the European salience of the ESC, can be assumed to result in a highly prototypical manifestation of European ELF.

We have already seen in the 2010 dataset that ELF plays the leading role at ESC press conferences, because it ensures wider intelligibility across Europe and enables participants to attenuate their national affiliations in front of the pan-European audience – a mechanism that carries high prestige in this community of practice. At the time of writing, the preparations for the ESC 2013 in Malmö are in full speed. And it seems that the growing importance of ELF both for cross-European understanding and cooperation has become even more prominent. Evidence for this can be gained from the official website of the ESC 2013 (www.eurovision.tv). In the press section of this website, journalists cannot just find information on how to receive an accreditation for the event. For the first time, press representatives are explicitly offered free English language courses in preparation for the event (see Eurovision.tv 2013). The text of the advertisement from the website is reproduced below:

> [headline, large font, bold print:] *Break down barriers at the Eurovision Song Contest 2013*
> [subheadline, bold print:] *Perfect your English with EF, the Official Language Learning Provider of the Eurovision Song Contest 2013*

[body copy:] *Enhance your experience covering the Eurovision Song Contest in Sweden with complimentary English lessons from EF Education First, the world's largest private education company. Founded in 1965 near Malmoe, EF has been breaking down barriers of language, geography and culture that divide us for nearly fifty years.*

As the Official Language Learning provider of the Eurovision Song Contest 2013, EF can help you prepare for the event by offering you a 3-month English course at EF's Englishtown, the world's largest online English school. You will even get three group lessons and one private lesson with a native speaker for free.

For your complimentary 3-month course, visit www.ef.com/eurovision and start advancing your English today.

[logo:] *EUROVISION SONG CONTEST MALMÖ 2013*

[slogan, large font, bold print:] *World leader in International Education/EF Education First*

The headline of the advertisement, *Break down barriers at the Eurovision Song Contest*, presupposes that there are in fact barriers within Europe. In the body copy, it is further specified which barriers are thought to exist. The types of barriers named clearly orient to the two central functions that ELF was found to fulfil at ESC press conferences, namely ensuring wider, cross-European communication (*barriers of language*) and toning down national affiliations in the service of European transnationalism (*barriers of geography and culture*). English is in this advertisement constructed as the means by which participants can break down these barriers. The directives *Perfect your English* (at the beginning of the subheadline) and *start advancing your English* (towards the end of the second paragraph of the body copy) presuppose that the addressee in fact already possesses a certain command of English, which, however, may be insufficient to fulfil the task of breaking down barriers. It is, therefore, evident that proficiency does play a role in this ELF context. Still, there is further evidence that proficiency is here not necessarily viewed in terms of native-likeness or grammatical correctness, because the services offered include only *one lesson with a native speaker*, whereas *three group lessons* are offered, which can be assumed to involve mainly non-native speakers. From the point of view of ELF communication, it is also interesting to note that the spelling ⟨*Malmoe*⟩ is used in the body copy (in contrast to the spelling in the unchangeable logo), probably in accommodation to readers whose L1 does not include the letter ⟨*ö*⟩, which is true for most European languages.

As suggested by the title of this book, the four preceding empirical chapters have shed new light on English as a European lingua franca by studying aspects of its usage that have so far received little (if any) research attention. The analysis of code choice patterns at ESC press conferences in Chapter 4 has documented that European ELF communication is per se not a puristically English form of communication but invariably involves the presence of other European languages that are activated as part of the participants' linguistic repertoires. Closer inspection of the circumstances under which language material traditionally considered non-English surfaces at the press conferences has shown that this material is usually employed to facilitate (rather than impede) communicative success and to cater for interactional functions for which ELF is not equipped (for example, cross-national solidarity-creation through tokenistic code switching in greetings). Linguistic diversity is here visible in two aspects: (a) the use of material stemming from European languages other than English in facilitative functions (for example, for clarification or as a means of crossing to enhance the interlocutor's face), and (b) the internal hybridity of ELF which results from the various linguacultural backgrounds of its users. These aspects distinguish ELF as a linguistic phenomenon from native and national uses of English.

Chapter 5 studied how participants describe their own linguistic practices. The bottom-up or folk-linguistic evidence provided by metalinguistic comments was at the same time inflected in a top-down fashion, namely by the centrality of Europeanness to the context, i.e. what was said and how it was said was decisively influenced by how participants want to be seen by the pan-European audience. Judging from the comments, English is in this community of practice widely constructed as an adequate medium for a transnational context, while other languages are more likely to be constructed as potentially impeding transnationalism and communicative efficiency.

The analysis of complimenting behaviour via ELF at ESC press conferences in Chapter 6 demonstrated that these (mainly non-native) ELF users are clearly not pragmatically deficient speakers. They form a community of competent language users who generally exhibit high abilities with respect to intercultural meaning negotiation. The complimenting practices observed pay witness to the operation of two sets of norms, namely those that seem to be typical of transnational ELF communication more generally (for example, the centrality of solidarity-creating compliments across national boundaries) and those that are more specific to the community of practice at hand (for example, the freedom from traditional gendered and sexual normativities connected to complimenting).

Finally, the documentation of relativisation practices in Chapter 7 yielded evidence for the internal structural hybridity of ELF and for the fact that ELF communication underlies a complex set of potentially influential factors – two aspects that contest the notion of (European) ELF as a "variety". Moreover, language typological considerations have opened up new ways of relating the structural diversity within ELF to Europeanness.

The following chapters discuss the implications of the findings in the empirical chapters in the light of the research questions outlined in Chapter 2.5. On a more general level, the question how to conceptualise ELF is discussed in Chapter 8.2. Chapter 8.3 concentrates on the connection between ELF and Europeanness as evident in the community of practice studied. Finally, Chapter 8.4 discusses the implications of the research findings presented in this book for ELF-oriented European language policies.

8.2   Conceptualising ELF

Despite the fact that ELF research has turned into a vibrant field of study during the last decade, it remains a field in which discussions of the conceptual status of ELF play a major role (see, for example, the debate published in recent editions of the *ELT Journal*: Cogo 2012b; Dewey 2013; Sewell 2013; Sowden 2012; Sung 2013). This is an outcome of at least two aspects. On the one hand, critics from non-ELF research backgrounds regularly misconstrue the basic tenets of the ELF paradigm, which in turn induces ELF researchers to correct these false assumptions and to clarify their positions. On the other hand, ELF theorisation has generally proven to be open for new theoretical influences and more specifically for recent postmodernist-minded developments in linguistics, which have necessitated a rethinking and adaptation of the basic tenets of earlier ELF research. The present chapter intends to contribute to this debate in the light of the Europe-based research findings presented in the previous chapters.

The empirical analyses of European ELF in Chapters 4 to 7 have yielded insights into the discursive formation of ELF from a range of different angles. What these various perspectives on ELF have documented is that a conceptualisation of ELF as a "variety" or "language", or as a form of language use connected to a "speech community" must be met with reservation, because these latter concepts build on notions of internal stability, homogeneity and purity, native speaker authority, geographical boundedness and national association that are neither borne out by ELF as a linguistic phenomenon nor are they particularly relevant for ELF communication (see James 2008; Modiano 2006; Seidlhofer 2010; see also Blommaert & Rampton 2011:5 for a similar argument about the status of the concepts "native speaker", "mother tongue", and "ethnolinguistic group"). While the participants at ESC press conferences clearly orient to such dominant discourses (as the analysis on metalinguistic comments in Chapter 5 illustrates) in order to make sense of the linguistic diversity they are faced with, it is at the same time also apparent that their linguistic practices frequently contradict such notions. The analysis of code choice practices at the press conferences suggests that ELF communication is in several respects not purely English communication, since the linguistic repertoires that ELF speakers draw on is per se a heterogeneous resource that is not restricted to the material of one "language". Moreover, although "English" is widely constructed as the default choice in this community of practice, this does not mean that it is English in its most traditional sense – namely as adhering to normative grammar, orienting to native speakers as role models and associated with Anglophone nations – that is perceived as the norm in this context. Here it is rather the non-native, non-national and transnational uses of English that are constructed as unproblematic and normal, and these do not fit into the systematic straitjacket of a "variety" or even a "language". "English" is in this context an inclusive medium that – in the service of cross-European communication – transcends traditional linguistic as well as national boundaries. Issues of native, national or linguistic exclusivity are strongly backgrounded in this phenomenon.

Widdowson (2012:9) describes concepts like "language" and "variety" as "convenient fictions", acknowledging that their use in linguistic research is a methodological necessity and therefore not reprehensible as such. But what Widdowson also is at pains to point out is that these concepts are certainly not neutral or objective tools – they rather work in the interest of certain groups of people (for example, native speakers of English and the ELT industry). To accept only one set of concepts that is based on native speakers as normative authorities is, therefore, clearly a matter of dominance, as research on ELF has increasingly demonstrated. Moreover, to cling to a set of concepts without being willing to adapt them to new social realities and needs is, of course, clearly up to criticism. It is a central motivation of ELF research as a critical paradigm to expose such dominant discourses associated with "English" as ideologically or politically charged (Sewell 2013:7). This can also be witnessed in Widdowson's recent account of the subject:

> We need abstract constructs, I have argued, because they represent our realities and without them we cannot make sense of the world. But these constructs represent different realities, different socio-cultural schemata, values, beliefs, ways of thinking that are appropriate to certain purposes, relevant to certain circumstances. One can see, of course, why it is politically and commercially expedient to represent a language, particularly English, as a well-defined and self-enclosed entity with fully competent native speakers to provide its norms of correctness. But these norms are determined by cultural and identity factors that no longer apply outside native-speaking communities. One can see that once such a construct of English is established as convenient fiction it becomes taken for granted and there is no need to question its validity: attitudes harden and the fiction takes on the force of fact. But when purposes and circumstances change, when English gets globalized as a lingua franca and becomes common property, and thus a means of expressing other cultural values, other identities, then there is the obvious need to adapt our representations of reality. The old conditions of relevance and appropriateness no longer apply.
> (Widdowson 2012:19)

It almost goes without saying that ELF is just as much ideologically charged as ENL. The two concepts can be seen as symptomatic of two competing ideologies, whose competition has recently become more lively (though not yet balanced) due to the strengthening of the ELF research paradigm.

As Sewell (2013:4) points out, the inclusivity of ELF is an aspect that current research on the topic is still struggling with, both methodologically and theoretically. ELF is commonly framed in terms of difference from ENL, a procedure that has an undesirable reifying effect and backgrounds both the internal hybridity of ELF and its extensive overlap with ENL. However, arguments connected to linguistic and/or geographical boundedness (as suggested by such difference-related discussions) are not applicable to ELF in the same way as they are to ENL. Moreover, Sewell (2013:6) adds that many features that are commonly claimed to be typical of ELF seem to by typical of human communication or language contact situations more generally (see also MacKenzie 2012:92). It follows that ELF research does not so much talk about entirely new phenomena but rather advances a recognition of these phenomena in a different light.

This does not mean that ELF is associated with an "anything goes" position. The analysis of metalinguistic comments on the use of English has shown that a certain degree of English proficiency is clearly expected, but this proficiency is not conceptualised in terms of adherence to normative grammar or native-likeness.[1] This is also highlighted by Seidlhofer:

> For non-native ELF speakers, being able to use the language like native speakers and without traces of their L1 is increasingly perceived as unnecessary, unrealistic, and, at least by some, as positively undesirable. Indeed, countless ELF speakers have begun to assert their identities and to operate according to their own 'commonsense' criteria. These relate not to externally defined native-speaker norms but to their emically perceived communicative needs and wants in the situation they find themselves in.
> (Seidlhofer 2011:50)

In ELF, communicative efficiency across national and L1 boundaries is the central factor determining who counts as a proficient speaker, and this does not just involve the use of linguistic forms that are widely intelligible but also the ability to negotiate meaning, to accommodate to the needs of one's interlocutors and, finally, an awareness of the social indexicality of one's linguistic choices.

As native speakers form a minority in most ELF contexts and are, as a consequence, not in the position to enforce their normative standards, ELF puts all participants on an equal footing. All participants in ELF interactions have to engage in the communcative negotiation that the local context demands. Even though the native acquisition of English generally involves less conscious effort than language learning in formal education, it is evident that native speakers are not per se "good" ELF communicators. Native speakers of English have traditionally been considered to have an unfair advantage compared to their non-native co-participants in ELF interactions. But (monolingual) native speakers who show no willingness to engage in the local linguistic negotiation processes that ELF interactions require lack a central cultural resource that non-native users of ELF generally have at their disposal, namely the use of English as a denationalised medium. This use is more compatible with transnational

---

1.   As Gal (2013:180) notes, grammatical correctness is also only rarely a key concern for native speakers.

communication than native uses of English, which are still conceptually firmly rooted in national affiliations. In fact, ELF is nobody's mother tongue and all users are required to make an effort to become efficient ELF communicators. This effort may even be harder for native English speakers, because they generally are less prototypical representatives of the category "ELF speaker" and therefore may be required to adjust their habitual modes of language production and reception in order to become more effective ELF communicators (Jenkins 2012: 487).

Taken together, the evidence adduced in Chapters 4 to 7 suggests a processual conceptualisation (Seidlhofer 2009b: 42), which does not view ELF in terms of a stable language system but rather as a matter of on-going change in situated performance (cf. also Canagarajah 2007) – a view that has gained more prominence in sociolinguistics more generally:

> But this commitment to system-in-language has been challenged by a linguistics of communicative practice, rooted in a linguistic-anthropological tradition running from Sapir through Hymes and Gumperz to Hanks (1996), Verschueren (1999) and Agha (2007). This approach puts situated action first, it sees linguistic conventions/ structures as just one (albeit important) semiotic resource among a number available to participants in the process of local language production and interpretation, and it treats meaning as an active process of here-and-now projection and inferencing, ranging across all kinds of percept, sign and knowledge.
>
> (Blommaert & Rampton 2011: 5)

For the study of ELF, the research focus must accordingly shift from describing a "variety" to describing "variation", and from describing codified linguistic norms to describing the contextual functions of linguistic features (cf. Seidlhofer 2011: 73). A processual view of language is also expressed in the concept of "languaging" (Møller & Jørgensen 2009), which has recently been connected to ELF theorisation (Ferguson 2009: 129; Seidlhofer 2009a: 242). In such an ELF conceptualisation, speakers are thought to exploit their linguistic resources without necessarily staying within the limits of "English" in the traditional sense. On the formal level, ELF instead turns out to be a hybrid formation involving communicative practices of which some are in accordance with normative English grammar (like most instances of relativisation in European ELF), some are non-standard from a traditional point of view (like the cases of relative *what* and *who-which* confusion), some are non-English (as, for example, L1 substrate influences or code switching within ELF talk), and some may constitute (pragmatically motivated) neologistic or nonce formations (which in turn may adhere to the word-formation patterns of any of the "languages" that form components in the ELF user's linguistic repertoire).

Even though ELF communication exhibits a high degree of linguistic creativity, this does not mean that it is completely abstract in its exploitation of linguistic resources. There are certain constraints at work, which locate ELF communication at the interface of structure and agency. These constraints cannot be sufficiently described with recourse to linguistic norm-dependency or orientation to native speakers of English as role models. By contrast, the factors restricting ELF usage are primarily local issues, such as the linguistic repertoires and ELF-related proficiency levels of the interactants, the generic conventions of the context of language use, locally ritualised practices (for example, the degree of European prominence) and the local require-ments of communicative efficiency. All of these influences work together to create a specific type of ELF culture in which participants construct identities that transcend their ethnic or national affiliations as L1 speakers of a certain "language". At ESC press conferences, for example, transnational European identities or the identities of inter-nationally oriented music and media professionals regularly take precedence over national identifications.

Due to its heterogeneity, instability and defiance of variety-formation, ELF repre-sents the epitome of language use in the postmodern world (cf. James 2008) and can be related to the notion of transcultural flows (Pennycook 2007b), which describes the travelling of English around the globe in the shape of local adaptations rather than as a monolithic, nationalist form of Anglophone colonialism. As has been shown by the empirical analyses in this book, the local context shapes concrete manifestations of ELF (see also Pölzl & Seidlhofer 2006).

The spread of English – in Europe and around the world – has in the past mainly been viewed from two perspectives: the homogeny position, which figures promi-nently in debates of linguistic imperialism (i.e. one language is said to spread and propagate an Anglo-American mindset; e.g. Phillipson 2008a/b), and the heterogeny position associated with the World Englishes paradigm, which describes new outer-circle Englishes in their own right to aid their emancipation from major reference varieties (Pennycook 2007a: 104). Both approaches have been criticised for their essentialist treatment of what is covered by the term "English" and for failing to enter an ontological debate of what it actually is that we call "English" (see Dewey 2007; Graddol 2006; Kirkpatrick 2006; Pennycook 2007a; Saraceni 2008).

Heterogeneity is indeed a useful concept to describe the various manifestations covered by the term "English". However, to base heterogeneity conceptually on the nation as a classificatory tool does no longer do justice to the complex, increas-ingly transnational realities in which "English" surfaces today. ELF research has in this respect substantially contributed to a reconceptualisation of linguistic diversity in an alternative way to variety pluralisation, namely as subject to local appropria-tion, contextual fluidity and internal hybridity (Cogo 2008: 58; Otsuji & Pennycook 2010: 251). These considerations are also in tune with recent discussions of language and "superdiversity" (as opposed to "multilingualism"; Blommaert & Rampton 2011; Creese & Blackledge 2010; Makoni & Pennycook 2012). In this line of research, the focus of attention shifts away from the question how many languages or varieties there are and whether we need to save or promote them to the power-related question to whose benefit and detriment such a pluralistic conceptualisation of linguistic diversity works. A pluralistic, nationally based classificatory system of linguistic diversity is first and foremost beneficial to those speaker groups that are traditionally considered to be the "owners" of the respective languages and varieties. More specifically, it enables them to employ gatekeeping strategies that exclude non-native and non-national users of English by degrading their language use to the status of non-standard, incorrect usage or interlanguage. With ELF realities in mind, it is inadequate to claim that the spread of English represents the spread of a homogeneous, Anglo-American phenomenon around the globe. One would rather have to concede that the label "English" covers highly heterogeneous phenomena, many of which cannot be neatly mapped onto nation states, and that traditional questions of ownership become less relevant for English in our postmodern world.

Pennycook links the criticism of the homogeny and heterogeny positions to his notion of "transcultural flows":

> English is closely tied to processes of globalization: a language of threat, desire, destruction and opportunity. It cannot be fully understood in modernist states-centric models of imperialism or world Englishes, or in terms of traditional, segregationist models of language. [...] [W]e need to move beyond arguments about homogeneity or heterogeneity, or imperialism and nation states, and instead focus on translocal and transcultural flows. English is a translocal language, a language of fluidity and fixity that moves across, while becoming embedded in, the materiality of localities and social relations. English is bound up with transcultural flows, a language of imagined communities and refashioning identities.   (Pennycook 2007b: 5–6)

The images evoked in this description clearly resonate with manifestations of European ELF at ESC press conferences, where ELF was shown to play a crucial role in the imagining of a Europeanness that transcends national boundaries.

Whereas earlier research strands informed by debates on linguistic imperialism and World Englishes treated European ELF as a (potentially) homogeneous entity, contemporary ELF research places greater emphasis on documenting the diversity inherent in ELF and how "English" is locally appropriated in transnational communication. For this purpose, the concept of the community of practice has turned out to be a useful tool for the description of the local linguistic practices in ELF communication, because it enables the researcher to grasp ELF as a phenomenon that cuts across more traditional macro-categories (such as nationalities or nativeness vs. non-nativeness). Future research will need to revise (or replace?) ENL-associated concepts to come up with theorisations (and methodologies) that correspond more closely to the current sociolinguistic realities of our increasingly transnational, globalised world. Studying ELF and its role in transnational European identity formation may prove a decisive step into this direction.

8.3   ELF and Europeanness

Discussing ELF in relation to Europeanness raises consequential questions about whether ELF can actually be viewed as a medium expressing culture and, if so, which cultures can be expressed by it (e.g. Baker 2009a/b). While especially early academic treatments of ELF used to conceptualise ELF as a medium of communication whose use is devoid of identificational values and governed by issues of transactional efficiency alone (e.g. House 2003; Hüllen 1992), more recent work on the topic has tended to acknowledge the identity indexing potential that ELF may possess for its users (e.g. Baker 2011). This move requires a renouncing of traditional discourses of linguistic diversity and identities along national or ethnic lines. In other words, ELF speakers are unlikely to attach a national, ethnic or even natively Anglophone identity to their use of ELF (even though they may readily orient to these identifications outside ELF contexts). The identification processes ELF users engage in may be multiple, subtle, emergent and temporary, but this does not justify the claim that ELF communication is identity- or culture-free.

What kinds of culture are potentially associated with ELF is still up to debate and, as pointed out by Baker (2011:35), needs further investigation, especially since the few previous discussions of ELF in relation to identity are mainly restricted to language teaching and learning contexts (e.g. Jenkins 2007; Pedrazzini & Nava 2011; Virkkula & Nikula 2010) and therefore deal with contexts that are less prototypical for ELF communication, in which participants are generally not teachers or learners. More identity-focused research on non-academic ELF contexts (such as ESC press conferences) is needed. In these contexts, the fact that speakers of various linguacultural backgrounds communicate with each other clearly foregrounds questions of identification (besides the need to be communicatively successful).

For ELF communication, some researchers propose the formation of an interculture resulting from a mixture of the participants' linguacultures (e.g. Meierkord 2002). In line with postmodernist approaches, others have proposed that the contact of cultures leads to new hybrid cultural formations whose ingredients are not necessarily separable into influences from specific (national/ethnic) linguacultures. Such formations have, for example, been described with the term "third place" (Kramsch 1993). The press conference data suggest that Europe, as jointly imagined via linguistic practices, may qualify as such a third space. European ELF does neither necessarily lack the "affective-emotive quality involved in identification", nor is it "bereft of collective cultural capital", as House (2003:560) puts it. Just because ELF speakers do not necessarily aim at assimilation to native English cultures, this does not automatically render their use of English devoid of identity values. In fact, ELF as a de-anglicised medium can take on a range of other identity values, with transnational European ones forming just a subset (see also Baker 2009b; Wolf & Polzenhagen 2006):

> In order for English as a Lingua Franca to fulfill the needs of its speakers, it does not need to become a culture-free communicative medium. Rather, it can be positioned as a culture-dependent tool which can be infused with identificatory meaning by the individual speaker who uses the language and, in the process, appropriates it. Users of English as a Lingua Franca will inevitably bring their own culture into the interaction, infusing the code with, for example, literal translations of culture-specific idioms. But the identity the language conveys is not prefabricated or adapted from native speakers but rather changeable according to the cultural and linguistic background of the particular speaker and thus open to a variety of identities.   (Dröschel 2011:136)

Acknowledging that ELF may be infused with various identities does not mean that it is a manifestation of distinct national identities such as German ELF or Greek ELF. The features exhibited by ELF are not usually systematic and specific enough to identify the national origin of a speaker. Dröschel (2011) shows for the use of ELF in SUI, for example, that those features in which Swiss ELF use may differ from native English patterns are anything but specifically Swiss but also occur in the English used by ELF speakers of other national backgrounds. ELF speakers are particularly unlikely to aim at a construction of national identities in intercultural communication. What ELF speakers in European contexts do is rather construct affiliations that transcend nationalities. "English" is losing much of its national indexical potential when used as a lingua franca in such contexts. In fact, it is arguable that such uses cross national boundaries and thereby de-essentialise the traditional relationship between the concepts "language" and "nation" (cf. Wright 2011). This can be seen as a decisive component in the formation of Europe – historically probably the most heavily nationalised territory in the world – as a transnational space.

The term "Europeanness" seems relatively vague and its usage in the present book begs the question why the term "European identity" is not instead used. A central motivation behind this choice is that the relationship between ELF and Europeanness is not invariably a matter of (fully-fledged) European identity construction. European identities are still in the making. Only few people would, for example, claim that their European identifications are more significant than their national identities as Dutch, Greek or Swiss, even though the number of people who would opt for such a self-description is rising. The term "Europeanness" is meant to cover the fact that European identifications may also come in more subtle shades than in the form of "I am a European" messages. These latter kinds of messages do play a role at ESC press conferences. But an exclusive concentration on these would lead to a relatively impoverished treatment of Europeanness in the data at hand and is less convincing if one focuses on the role of ELF alone as a matter of European identity construction. ELF is but one of many components involved in the complex construction of European identities (see Motschenbacher 2010, 2012a/b, 2013, forthcoming). When viewed in isolation, as in this book, its European identity indexical potential is more limited.

A more adequate conceptualisation of the relationship between ELF and Europeanness may be a description in terms of "belonging" (cf. Meinhof & Galasiński 2005; Sandvoss 2008). When applied to the current interactional context, this concept represents a useful tool for understanding the use of ELF at ESC press conferences as a means of producing "Europeanness" rather than of reflecting European identities, i.e. it is less a matter of "I am European" than of "I want to be/become/remain a part of Europe". A belonging of this kind also has to be performed by speakers coming from native Anglophone cultures within Europe. If these speakers use ENL without accommodating to their non-native European fellow citizens at ESC press conferences, this can be considered an act of prioritising national over European affiliations, which carries little prestige in this transnational European community of practice. For example, a reliance on native English idioms which are semantically less transparent to non-native ELF users can, in transnational contexts, be perceived as a gatekeeping strategy that endangers communicative success (cf. Seidlhofer 2009c).

As discussed by Meinhof and Galasiński (2005), the construction of belonging is not a one-dimensional process. It is normally a process orienting to multiple levels of identification (local, regional, national, transnational) that may intersect, overlap or challenge each other (see also Baker 2011:46). The different layers of identity are not invariably salient. They may in a given context be backgrounded or treated as irrelevant. This is also true for ESC press conferences, in which local and regional identifications are rarely oriented to by the participants. What one finds predominantly in this context is a lively competition between national and transnational European identifications, which, maybe as a result of the European salience of the context, is in most cases won by the the latter form of identification. This is a highly context-dependent finding. In the German and Polish contexts studied by Meinhof and Galasiński, for example, European identifications were notably absent from the data, except when subjects were prompted to orient to them (Meinhof & Galasiński 2005:181). In other words, local, regional and national identifications took precedence in these contexts. At ESC press conferences, by contrast, orienting to Europeanness is clearly the salient type of identification.

It adds to the complexity of the issue that "Europe" is a prototypical case of an imagined community (Anderson 1991), i.e. a discursive formation that requires significant collaborative effort to construct. It is notoriously difficult to define what "Europe" is. Answers vary depending on the basis that is adopted for making such definitions. For example, defining Europe along geographic, cultural, religious or economic lines will invariably lead to different, though substantially overlapping, results. The same can be said for attempts to define Europe linguistically or, more specifically, in relation to ELF. As has been shown in the empirical chapters of this book, the "Europeanness" of ELF manifests itself in partly different ways at the various linguistic levels. Language choice, metalinguistic comments, complimenting behaviour and relativisation in the ELF communication at ESC press conferences all exhibit their own picture of what constitutes Europeanness, and it may be argued that it is the combination of these four levels (rather than a one-dimensional view) that facilitates a more comprehensive description of the complexity of European ELF as a form of situated linguistic practice.

On the level of code choice, Europeanness surfaces in the default status of English as a medium of transnational European communication and the simultaneous activation of other European languages as part of the participants' linguistic repertoires. It is especially non-native uses of ELF that dominate the European stage in this community of practice. These enable the community members to guarantee communicative efficiency across Europe and to tone down national affiliations. This latter linguistic mechanism of denationalisation via ELF is compatible with European transnationalism, for which national demands must, to a certain degree, be subdued. What one finds is a connection between Europeanness and (linguistic) inclusiveness via ELF, while a highlighting of national issues (for example, through the choice of national languages) would rather have to be considered as excluding large parts of the pan-European population and as prioritising a nationalist motivation.

On the level of metalinguistic comments, the use of ELF was constructed as a means of transcending language-related communication boundaries within Europe, while a reliance on national languages was perceived as endangering successful European cooperation. It was also apparent that the participants increasingly take on a self-confident stance in relation to non-native accents, which are widely viewed as normal, legitimate and at times even desired in this transnational European community of practice. At the same time, it is evident that Europeanness is not connected to an English-only policy. Despite the fact that English was the language predominantly used at the press conferences, participants generally also acknowledged the presence of speakers of L1s other than English. In other words, even though languages other than English may sometimes be treated as of secondary importance to the transactional business at the press conferences, showing awareness of and concern for speakers of other languages generally also enjoys high prestige in this European community of practice. Overall, one could witness a lively competition of discourses, some of which favour ELF while others favour the use of national languages. However, it was revealed that ELF prevails more and more often in this competition and that the use of national languages is at times treated as a piece of European (and Eurovision) nostalgia.

The complimenting behaviour observed at the press conferences showed quite different aspects of what Europeanness may mean. The European ELF users in this community of practice are clearly not pragmatically deficient speakers. By contrast, they generally adhere to ritualised pragmatic norms that see cross-national compliments as valuable and compliments targeting one's own nation or national team as more problematic. The high frequency of compliments across national boundaries indicates that this speech act type plays a prominent role for cross-European solidarity-creation. In most cases, such compliments save an interlocutor's positive face (Brown & Levinson 1987), i.e. in the community of practice at hand they convey the message that the complimentees (and by extension the nations they represent) are accepted as members of the European "family" (an image sometimes evoked by the participants themselves). This mechanism seems particularly relevant in the face of Europe's heavily nationalised history and the superficial structure of the contest as a competition between nations – a notion that would normally stand in the way of a transnational Europeanness. On the sociolinguistic level, it was found that the Europeanness of the context was associated with a notable absence of the social compliment restrictions amply documented in other (native/national) contexts. The ritualised practices at ESC press conferences rather show gender equality and tolerance of non-heteronormative identities and desires as the norm. Taken together, the analysis of complimenting behaviour at ESC press conferences illustrates that the use of English is in this context associated with a range of identifications, among which national identifications play only a subdued role. It is rather the performance of transnational Europeanness, professionality at the international level and less traditional gender and sexual identities via ELF that predominates in this community of practice.

Finally, on the structural level, the relativisation patterns identified in ESC-PC document the internal hybridity of European ELF as a form of language use exhibiting complex patterns of variation that are potentially influenced by a range of factors. This, in turn, prohibits labelling the linguistic practices observed "Euro-English". Relevant factors include structural aspects that have also been shown to play a prominent role in native varieties of English and that ELF speakers are likely to have internalised through formal education. However, there are other factors that are more directly linked to the Europeanness of the context, such as the European languages forming parts of the participants' linguistic repertoires, European region and EU status. The link between language typology and Europeanness used as the basis for the analysis suggests that the structural Europeanness of ELF is not a stable category or a binary matter of European versus non-European but rather a matter of higher or lower prototypicality. It is, therefore, more adequate to say that certain speakers or speaker groups use English in more prototypically European ways than others, with the latter still being perceived as (potentially) belonging to Europe. Europeanness is in this respect a highly inclusive concept that is not determined by the presence of certain linguistic features.

The present study is witness to the fact that the status of English in Europe is currently changing, and that on a number of levels. Six of these (intersecting) dimensions are the following:

1. Research is moving from seeing English in Europe in (purely) structural terms as a potential variety to a performative notion of European ELF as internally heterogeneous and pragmatically governed ("form follows function").
2. English is today less seen as a "killer" language ousting other languages and leading to Anglophone homogenisation across Europe, but more in terms of a medium whose internal hybridity causes new forms of linguistic variation and diversity.

3. In cross-European communication, the traditional, binary status of English as a language of (British, Irish, Maltese) national belonging vs. as a foreign language across mainland Europe is giving way to the notion of ELF as a de-anglicised, transnational European medium of communication.
4. There is an increasing trend for English to be no longer exclusively learnt as a foreign language in formal secondary education across Europe. English is today largely introduced already in primary education, and Europeans increasingly find themselves in ELF contexts in which an additional informal acquisition through communication with other Europeans is possible. This latter development caters more specifically for ELF-related communicative needs.
5. Transnational uses of English as a European lingua franca are emancipating themselves from the native-speaker orientation propagated by traditional ELT. They are increasingly perceived to be less governed by normative standards and native role models, and more by the local communicative requirements of the participants in a certain context.
6. European ELF is turning from a "language of communication" into a "language of identification" for many Europeans. These identifications go well beyond learner identities or ethnic/national identifications and potentially include socially progressive identifications (such as a transnational European belonging).

At present, there is no complete switch to the more recent developments, and traditional views still have an impact on how English in Europe is conceptualised. However, it can easily be predicted that the future will see a further decrease in the influence that the traditional discourses revolving around ELF will have.

From a postmodernist point of view, the use of the term "language" in relation to European ELF has to be viewed critically. It may have some legitimacy when viewed from a bottom-up or anthropological perspective, because ELF speakers generally are of the opinion that they speak a certain "language", namely "English", when they use ELF. Nevertheless, calling European ELF "a language" remains problematic on at least two grounds. Firstly, the term "language" suggests a high degree of stability and internal homogeneity that European ELF as a hybrid medium does not exhibit. And secondly, the term "language" is so deeply tied to nationalist thinking that ELF as a transnational medium of communication cannot be adequately described within this paradigm.

A performative conceptualisation no longer sees European ELF as strictly or ideally tied to reflecting or orienting to Anglo-American cultural values but as an efficient means of "doing Europe" and constructing transnational affiliations. This begs the question of what should be considered specifically European in European ELF interactions. Obviously "European ELF" is a de-essentialised, fuzzy concept without fixed boundaries. This kind of reasoning has become highly popular in contemporary gender studies, for example, where it is increasingly acknowledged that there is no characteristic that is shared by all people identifying as "women". Still, the category "woman" is far from empty or meaningless. Transferred to the object of the present study, this means that there is no essence that all European ELF interactions share and that these interactions exhibit considerable overlap with other types of ELF interactions. Still, the term "European ELF" is not entirely pointless because it is associated with certain prototypical notions, which in turn need not invariably manifest themselves in all European ELF interactions.

Central prototypical aspects of European ELF include some that are relevant for ELF interactions in general, such as consensus-orientedness, the predominance of non-native participants and a concomitant decrease in the orientation to normative standards, local meaning negotiation and speakers' wish to use language to communicate with people from other linguacultural backgrounds (rather than to exclude). Others are more specific to Europe. Among these is the increasingly high proficiency level as a result of the English input provided by formal education across Europe, the European languages forming components in the participants' linguistic repertoires (which exhibit typological differences from languages in other parts of the world), speakers' motivations to be "good Europeans" and to be effective communicators in intra-European transnational contexts, or the increased perception of English as a denationalised medium (which is maybe more easily feasible in mainland Europe as an area that does not look back on a history of British colonialism).

8.4   Implications for European language policies

The data analysed in the present book indicates that ELF plays an essential role in contexts where Europeans from various linguacultural backgrounds get together. A feasible European language policy must acknowledge this fact and recognise that the use of English in Europe is no longer exclusively associated with national British, Irish or Maltese identities or, more generally speaking, Anglo-American values. A sole equalisation of "English" with ENL (and maybe ESL) together with a deliberate ignorance of the fundamental role that ELF plays for cross-European communication is the problem at the very heart of current EU language policies (see Chapters 2.1 and 4.2). Such official policies reinforce nationalist discourses that privilege the British and the Irish as owners of "English" and disadvantage non-native European speakers (Seidlhofer 2011:55). A similar problem has been noted by Jenkins (2011) in relation to the language policies of internationally oriented universities, whose focus on AmE and BrE as reference varieties contradicts the fact that international academic communication is today hardly ever native English communication.

A language policy that fosters the use of English as a European lingua franca may at first glance be thought to give an unfair advantage to native speakers of English.

This would clearly be the case if British or Irish English were officially implemented for cross-European communication. However, as cross-cultural interactions in English are prototypically associated with communication among (mainly) non-native speakers, the implementation of native standard varieties remains questionable for such contexts.

As has been shown in the empirical sections of this book, it is the non-national and non-native uses of English that dominate the picture in transnational European communication. This dominance is first of all a quantitative matter, with intra-European interactions across national boundaries being more often conducted in ELF than in any other lingua franca, and with most of these interactions showing a greater number of non-native than native speakers. However, there is increasing evidence that this dominance is also becoming a qualitative matter. This was in the present study, for example, indicated by the fact that non-standard and non-native usage patterns were generally not treated as problematic and by the self-confident attitude with which some of the press conference participants viewed their own non-native accents. These developments contribute to the de-essentialisation of traditional "language-equals-nation" discourses in the service of cross-European communication.

If one compares the situation at the press conferences to that of EU institutions, one is tempted to argue that the strong internal reliance on national structures of the latter may stand in the way of a deeper Europeanisation process. More specifically, a clinging to nationalist linguistic essentialisms prevents a greater openness in the conceptualisation of "English", thereby restricting it to the function of a medium of national identity construction and ignoring (or not officially recognising) the non-native/non-national uses of English that ensure cross-European understanding and provide speakers with a means of indexing transnational European affiliations. Where "English" is conceptually tied to those nations in which it plays an official function, there is no space for granting it any wider potential for Europeanisation, simply because a promotion of English would then invariably be tantamount to a promotion of these very nations – a development that, in turn, runs counter to the principle of cross-European egalitarianism.

Promoting the use of a native English standard for cross-European communication would correspond with the homogeny position, because the national language of one particular culture would spread. It is immediately understandable that such a scenario draws criticism, and legitimately so (with accusations of linguistic imperialism being among the strongest types of criticism that have been voiced). However, it is decisive to make a distinction between the use of ELF and native/national Englishes in Europe. While a propagation of the latter would indeed foster linguistic homogenisation, European ELF exhibits its own kind of internal heterogeneity, which in fact dovetails quite neatly with the European slogan "unity in diversity". The "unity" part in this slogan points to the use of "English" – a medium of communication that has

traditionally evolved in Anglophone cultures but is nowadays appropriated by speakers all over the world for their communicative needs. The "diversity" part refers to the
internal hybridity of ELF as a contextually shaped linguistic phenomenon. This entails
a reconceptualisation of linguistic diversity: from a plurilinguistic conceptualisation
based on the enumeration of "languages" and "varieties" to a conceptualisation that
recognises the internal hybridity under the surface of the umbrella term "English"
and views the latter as a European cultural asset rather than as a sign of corruption or
deviance from native and national varieties.

The way English is used at ESC press conferences is far away from the notion of
a "lingua bellica of wars between states", as Phillipson (2008a: 250) wants to make us
believe. Participants at ESC press conferences never orient to such opinions about their
use of English and rather indicate that they see English as a valuable means of communicating with Europeans from other linguacultural backgrounds. As far as Europe
is concerned, one is probably safe to assume that English today opens more doors
than it closes, and this quality becomes especially important in comparison to other
European languages. Moreover the fact that Europeans increasingly attach identity
values other than Anglo-American ones to their use of ELF contrasts markedly with
the hostile picture drawn by linguistic imperialism scholars, who generally seem to
suggest that users of English are swept over by Anglo-Americanisation. As Seidlhofer
points out, such dominance-oriented readings of the spread of English make little
sense in relation to ELF:

> [T]he claim that English is necessarily and generally a threat to other languages [...]
> seems to be based on the assumption that languages are complete and functionally
> comprehensive entities and that they are bound to compete with each other for the
> same communicative space and cannot peacefully co-exist as parts of a more general
> linguistic repertoire to be exploited as appropriate in different domains of use. When
> this assumption is compounded by the belief that different languages necessarily
> belong to different nation states and represent their values and interests, it is not
> surprising that the *dominance* of English is taken to imply *domination* by its native
> speakers. But once one denies this right of exclusive ownership and dissociates the
> language from its native speakers and recognizes it as a partial and expedient resource
> that anyone can make use of – in other words, once one thinks of English as ELF, then
> the language obviously no longer poses the same threat of domination.
>
> (Seidlhofer 2011: 68; italics as in the original)

The use of ELF in Europe does not necessarily work to the detriment of other languages. In their ethnic or national functions, the latter are unlikely to be threatened
by the use of ELF in transnational communication. The threat of ELF can maximally be said to affect the transnational communicative level, where only few other
European languages are in fact used (French, and German; to some extent Italian,
Russian and Spanish). What makes these latter languages less well equipped for the

role of European lingua franca (apart from their lower degree of institutionalisation in European foreign language education) is the fact that they seem to be much more strongly nationally associated than English today, whose default use in transnational communication contributes to its de-anglicisation, thereby opening up some space for the expression of alternative, non-national identity values. At ESC press conferences, for example, the use of ELF is not just a means of effective cross-European communication but also a way of toning down national affiliations that may stand in the way of reaching any deeper levels of Europeanisation. A Europe in which all nations aim at enforcing their own national issues (including languages) is bound to fail. Europeanness is an achievement that can only be reached when such national interests are minimised, and non-national uses of English are very well compatible with such a goal, because they require all participants to make adjustments. Anchoring ELF within a European language policy, therefore, means sacrifices on both sides. An implementation of ELF would require non-native speakers to give up promoting their own national languages on the transnational European level and native speakers to give up their status as normative linguistic authorities and role models who do not need to adjust their linguistic behaviour. It is doubtful whether a promotion of English as a European lingua franca would in fact privilege native speakers of English (see Busse 2007: 170). They would first of all have to live with the situation that their national uses of English are downgraded from normative teaching standards across Europe to just one of many aspects causing the hybridity of European ELF. Secondly, they would – like all Europeans – have to develop accommodative skills that enable them to function in cross-European communication. Monolingual English speakers will automatically make a pragmatically impoverished impression if they are not able to adapt to the local requirements in ELF interactions, self-sufficiently relying on the fact that the others speak "their language".

As lamentable as the adoption of English to the detriment of other languages may be on the surface – and on the transnational level ELF indeed ousts other European languages of wider communication –, one must not forget that adoption processes like these also tell us something about people's desired identities, i.e. how they see themselves or want to be seen by others. The increasing use of ELF is today more or less a bottom-up phenomenon, and therefore by far more successful than any top-down attempts to install large-scale European multilingualism (the declared aim of the EU).

The crucial question remains whether ELF as a medium of cross-European communication can be severed from its traditional association with Anglophone nations. For obvious reasons, no natural language can serve as a completely neutral means of communication because all languages have evolved in concrete cultural contexts. However, this original cultural connection may become darkened or less relevant throughout time. This is a mechanism that is generally attested for the geographical spread of languages. For example, the modern Romance languages can be traced back

to Vulgar Latin, which in turn is a result of the spread of Latin to the various territories of the Roman Empire. This historical connection with the Romans, however,
is nowadays of only limited import: speakers of Romanian in ROM or of Spanish in
ESP would consider their language as a means of national Romanian/Spanish identity
expression and not as a manifestation of Roman imperialism. For mainland Europe, a
history of Anglo-American colonisation does not even exist, which makes accusations
of linguistic imperialism still more difficult to substantiate.

It is today hardly conceivable that a European affiliation can be constructed without any recourse to ELF. The status of English as a "foreign" language in the literal sense
of the word is therefore clearly under attack in Europe. A European language policy
should not try to impede this development (a regulatory undertaking that is ultimately
bound to fail) but rather foster, or at least tolerate, the conceptual de-anglicisation of
ELF and its concomitant association with identity values beyond Anglophone nations.

At the same time, an efficient European language policy should not uncritically
endorse multilingualism but recognise the multidiversity within ELF as a potentially
European value. Language pluralisation mainly boils down to an often hostile competition between a range of incompatible nationalist goals and, as a consequence,
impedes rather than fosters deeper Europeanisation processes. Top-down regulations
of European multilingualism (such as those of the EU) must therefore be replaced
by bottom-up approaches (Seidlhofer 2010) that acknowledge the increasing importance of ELF as a powerful means of cross-European communication. It is unhelpful
to condemn all uses of English outside ENL societies as instances of Anglo-American
power-wielding (see also Friedrich 2009 for an alternative discussion of English in
relation to Peace Sociolinguistics). If its internal heterogeneity and local negotiability are taken into account, the spread of ELF cannot be seen as advancing linguistic
and cultural homogeneity (Pennycook 2011:516). Furthermore, placing less emphasis on individual national languages and more emphasis on ELF as a transnational
European formation avoids the undesirable effect of creating power imbalances
between (speakers of) larger and smaller European languages. It is here not suggested
that the promotion of national languages is an undertaking that should be given up.
Still, it may be less contradictive to locate this task on the national rather than on the
European level. The European level would then be responsible for pan-European as
well as minority language policies, i.e. issues that tend to be not or sometimes only
insufficiently dealt with on the national level.

However, it is not enough to sever ELF from its traditional association with native
English cultures. An ELF-oriented European language policy also needs to take care
not to re-import traditional ELT thinking into its discussions of ELF. This means,
for example, that ELF should not be subjected to attempts of neo-standardisation
and -codification – steps that may be deemed necessary to facilitate teaching ELF
(cf. Burger 2000; R. Walker 2010). However, ELF cannot per se be adequately taught

in the EFL classroom. ELF-relevant competences are rather acquired in concrete ELF communication contexts that confront speakers with locally diverse communicative requirements and thereby help them to build up the necessary linguistic flexibility in both production and reception. A standardisation of ELF may be a development on which ELT curricula can be based, but it also stratifies speakers by excluding those who do not fully meet the new standard (Gal 2013). This runs counter to ELF as a linguistic phenomenon that is conceptually based on notions of inclusivity rather then exclusivity. In other words, the design of effective, socially realistic European language policies must not just involve an acknowledgement of the existence of ELF but also should be guided by the challenges that ELF and ELF research pose to more traditional language-oriented conceptualisations.

Chapter 9

Appendix

9.1 Transcription conventions: ESC press conferences corpus [ESC-PC]

(A) MARK-UP CONVENTIONS

1. SPEAKER ABBREVIATIONS

KS:	"Kristian Strand", the press conference moderator
FA1:, FA2: etc.	"Female delegate 1", "female delegate 2" etc.
MA1:, MA2: etc.	"Male delegate 1", "male delegate 2" etc. (in order of speaking)
FP1:, FP2: etc.	"Female press representative 1", female press representative 2"
MP1:, MP2: etc.	"Male press representative 1", "male press representative 2" etc. (in order of speaking)
Group:	Utterances performed by a group of people simultaneously
FA2:, *MP3*: etc.	ENL/ESL speakers are additionally marked with asterisks.

2. RISING INTONATION

Example: *MA1: you don't understand what i me- mean no?*	A question mark (?) indicates rising intonation.

3. EMPHASIS

Examples: *KS: so why did you wanna put **THESE** two band together* *MA1: ⟨3⟩ it's ⟨/3⟩ **RAINing** gold=*	Syllables or words with particular emphasis are capitalised.

4. PAUSES

Example: *KS: and the (.) just show us your routine*	A full stop in parentheses (.) marks brief pauses of 1 second or less.
Example: *KS: questions? (**3**) i know that you guys wanna perform a little bit for us*	Longer pauses are noted as the number of seconds in parentheses.

(Continued)

9.1 Transcription conventions: ESC press conferences corpus [ESC-PC] (Continued)

5. OVERLAPS

Example: *FA1: you cannot ⟨2⟩ @@@ ⟨/2⟩* *MA1: ⟨2⟩ **no no comparing** ⟨/2⟩ @@ (.)* *there is no comparing @@*	Overlapping utterances are marked with numbered tags: ⟨1⟩ ⟨/1⟩, ⟨2⟩ ⟨/2⟩, etc.

6. LATCHING

Example: *MP2: hello (.) morten from **norway**=* *FA1: =**hello***	Latching is marked by means of an equals sign (=).

7. LENGTHENING

Example: *FA1: two year- **no:** {laughter} (.)*	Lengthened sounds are marked with a colon (:).
Example: *FA1: **u::hm** i'm gonna wear a dress a long dress*	For exceptionally long sounds, several colons are used.

8. REPETITION

Example: *MA1: uh **it** it's it's a- **actually** it still feels* *live because **i i** have it in my hands*	Accidental repetitions and false starts are included in the transcript.

9. WORD FRAGMENTS

Example: *FA1: uh well it's actually it's **o-** okay because i mean people uh*	Missing parts of words are indicated with a hyphen.

10. LAUGHTER

Example: *MA1: it was my dream @@@@@*	Laughter is transcribed using the @ symbol. The number of signs approximates the number of syllables.
Example: *FA1: the performance is about spreading* *happiness joy and love all over europe* *{**laughter**} (.) along with a little bit of ash sorry*	Laughter which cannot be attributed to a single person but rather involves large parts of the audience is indicated in curly brackets. The occurrence of {laughter}, in the running text or between turns, marks the starting point of the laughter in question.
Example: *MP6: thank you very much i stay at room four one seven* *{**laughter** (4)}* *KS: @@ do we ha- we ha- we have another* *one there you go please*	If audience laughter extends over two seconds or longer without anybody speaking, the duration is marked in parentheses.

11. INNOVATIONS

Example: *FA1: we're also ⟨pvc⟩ **rehearsaling** ⟨/pvc⟩* *a lot*	Linguistic innovations are marked using the tag ⟨pvc⟩ ⟨/pvc⟩ and are spelled in accordance with general principles of English orthography. (pvc is short for "pronunciation variations and coinages".)

12. NON-ENGLISH SPEECH

Example: *FA1: uhm (.) ⟨German⟩ **gegenfrage** ⟨/German⟩* *how would YOU describe my image*	Passages in languages other than English are specifically marked.
Example: *MA1: there it's this (.) ⟨Greek⟩ **xxxx** ⟨/Greek⟩*	If a non-English passage is not decodable and of short length, the number of syllables is indicated using x's.
Example: *{FA2 speaks Greek (39)}*	If a non-English passage is not decodable and constitutes a longer turn, it is given in curly brackets with duration information in parentheses.

13. ALPHABETISMS

Example: *MP1: hello uh roy bennett from* *⟨spel⟩ **esc** ⟨/spel⟩ today dot com*	Alphabetisms are transcribed using the ⟨spel⟩ ⟨/spel⟩ tag to indicate that their constituents are pronounced as individual letters.
Example: cee dees (instead of "⟨spel⟩ cd ⟨/spel⟩s")	In cases where alphabetisms carry an additional inflectional marker, the spelling tags are not used. Instead, the individual letters are represented as words.

14. SPEAKING MODES

Example: *FA1: ⟨singing⟩ under pressure ⟨/singing⟩* Others include: ⟨fast⟩ ⟨/fast⟩ ⟨slow⟩ ⟨/slow⟩ ⟨loud⟩ ⟨/loud⟩ ⟨whispering⟩ ⟨/whispering⟩	Utterances that are spoken in a particular mode and are notably different from the speaker's normal speaking style are marked accordingly.

15. BREATH

Example: *MA2: uh first of all i (.) **hh** try not to think* *about winning or or getting good place*	Noticeable breathing in or out is represented as hh.

16. NON-VERBAL ACTIONS AND EVENTS

Examples: *FA1: o:h (.) yes @@@@ (.) okay* *⟨clears throat⟩ (.) you can help me* *KS: ⟨addresses other group members⟩ have* *you have YOU guys also dreamt about* *the eurovision?* *MA1: huh (.) i don't know we see with my* *met uh wi- with my composer (.) kristian* *gabroski u:h he: ⟨talks to FA1 (2)⟩*	Actions performed by a person who is speaking are transcribed in angled brackets as part of the running text. This may also include information on whom a speaker is addressing or instances of the speaker inaudibly talking to somebody. If such actions take two seconds or longer, this is indicated by numbers in parentheses.

(Continued)

9.1 Transcription conventions: ESC press conferences corpus [ESC-PC] (Continued)

Examples: *{person comes and places Swiss flag in front* *of MA1, laughter (9)}* MA1: no i do- i hope not @@@@ *{thunder in the background}* KS: oh what a thunder woah	Actions and contextual events that cannot be attributed to the current speaker are only transcribed where relevant. They are noted in curly brackets {} with the duration indicated in parentheses if two seconds or longer.

17. UNTRANSCRIBED PASSAGES

Example: *{FA1 performs "drip drop" (51)}*	Lyrics of musical performances are not transcribed. Instead, such performances are noted in curly brackets, with information on duration and, if known, song title.
Example: *{Norwegian quiz (56)}*	The "Norwegian quiz" is also not transcribed. It is indicated in curly brackets with information on duration in parentheses.
Examples: *{MA1 translates, FA1 answers in Russian (14)}* *{MP1 asks question in French (20)}*	Longer non-English passages are left untranscribed. These include passages in which an interpreter translates into the interviewee's L1 (often inaudible), in which the interviewee answers in his or her L1 or in which journalists ask questions in languages other than English.

18. APPLAUSE

Example: KS: sha-la-lie yeah that's right @@@@ *{applause}* (.) that's a good ending sha-la-lie	For applause, the starting point is indicated by the word "applause" in curly brackets.
Example: KS: no you're very good (.) v- very good *{applause (6)}*	For longer stretches of applause during which none of the participants is speaking, the duration is also indicated.

19. DISCOURSE MARKERS

yes, yeah *okay* *mhm, hm, aha, uhu*	All types of discourse markers are represented in the transcript, e.g.: Backchannels and positive minimal feedback
no *uh-uh*	Negative minimal feedback
uh (hesitation/filler) *huh?* *whoo, mm:* *ah, oh* *wow*	Other common discourse markers

20. UNINTELLIGIBLE SPEECH

Example:
MA1: we like uh ⟨un⟩ xx ⟨/un⟩
we like one song lithuania

Unintelligible speech is represented by x's approximating syllable number and placed between ⟨un⟩ ⟨/un⟩ tags.

(B) SPELLING CONVENTIONS

21. CHARACTERS

Roman characters are used for the transcriptions of English passages. Nonroman characters may occur in non-English passages and names.

22. DECAPITALISATION

Example:
FA3: well i don't even remember that was around ten years ago when (.) we were watching ⟨spel⟩ tv ⟨/spel⟩ and seeing people from all the different countries

No capital letters are used except for marking emphasis (cf. mark-up conventions).

23. BRITISH ENGLISH SPELLING

British English spelling is used throughout the corpus.

24. NON-ENGLISH WORDS

Example:
MA1: uh maybe something from (.) new musical ⟨French⟩ les misérables ⟨/French⟩

Non-English words are rendered in the standard orthography of the respective language. Decapitalisation applies throughout.

25. NON-NATIVE ACCENTS

Example:
Native speakers of French may drop word-initial /h-/ when speaking English, but this is not reflected in the transcription.

Although words may be pronounced with a non-native accent, they are generally represented in their standard orthographic form.

26. NUMBERS, TITLES & ABBREVIATIONS

Examples:
one, two, three, …
nineteen sixty-three,
one hundred, two thousand etc.

Numbers are spelled out as whole words.

Examples:
misses (for Mrs), *mister* (for Mr)

Titles and terms of address are fully spelled out.

Example:
FA1: and i would also like to thank to the ogae journalist and to the ogae which are here

Acronyms (i.e. abbreviations pronounced like one word) are transcribed as words.

(Continued)

9.1 Transcription conventions: ESC press conferences corpus [ESC-PC] (Continued)

27. CONTRACTIONS

Examples: *i'm, you're, he's, she's, it's, we're, they're* *i've, you've, he's, she's*, etc. *i'd, you'd, she'd, we'd*, etc. *i'll, you'll*, etc. *aren't, isn't, won't, don't, doesn't, didn't* etc. *let's* *gonna, wanna*	Transcriptions include standard contractions. These mainly involve verb contractions with *be* (*am, is are*), *have* (*have, has, had*), *will* and *would* as well as *not*-contractions.

9.2   List of press conferences in ESC-PC

* = speaker from the UK; ** = speaker from IRL; *** = speaker from Australia; **** = speaker from the US; ***** = speaker from Malta;
() = speakers using a language other than English;
KS = Kristian Strand, the moderator;
FA/MA = female/male delegate;
FP/MP = female/male press representative

Factors in factor group "active speaker participation" (last column):
n = mainly ENL/ESL speakers involved (8)
2 = mainly ELF speakers, with two or more ENL/ESL speakers involved (14)
1 = mainly ELF speakers, with one ENL/ESL speaker involved (43)
f = exclusively ELF speakers involved (13)

#	Press conference	Date	Time	Duration	Active participants	Factor
1.	MOL1	16.05.2010	10:50h	22:22	KS FA1, MA1, MA2 MP1***, MP2, MP3, MP4	1
2.	RUS1	16.05.2010	11:30h	29:06	KS MA1, MA2, MA3, MA4 MP1, MP2, MP3***, MP4, MP5, (MP6)	1
3.	EST1	16.05.2010	12:10h	29:30	KS MA1, MA2, MA3, MA4 MP1, MP2***, MP3	1
4.	SLK1	16.05.2010	13:40h	30:40	KS FA1, MA1 FP1, MP1, MP2***, MP3, MP4	1
5.	FIN1	16.05.2010	14:30h	30:37	KS FA1, FA2, FA3 MP1***, MP2, MP3	1
6.	LAT1	16.05.2010	15:10h	25:30	KS FA1, FA2, FA3, FA4, FA5 MP1, MP2, MP3, MP4***	1
7.	SER1	16.05.2010	16:10h	28:32	KS FA1, FA2, MA1, MA2, MA3 FP1, FP2, MP1, MP2***	1
8.	BOS1	16.05.2010	16:50h	24:28	KS FA1, FA2, MA1, MA2 FP1, MP1***, MP2	1

(Continued)

9.2 List of press conferences in ESC-PC (Continued)

#	Press conference	Date	Time	Duration	Active participants	Factor
9.	POL1	17.05.2010	10:55h	23:13	KS FA1, FA2, (FA3), MA1 MP1, MP2***	1
10.	BEL1	17.05.2010	11:35h	22:04	KS MA1, MA2, MA3 MP1, MP2***, MP3	1
11.	MAL1	17.05.2010	12:10h	23:46	KS FA1*****, FA2*****, FA3*****, MA1*****, MA2*****, MA3*****, MA4***** MP1, MP2, MP3, MP4, MP5	n
12.	ALB1	17.05.2010	13:50h	31:47	KS FA1, FA2****, FA3****, FA4****, MA1, MA2 MP1, MP2, MP3, MP4, MP5***	2
13.	GRE1	17.05.2010	14:30h	12:53	KS FA1, MA1, MA2, MA3, MA4 MP1***, MP2	1
14.	POR1	17.05.2010	15:10h	25:43	KS FA1, FA2, MA1, MA2 MP1, MP2, MP3, MP4	f
15.	MAC1	17.05.2010	16:10h	18:53	KS FA1, FA2, FA3, FA4, FA5, MA1, MA2, MA3 MP1***, MP2, MP3	1
16.	BLR1	17.05.2010	16:50h	25:21	KS FA1, FA2, FA3, MA1, MA2, (MA3) MP1, (MP2), MP3***	1
17.	ISL1	17.05.2010	17:30h	24:40	KS FA1, FA2, FA3, FA4, MA1 FP1, MP1, MP2***, MP3	1
18.	LIT1	18.05.2010	10:50h	20:19	KS MA1, MA2, MA3, MA4 FP1*, MP1, MP2***	2
19.	ARM1	18.05.2010	11:30h	24:03	KS FA1, FA2 MP1***, MP2*, MP3, MP4, MP5, MP6, MP7	2
20.	ISR1	18.05.2010	12:10h	18:53	KS MA1, MA2, MA3 MP1, MP2, MP3, MP4***, MP5, MP6	1

#	Press conference	Date	Time	Duration	Active participants	Factor
21.	DAN1	18.05.2010	13:50h	15:14	KS FA1, MA1 MP1, MP2, MP3***, MP4	1
22.	SUI1	18.05.2010	14:30h	20:44	KS FA1****, FA2, FA3, MA1, MA2 MP1***, MP2, MP3	2
23.	SWE1	18.05.2010	15:10h	10:49	KS FA1 MP1, (MP2), MP3*	1
24.	AZE1	18.05.2010	16:10h	20:19	KS (FA1), MA1, MA2****, MA3 MP1, MP2, MP3, MP4*, MP5, MP6, MP7	2
25.	UKR1	18.05.2010	16:50h	16:03	KS FA1, FA2, MA1, (MA2) MP1***, MP2*	2
26.	NED1	19.05.2010	10:50h	06:12	KS FA1, MA1 MP1, MP2***, MP3	1
27.	ROM1	19.05.2010	11:30h	19:20	KS FA1, MA1 MP1, MP2***, MP3	1
28.	SLO1	19.05.2010	12:10h	18:22	KS (FA1), MA1, MA2, MA3 MP1***, MP2	1
29.	IRL1	19.05.2010	13:40h	22:46	KS FA1** MP1, MP2, MP3, MP4***, MP5**, MP6**, MP7*	n
30.	BUL1	19.05.2010	14:30h	21:26	KS FA1, MA1, MA2* MP1, MP2, MP3, MP4***, MP5, MP6	2
31.	CYP1	19.05.2010	15:10h	25:43	KS FA1, FA2*, MA1*, MA2*, MA3, MA4, MA5* FP1*, MP1***, MP2**, MP3, MP4*	n
32.	CRO1	19.05.2010	16:10h	21:01	KS FA1, FA2, FA3, MA1, MA2 MP1, MP2***	1
33.	GEO1	19.05.2010	16:50h	23:16	KS FA1, FA2, FA3, FA4, MA1 FP1, FP2, MP1, MP2***, MP3	1

(*Continued*)

9.2 List of press conferences in ESC-PC (Continued)

#	Press conference	Date	Time	Duration	Active participants	Factor
34.	TUR1	19.05.2010	17:30h	16:32	KS FA1, MA1, MA2, MA3, MA4, MA5 FP1, MP1, MP2*, MP3	1
35.	MOL2	20.05.2010	12:10h	17:30	KS FA1, MA1, MA2, MA3 FP1, MP1, MP2***, MP3, MP4, MP5	1
36.	RUS2	20.05.2010	12:40h	14:37	KS MA1, MA2 (FP1), FP2, FP3, (FP4), MP1, MP2***, MP3, MP4	1
37.	EST2	20.05.2010	13:10h	10:37	KS MA1, MA2, MA3, MA4, MA5 MP1, MP2*	1
38.	SLK2	20.05.2010	14:40h	17:52	KS FA1, FA2, MA1 FP1, FP2, FP3, FP4, MP1, MP2	f
39.	FIN2	20.05.2010	15:10h	15:03	KS FA1, FA2, FA3, MA1, MA2 MP1, MP2, MP3***, MP4, MP5	1
40.	LAT2	20.05.2010	15:40h	17:57	KS FA1, FA2, FA3, FA4, FA5 MP1***, MP2, MP3, MP4	1
41.	SER2	20.05.2010	16:10h	18:05	KS FA1, FA2, MA1, MA2 FP1, MP1**	1
42.	BOS2	20.05.2010	16:55h	18:05	KS FA1, MA1, MA2, MA3, MA4 FP1, MP1, MP2	f
43.	POL2	20.05.2010	17:25h	21:15	KS MA1, MA2, MA3, MA4 FP1, MP1***, MP2, MP3, MP4, MP5	1
44.	BEL2	20.05.2010	17:55h	12:47	KS MA1 MP1***, MP2**, MP3, MP4, MP5	2
45.	MAL2	20.05.2010	18:25h	12:14	KS FA1*****, MA1*****, MA2***** MP1, MP2, MP3***, MP4, MP5*	n

#	Press conference	Date	Time	Duration	Active participants	Factor
46.	ALB2	21.05.2010	12:10h	17:45	KS FA1, FA2****, FA3****, FA4****, MA1 MP1, MP2, MP3, MP4, MP5**, MP6, MP7	2
47.	GRE2	21.05.2010	12:40h	24:35	KS FA1, (FA2), MA1, MA2, MA3, MA4, MA5, MA6 MP1, MP2, MP3, MP4, MP5***	1
48.	POR2	21.05.2010	13:10h	18:00	KS FA1, FA2, FA3, MA1 MP1, MP2, MP3, MP4**	1
49.	MAC2	21.05.2010	13:40h	12:42	KS FA1, FA2, MA1, MA2, MA3 MP1, MP2	f
50.	BLR2	21.05.2010	15:10h	19:14	KS FA1, FA2, FA3, MA1, MA2, MA3 MP1*	1
51.	ISL2	21.05.2010	15:40h	22:12	KS FA1, FA2, FA3, FA4, MA1, MA2, MA3, MA4 MP1, MP2, MP3***, MP4**, MP5, MP6*	2
52.	LIT2	21.05.2010	16:10h	17:10	KS MA1, MA2 MP1, MP2, MP3	f
53.	ARM2	21.05.2010	16:40h	18:11	KS FA1, FA2, MA1 MP1, MP2, MP3, MP4	f
54.	ISR2	21.05.2010	17:25h	15:41	KS MA1, MA2, MA3 FP1, MP1***, MP2, MP3, MP4	1
55.	DAN2	21.05.2010	17:55h	06:41	KS FA1, MA1 FP1	f
56.	SUI2	21.05.2010	18:25h	15:51	KS FA1, MA1, MA2 FP1, MP1, MP2, MP3, MP4	f
57.	SWE2	21.05.2010	18:55h	15:31	KS FA1, FA2, MA1, MA2 MP1, MP2, MP3, MP4, MP5, MP6	f

(Continued)

9.2 List of press conferences in ESC-PC (Continued)

#	Press conference	Date	Time	Duration	Active participants	Factor
58.	AZE2	22.05.2010	12:10h	17:54	KS FA1, FA2, FA3, FA4*, FA5, FA6, MA1 FP1, MP1, MP2, MP3, MP4*	2
59.	UKR2	22.05.2010	12:40h	17:49	KS FA1, FA2, MA1 MP1, MP2*****, MP3, MP4, MP5***	2
60.	NED2	22.05.2010	13:10h	16:30	KS FA1, FA2 MP1, MP2*, MP3, MP4***, MP5, MP6*, MP7	2
61.	ROM2	22.05.2010	14:35h	19:08	KS FA1, MA1 MP1, MP2, MP3, MP4, MP5, MP6*, MP7	1
62.	SLO2	22.05.2010	15:10h	13:00	KS FA1, MA1, MA2, MA3, MA4, MA5, MA6, MA7 MP1	f
63.	ESP1	22.05.2010	15:50h	28:06	KS FA1, MA1, MA2, MA3 MP1, (MP2), (MP3), MP4, MP5, MP6***, (MP7)	1
64.	NOR1	22.05.2010	16:30h	29:42	KS FA1, FA2, MA1, MA2, MA3 (MP1), MP2, (MP3), MP4, (MP5), MP6***, MP7, MP8, MP9, MP10, MP11, MP12, MP13, (MP14), MP15	1
65.	UK1	22.05.2010	17:30h	19:54	KS MA1*, MA2* FP1*, MP1*, MP2*, MP3***, MP4*, MP5*, MP6**, MP7*, MP8*, MP9*, MP10*, MP11*	n
66.	FRA1	22.05.2010	18:10h	23: 50	KS MA1, MA2, MA3 (FP1), (MP1), MP2, MP3, MP4**, MP5, MP6***, MP7	2
67.	GER1	22.05.2010	18:50h	29:09	KS FA1, MA1, MA2, MA3 FP1, (FP2), FP3, MP1, (MP2), MP3, MP4***, MP5, MP6, MP7, (MP8), (MP9), MP10, MP11, MP12	1

#	Press conference	Date	Time	Duration	Active participants	Factor
68.	IRL2	23.05.2010	12:10h	19:16	KS FA1**, FA2**, FA3**, MA1**, MA2** MP1*, MP2, MP3**, MP4**, MP5, MP6**, MP7**, MP8	n
69.	BUL2	23.05.2010	12:40h	14:32	KS FA1, FA2, MA1 FP1, MP1, MP2, MP3	f
70.	CYP2	23.05.2010	13:10h	17:40	KS FA1, FA2, FA3*, MA1*, MA2*, MA3* FP1, FP2, MP1*, MP2***, MP3	n
71.	CRO2	23.05.2010	14:10h	17:35	KS FA1, FA2, FA3, MA1 MP1, MP2, MP3***	l
72.	GEO2	23.05.2010	15:10h	17:43	KS FA1, FA2, FA3, FA4, MA1, MA2 MP1, MP2, MP3***, MP4	l
73.	TUR2	23.05.2010	15:40h	15:15	KS FA1, FA2, MA1, MA2, MA3 MP1, MP2, MP3, MP4, MP5, MP6, MP7	f
74.	ESP2	28.05.2010	16:30h	13:36	KS MA1, MA2 FP1, FP2, FP3, MP1*, (MP2), MP3	l
75.	NOR2	28.05.2010	16:55h	19:55	KS FA1, FA2, MA1, MA2 (FP1), (FP2), (FP3), FP4, MP1, MP2, MP3, MP4, MP5, MP6, MP7	f
76.	UK2	28.05.2010	17:20h	19:40	KS MA1*, MA2**, MA3**, MA4*, MA5* FP1, FP2*, FP3*, FP4, MP1*, MP2*, MP3**, MP4*, MP5, MP6, MP7*, MP8*, MP9*	n
77.	FRA2	28.05.2010	17:45h	21:02	KS MA1, MA2, (MA3), (MA4), MA5, (MA6) FP1, MP1*, MP2, MP3	l
78.	GER2	28.05.2010	18:10h	20:43	KS FA1, MA1, MA2 FP1, FP2, FP3, FP4, MP1, MP2, (MP3), MP4, MP5, (MP6), MP7*, MP8, (MP9), MP10, MP11	l

References

Aarts, Flor. 1993. *Who, whom, that* and Ø in two corpora of spoken English. *English Today* 9(3): 19–21.

Aarts, Flor. 1994. Relative *who* and *whom*: Prescriptive rules and linguistic reality. *American Speech* 69(1): 71–79.

Adolphs, Svenja. 2005. 'I don't think I should learn all this' – A longitudinal view of attitudes towards 'native speaker' English. In *The Globalisation of English and the English Language Classroom*, Claus Gnutzmann & Frauke Intemann (eds), 119–131. Tübingen: Gunter Narr.

Ammon, Ulrich. 2000. Towards more fairness in International English: Linguistic rights of non-native speakers? In *Rights to Language. Equity, Power, and Education*, Robert Phillipson (ed.), 111–116. Mahwah, NJ: Lawrence Erlbaum Associates.

Ammon, Ulrich. 2003. Present and future language conflicts as a consequence of the integration and expansion of the European Union (EU). In *Ecologia Linguistica. Atti del XXXVI Congresso Internazionale di Studi della Società di Linguistica Italiana (SLI), Bergamo, 26–28 Settembre 2002*, Ada Valentini, Piera Molinelli, Pierluigi Cuzzolin & Giuliano Bernini (eds), 393–405. Roma: Bulzoni.

Ammon, Ulrich. 2006a. Language conflicts in the European Union. *International Journal of Applied Linguistics* 16(3): 319–338.

Ammon, Ulrich. 2006b. The dominance of languages and language communities in the European Union (EU) and the consequences. In *'Along the Routes to Power'. Explorations of Empowerment through Language*, Martin Pütz, Joshua A. Fishman & JoAnne Neff-van Aertselaer (eds), 217–238. Berlin: Mouton de Gruyter.

Ammon, Ulrich. 2008. Über die Dilemmata jeglicher EU-Sprachenpolitik. In *National and European Language Policies: Contributions to the Annual Conference 2007 of EFNIL in Riga*, Gerhard Stickel (ed.), 19–34. Frankfurt: Peter Lang.

Anderson, Benedict. 1991. *Imagined Communities. Reflections on the Origin and Spread of Nationalism*. London: Verso.

Andrews, Avery D. 2007. Relative clauses. In *Language Typology and Syntactic Description. Volume II: Complex Constructions*, Timothy Shopen (ed.), 206–236. Cambridge: Cambridge University Press.

Baker, Will. 2009a. Language, culture and identity through English as a lingua franca in Asia: Notes from the field. *Linguistics Journal* 4: 8–35.

Baker, Will. 2009b. The cultures of English as a lingua franca. *TESOL Quarterly* 43(4): 567–592.

Baker, Will. 2011. Culture and identity through ELF in Asia: Fact or fiction? In *Latest Trends in ELF Research,* Alasdair Archibald, Alessia Cogo & Jennifer Jenkins (eds), 35–51. Newcastle upon Tyne: Cambridge Scholars.

Ball, Catherine N. 1996. A diachronic study of relative markers in spoken and written English. *Language Variation and Change* 8(2): 227–258.

Bayley, Robert. 1999. Relativization strategies in Mexican-American English. *American Speech* 74(2): 115–139.

Bell, Allan. 1999. Styling the other to define the self: A study in New Zealand identity making. *Journal of Sociolinguistics* 3(4): 523–541.

Berlant, Lauren & Warner, Michael. 1998. Sex in public. *Critical Inquiry* 24(2): 547–566.

Berlin, Lawrence N. 1997. The role of gender in complimenting in American English: Implications for second language learning. *Arizona Working Papers in Second Language Acquisition and Teaching* 5: 46–58.

Berns, Margie. 2008. World Englishes, English as a lingua franca, and intelligibility. *World Englishes* 27(3–4): 327–34.

Berns, Margie. 2009. English as lingua franca and English in Europe. *World Englishes* 28(2): 192–199.

Berry, Roger. 2005. Making the most of metalanguage. *Language Awareness* 14(1): 3–20.

Bhatia, Aditi. 2006. Critical discourse analysis of political press conferences. *Discourse & Society* 17(2): 173–203.

Biancolini Decuypère, Paola. 2000. Can we trust compliments? A contrastive analysis of compliments in English and Italian. In *Semiotics as a Bridge Between the Humanities and the Sciences*, Paul Perron, Leonard G. Sbrocchi, Paul Colilli & Marcel Danesi (eds), 585–592. New York: Legas.

Block, David. 2007. *Second Language Identities*. London: Continuum.

Blommaert, Jan & Rampton, Ben. 2011. Language and superdiversity. *Diversities* 13(2): 1–21.

Bonnici, Lisa M. 2009. Maltese English: History of use, structural variation and sociolinguistic status. In *Introducing Maltese Linguistics. Selected Papers from the 1st International Conference on Maltese Linguistics, Bremen, 18–20 October,* 2007, Bernard Comrie, Ray Fabri, Elizabeth Hume, Manwel Mifsud, Thomas Stolz & Martine Vanhove (eds), 393–414. Amsterdam: John Benjamins.

Bousfield, Derek. 2008. *Impoliteness in Interaction*. Amsterdam: John Benjamins.

Boyle, Ronald. 2000. 'You've worked with Elizabeth Taylor!': Phatic functions and implicit compliments. *Applied Linguistics* 21(1): 26–46.

Bradac, James J., Mulac, Anthony & Thompson, Sandra A. 1995. Men's and women's use of intensifiers and hedges in problem-solving interaction: Molar and molecular analyses. *Research on Language and Social Interaction* 28(2): 93–116.

Braselmann, Petra. 2005. 'Killersprache' Englisch: Europäische Sprachpolitik und 'Globalisierung'. In *Translationswissenschaft im interdisziplinären Dialog. Innsbrucker Ringvorlesungen zur Translationswissenschaft III*, Lew N. Zybatow (ed.), 151–169. Frankfurt: Peter Lang.

Breiteneder, Angelika. 2009. English as a lingua franca in Europe: An empirical perspective. *World Englishes* 28(2): 256–269.

Breiteneder, Angelika, Pitzl, Marie-Luise, Majewski, Stefan & Klimpfinger, Theresa. 2006. VOICE recording – Methodological challenges in the compilation of a corpus of spoken ELF. *Nordic Journal of English Studies* 5(2): 161–187.

Brown, Penelope & Levinson, Stephen C. 1987. *Politeness. Some Universals in Language Usage*. Cambridge: Cambridge University Press.

Brumfit, Christopher. 2006. A European perspective on language as liminality. In *Language Ideologies, Policies and Practices. Language and the Future of Europe*, Clare Mar-Molinero & Patrick Stevenson (eds), 28–43. Basingstoke: Palgrave Macmillan.

Bruthiaux, Paul. 2003. Squaring the circles: Issues in modeling English worldwide. *International Journal of Applied Linguistics* 13(2): 159–178.

Bucholtz, Mary & Hall, Kira. 2005. Identity and interaction: A sociocultural linguistic approach. *Discourse Studies* 7(4–5): 585–614.

Bucholtz, Mary & Hall, Kira. 2010. Locating identity in language. In *Language and Identities*, Carmen Llamas & Dominic Watt (eds), 18–28. Edinburgh: Edinburgh University Press.

Burger, Günter. 2000. Englisch als globale lingua franca: Überlegungen zu einer notwendigen Neuorientierung des Englischunterrichts. *Fremdsprachenunterricht* 53(1): 9–14.

Busse, Ulrich. 2007. Englisch als Lingua Franca: Fluch oder Segen für Englisch und andere Sprachen? *Muttersprache* 117(2): 154–173.

Bybee, Joan & Hopper, Paul. 2001. Introduction to frequency and the emergence of linguistic structure. In *Frequency and the Emergence of Linguistic Structure*, Joan Bybee & Paul Hopper (eds), 1–24. Amsterdam: John Benjamins.

Cameron, Deborah. 2001. *Working with Spoken Discourse*. London: Sage.

Cameron, Deborah. 2004. Out of the bottle: The social life of metalanguage. In *Metalanguage: Social and Ideological Perspectives*, Adam Jaworski, Nikolas Coupland & Dariusz Galasiński (eds), 311–321. Berlin: Mouton de Gruyter.

Canagarajah, A. Suresh. 2007. The ecology of global English. *International Multilingual Research Journal* 1(2): 89–100.

Caviedes, Alexander. 2003. The role of language in nation-building within the European Union. *Dialectical Anthropology* 27: 249–268.

Chen, Rong. 2010. Compliment and compliment response research: A cross-cultural survey. In *Pragmatics Across Languages and Cultures*, Anna Trosborg (ed.), 79–101. Berlin: Mouton de Gruyter.

Cheng, Liying. 2012. The power of English and the power of Asia: English as lingua franca and in bilingual and multilingual education. *Journal of Multilingual and Multicultural Development* 33(4): 327–330.

Christiansen, Pia Vanting. 2006. Language policy in the European Union: European/English/Elite/ Equal/Esperanto Union? *Language Problems & Language Planning* 30(1): 21–44.

Cogo, Alessia. 2008. English as a lingua franca: Form follows function. *English Today* 24(3): 58–61.

Cogo, Alessia. 2012a. ELF and super-diversity: A case study of ELF multilingual practices from a business context. *Journal of English as a Lingua Franca* 1(2): 287–313.

Cogo, Alessia. 2012b. English as a lingua franca: Concepts, use, and implications. *ELT Journal* 66(1): 97–105.

Cogo, Alessia & Dewey, Martin. 2012. *Analysing English as a Lingua Franca: A Corpus-Driven Investigation*. London: Continuum.

Comrie, Bernard. 1998. Rethinking the typology of relative clauses. *Language Design* 1: 59–85.

Comrie, Bernard. 1999. Relative clauses. Structure and typology on the periphery of standard English. In *The Clause in English. In Honour of Rodney Huddleston*, Peter Collins & David Lee (eds), 81–91. Amsterdam: John Benjamins.

Comrie, Bernard. 2006. Syntactic typology: Just how exotic are European-type relative clauses? In *Linguistic Universals*, Ricardo Mairal & Juana Gil (eds), 130–154. Cambridge: Cambridge University Press.

Comrie, Bernard & Kuteva, Tania. 2005. Relativization strategies. In *The World Atlas of Language Structures*, Martin Haspelmath, Matthew S. Dryer, David Gil & Bernard Comrie (eds), 494–501. Oxford: Oxford University Press.

Cooke, Sheryl. 1999. Street remarks: A cross cultural study. *Language Matters* 30: 171–196.

Cordella, Marisa, Large, Heather & Pardo, Verónica. 1995. Complimenting behavior in Australian English and Spanish speech. *Multilingua* 14(3): 235–252.

Coupland, Nikolas & Jaworski, Adam. 2004. Sociolinguistic perspectives on metalanguage: Reflexivity, evaluation and ideology. In *Metalanguage: Social and Ideological Perspectives*, Adam Jaworski, Nikolas Coupland & Dariusz Galasiński (eds), 15–51. Berlin: Mouton de Gruyter.

Creese, Angela. 1991. Speech act variation in British and American English. *Working Papers in Educational Linguistics* 7(2): 37–58.

Creese, Angela & Blackledge, Adrian. 2010. Towards a sociolinguistics of superdiversity. *Zeitschrift für Erziehungswissenschaft* 13(4): 549–572.

Cristofaro, Sonia & Giacalone Ramat, Anna. 2007. Relativisation strategies in the languages of Europe. In *Europe and the Mediterranean as Linguistic Areas. Convergencies from a Historical and Typological Perspective*, Paolo Ramat & Elisa Roma (eds), 63–93. Amsterdam: John Benjamins.

Curzan, Anne. 2003. *Gender Shifts in the History of English*. Cambridge: Cambridge University Press.

D'Arcy, Alexandra & Tagliamonte, Sali. 2010. Prestige, accommodation, and the legacy of relative *who*. *Language in Society* 39(3): 383–410.

Davidson, Keith. 1996. The Malta experience. *English Today* 12(4): 15–23.

de Swaan, Abram. 2001. *Words of the World*. Cambridge: Polity Press.

Demont-Heinrich, Christof. 2005. Language and national identity in the era of globalization: The case of English in Switzerland. *Journal of Communication Inquiry* 29(1): 66–84.

Dewey, Martin. 2007. English as a lingua franca and globalization: An interconnected perspective. *International Journal of Applied Linguistics* 17(3): 332–354.

Dewey, Martin. 2011. Accommodative ELF talk and teacher knowledge. In *Latest Trends in ELF Research*, Alasdair Archibald, Alessia Cogo & Jennifer Jenkins (eds), 205–227. Newcastle upon Tyne: Cambridge Scholars.

Dewey, Martin. 2013. The distinctiveness of English as a Lingua Franca. *ELT Journal* 67(3): 346–349.

Doohan, Eve-Anne M. & Manusov, Valerie. 2004. The communication of compliments in romantic relationships: An investigation of relational satisfaction and sex differences and similarities in compliment behavior. *Western Journal of Communication* 68(2): 170–194.

Dröschel, Yvonne. 2011. *Lingua Franca English: The Role of Simplification and Transfer*. Bern: Peter Lang.

Dryer, Matthew S. 2005. Order of relative clause and noun. In *The World Atlas of Language Structures*, Martin Haspelmath, Matthew S. Dryer, David Gil & Bernard Comrie (eds), 366–369. Oxford: Oxford University Press.

Durham, Mercedes. 2007. *English in Switzerland: Inherent Variation in a Non-Native Speech Community*. Fribourg: Université de Fribourg.

Duttlinger, Claudia. 1999. *Komplimente im Spanischen*. Freiburg im Breisgau: Hochschul Verlag.

Eckert, Penelope & McConnell-Ginet, Sally. 1992. Think practically and look locally: Language and gender as community-based practice. *Annual Review of Anthropology* 21: 461–490.

Eckert, Penelope & McConnell-Ginet, Sally. 2007. Putting communities of practice in their place. *Gender and Language* 1(1): 27–37.

Ehrenreich, Susanne. 2009. English as a lingua franca in multinational corporations – Exploring business communities of practice. In *English as a Lingua Franca: Studies and Findings*, Anna Mauranen & Elina Ranta (eds), 126–151. Newcastle upon Tyne: Cambridge Scholars.

Ehrenreich, Susanne. 2011. The dynamics of English as a lingua franca in international business: A language contact perspective. In *Latest Trends in ELF Research*, Alasdair Archibald, Alessia Cogo & Jennifer Jenkins (eds), 11–34. Newcastle upon Tyne: Cambridge Scholars.

European Commission. 2006. *Special Eurobarometer 243: Europeans and their Languages (Summary)*. ⟨http://ec.europa.eu/public_opinion/archives/ebs/ebs_243_sum_en.pdf⟩ (4 November 2011).

Eurovision.tv. 2013. *Break Down Barriers at the Eurovision Song Contest 2013*. ⟨http://www.eurovision.tv/upload/press-downloads/2013/Eurovision_A4_Journalists_low_res.pdf.pdf⟩ (20 October 2013).

Extra, Guus & Gorter, Durk. 2008. The constellation of languages in Europe: An inclusive approach. In *Multilingual Europe: Facts and Policies*, Guus Extra & Durk Gorter (eds), 3–60. Berlin: Mouton de Gruyter.

Fenet, Alain. 2004. Difference rights and language in France. In *Language, Nation, and State: Identity Politics in a Multilingual Age*, Tony Judt & Denis Lacorne (eds), 19–61. Basingstoke: Palgrave Macmillan.

Ferguson, Gibson. 2009. Issues in researching English as a lingua franca: A conceptual enquiry. *International Journal of Applied Linguistics* 19(2): 117–135.

Ferguson, Gibson. 2012. The practice of ELF. *Journal of English as a Lingua Franca* 1(1): 177–180.

Fiedler, Sabine. 2010. The English-as-a-lingua-franca approach: Linguistic fair play? *Language Problems & Language Planning* 34(3): 201–221.

Fiedler, Sabine. 2011. English as a lingua franca – a native-culture-free code? Language of communication vs. language of identification. *Apples – Journal of Applied Language Studies* 5(3): 79–97.

Fiorentino, Giuliana. 2007. European relative clauses and the uniqueness of the relative pronoun type. *Italian Journal of Linguistics* 19(2): 263–291.

Firth, Alan. 1996. The discursive accomplishment of normality: On 'lingua franca' English and conversation analysis. *Journal of Pragmatics* 26(2): 237–259.

Firth, Alan. 2009. The lingua franca factor. *Intercultural Pragmatics* 6(2): 147–170.

Flanigan, Beverly Olson & Inal, Emel. 1996. Object relative pronoun use in native and non-native English: A variable rule analysis. *Language Variation and Change* 8(2): 203–226.

Fox, Barbara A. 2007. Principles shaping grammatical practices: An exploration. *Discourse Studies* 9(3): 299–318.

Fox, Barbara A. & Thompson, Sandra A. 2007. Relative clauses in English conversation: Relativizers, frequency, and the notion of construction. *Studies in Language* 31(2): 293–326.

Friedrich, Patricia. 2007. English for peace: Toward a framework of Peace Sociolinguistics. *World Englishes* 26(1): 72–83.

Friedrich, Patricia. 2009. World Englishes and Peace Sociolinguistics. Towards a common goal of linguistic understanding. In *World Englishes – Problems, Properties and Prospects*, Thomas Hoffmann & Lucia Siebers (eds), 407–414. Amsterdam: John Benjamins.

Gal, Susan. 2013. A linguistic anthropologist looks at English as a lingua franca. *Journal of English as a Lingua Franca* 2(1): 177–183.

Geisler, Christer & Johansson, Christine. 2002. Relativization in formal spoken American English. In *Studies in Mid-Atlantic English*, Marko Modiano (ed.), 87–109. Gävle: Högskolan i Gävle.

Giles, Howard, Scholes, Janet & Young, Louis. 1983. Stereotypes of male and female speech: A British study. *Central States Speech Journal* 34: 255–256.

Gnutzmann, Claus. 2005. 'Standard English' and 'World Standard English'. Linguistic and pedagogical considerations. In *The Globalisation of English and the English Language Classroom*, Claus Gnutzmann & Frauke Intemann (eds), 107–118. Tübingen: Gunter Narr.

Gnutzmann, Claus. 2008. Fighting or fostering the dominance of English in academic communication? In *English in Academia: Catalyst or Barrier?*, Claus Gnutzmann (ed.), 73–91. Tübingen: Gunter Narr.

Golato, Andrea. 2005. *Compliments and Compliment Responses: Grammatical Structure and Sequential Organization*. Amsterdam: John Benjamins.

Görlach, Manfred. 2001. *A Dictionary of European Anglicisms. A Usage Dictionary of Anglicisms in Sixteen European Languages*. Oxford: Oxford University Press.

Görlach, Manfred. 2002. *Still More Englishes*. Amsterdam: John Benjamins.

Gottburgsen, Anja. 2000. *Stereotype Muster des sprachlichen Doing Gender. Eine empirische Untersuchung*. Wiesbaden: Westdeutscher Verlag.

Graddol, David. 2001. The future of English as a European language. *European English Messenger* 10(2): 47–55.

Graddol, David. 2006. *English Next. Why Global English May Mean the End of 'English as a Foreign Language'*. London: British Council.

Grein, Marion. 2008. Der Sprechakt des Kompliments im interkulturellen Vergleich. In *Dialogue In and Between Different Cultures*, Marion Grein (ed.), 15–32. Mainz: University of Mainz.

Grimm, Anne. 2008. 'Männersprache' – 'Frauensprache'? Eine korpusgestützte empirische Analyse des Sprachgebrauchs britischer und amerikanischer Frauen und Männer hinsichtlich Geschlechtsspezifika. Hamburg: Dr. Kovač.

Gubbins, Paul. 2002. Lost in translation: EU language policy in an expanded Europe. In *Beyond Boundaries. Language and Identity in Contemporary Europe*, Paul Gubbins & Mike Holt (eds), 46–58. Clevedon: Multilingual Matters.

Guy, Gregory G. & Bayley, Robert. 1995. On the choice of relative pronouns in English. *American Speech* 70(2): 148–162.

Hadic Zabala, Loreley Marie. 2004. Functional factors in the production of relative clauses by native and non-native speakers of English. *University of Washington Working Papers in Linguistics* 23: 362–376.

Harvey, Keith. 2002. Camp talk and citationality: A queer take on 'authentic' and 'represented' utterance. *Journal of Pragmatics* 34(9): 1145–1165.

Haspelmath, Martin. 2001. The European linguistic area: Standard Average European. In *Language Typology and Language Universals: An International Handbook,* Vol. 2, Martin Haspelmath, Ekkehard König, Wulf Oesterreicher & Wolfgang Raible (eds), 1492–1510. Berlin: Walter de Gruyter.

Haugh, Michael. 2010. Intercultural (im)politeness and the micro-macro issue. In *Pragmatics Across Languages and Cultures*, Anna Trosborg (ed.), 139–166. Berlin: De Gruyter Mouton.

Heller, Monica. 2011. *Paths to Post-Nationalism. A Critical Ethnography of Language and Identity.* Oxford: Oxford University Press.

Herbert, Robert K. 1989. The ethnography of English compliment and compliment responses: A contrastive sketch. In *Contrastive Pragmatics*, Wieslaw Oleksy (ed.), 3–35. Amsterdam: John Benjamins.

Herbert, Robert K. 1990. Sex-based differences in compliment behavior. *Language in Society* 19(2): 201–224.

Herbert, Robert K. 1991. The sociology of compliment work: An ethnocontrastive study of Polish and English compliments. *Multilingua* 10(4): 381–402.

Herrmann, Tanja. 2005. Relative clauses in English dialects of the British Isles. In *A Comparative Grammar of British English Dialects. Agreement, Gender, Relative Clauses*, Bernd Kortmann, Tanja Herrmann, Lukas Pietsch & Susanne Wagner (eds), 21–123. Berlin: Mouton de Gruyter.

Hickey, Leo. 2005. Politeness in Spain: Thanks but no 'thanks'. In *Politeness in Europe*, Leo Hickey & Miranda Stewart (eds), 317–330. Clevedon: Multilingual Matters.

Hickey, Leo & Stewart, Miranda (eds). 2005. *Politeness in Europe*. Clevedon: Multilingual Matters.

Hobbs, Pamela. 2003. The medium is the message: Politeness strategies in men's and women's voice mail messages. *Journal of Pragmatics* 35(2): 243–262.

Hoffmann, Thomas. 2007. 'I need data which I can rely on': Corroborating empirical evidence on preposition placement in English relative clauses. In *Roots: Linguistics in Search of its Evidential Base*, Sam Featherston & Wolfgang Sternefeld (eds), 161–183. Berlin: Mouton de Gruyter.

Holmes, Janet. 1986. Compliments and compliment responses in New Zealand English. *Anthropological Linguistics* 28(4): 485–508.

Holmes, Janet. 1988. Paying compliments: A sex-preferential politeness strategy. *Journal of Pragmatics* 12(4): 445–465.

Holmes, Janet. 1995. *Women, Men and Politeness*. London: Longman.

Holmes, Janet & Brown, Dorothy F. 1987. Teachers and students learning about compliments. *TESOL Quarterly* 21(3): 523–546.

Hopper, Paul J. 1998. Emergent grammar. In *The New Psychology of Language. Cognitive and Functional Approaches to Language Structure*, Michael Tomasello (ed.), 155–175. Mahwah, NJ: Lawrence Erlbaum Associates.

Hornscheidt, Antje. 1998. Grammatik als Ort von Geschlechterkonstruktion. Eine kritische Analyse. In *Kritische Differenzen – geteilte Perspektiven. Zum Verhältnis von Feminismus und Postmoderne*, Antje Hornscheidt, Gabriele Jähnert & Annette Schlichter (eds), 140–173. Opladen: Westdeutscher Verlag.

House, Juliane. 2003. English as a lingua franca: A threat to multilingualism? *Journal of Sociolinguistics* 7(4): 556–578.

House, Juliane. 2008a. English as lingua franca in Europe today. In *Multilingual Europe: Facts and Policies*, Guus Extra & Durk Gorter (eds), 63–85. Berlin: Mouton de Gruyter.

House, Juliane. 2008b. (Im)politeness in English as a lingua franca discourse. In *Standards and Norms in the English Language*, Miriam A. Locher & Jürg Strässler (eds), 351–366. Berlin: Mouton de Gruyter.

Hüllen, Werner. 1992. Identifikationssprachen und Kommunikationssprachen. *Zeitschrift für germanistische Linguistik* 20: 298–317.

Hülmbauer, Cornelia. 2011. Old friends? Cognates in ELF communication. In *Latest Trends in ELF Research*, Alasdair Archibald, Alessia Cogo & Jennifer Jenkins (eds), 139–161. Newcastle upon Tyne: Cambridge Scholars.

Jacobs, Geert. 2011. Press conferences on the Internet: Technology, mediation and access in the news. *Journal of Pragmatics* 43(7): 1900–1911.

Jacquemet, Marco. 2005. Transidiomatic practices: Language and power in the age of globalization. *Language & Communication* 25(3): 257–277.

James, Allan. 2005. The challenges of the lingua franca: English in the world and types of variety. In *The Globalisation of English and the English Language Classroom*, Claus Gnutzmann & Frauke Intemann (eds), 133–144. Tübingen: Gunter Narr.

James, Allan. 2008. New Englishes as post-geographic Englishes in lingua franca use. Genre, interdiscursivity and late modernity. *European Journal of English Studies* 12(1): 97–112.

Jaworski, Adam. 1995. 'This is not an empty compliment!' Polish compliments and the expression of solidarity. *International Journal of Applied Linguistics* 5(1): 63–94.

Jaworski, Adam, Coupland, Nikolas & Galasiński, Dariusz. 2004. Metalanguage: Why now? In *Metalanguage: Social and Ideological Perspectives*, Adam Jaworski, Nikolas Coupland & Dariusz Galasiński (eds), 3–13. Berlin: Mouton de Gruyter.

Jenkins, Jennifer. 2000. *The Phonology of English as an International Language. New Models, New Norms, New Goals*. Oxford: Oxford University Press.

Jenkins, Jennifer. 2003. *World Englishes: A Resource Book for Students*. London: Routledge.

Jenkins, Jennifer. 2005. Teaching pronunciation for English as a lingua franca: A sociopolitical perspective. In *The Globalisation of English and the English Language Classroom,* Claus Gnutzmann & Frauke Intemann (eds), 145–158. Tübingen: Gunter Narr.

Jenkins, Jennifer. 2006. English pronunciation and second language speaker identity. In *The Sociolinguistics of Identity*, Tope Omoniyi & Goodith White (eds), 75–91. London: Continuum.

Jenkins, Jennifer. 2007. *English as a Lingua Franca: Attitude and Identity*. Oxford: Oxford University Press.

Jenkins, Jennifer. 2009. English as a lingua franca: Interpretations and attitudes. *World Englishes* 28(2): 200–207.

Jenkins, Jennifer. 2011. Accommodating (to) ELF in the international university. *Journal of Pragmatics* 43(4): 926–936.

Jenkins, Jennifer. 2012. English as a Lingua Franca from the classroom to the classroom. *ELT Journal* 66(4): 486–494.

Jenkins, Jennifer, Cogo, Alessia & Dewey, Martin. 2011. Review of developments in research into English as a lingua franca. *Language Teaching* 44(3): 281–315.

Jenkins, Jennifer, Modiano, Marko & Seidlhofer, Barbara. 2001. Euro-English. *English Today* 17(4): 13–19.

Jessner, Ulrike. 2006. *Linguistic Awareness in Multilinguals. English as a Third Language*. Edinburgh: Edinburgh University Press.

Johnson, Donna M. & Roen, Duane H. 1992. Complimenting and involvement in peer reviews: Gender variation. *Language in Society* 21(1): 27–57.

Jørgensen, J. Normann. 2004. Languaging and languagers. *Copenhagen Studies in Bilingualism* 36: 5–22.

Jørgensen, J. Normann. 2008. Polylingual languaging around and among children and adolescents. *International Journal of Multilingualism* 5(3): 161–176.

Jucker, Andreas H. 2009. Speech act research between armchair, field and laboratory: The case of compliments. *Journal of Pragmatics* 41(8): 1611–1635.

Jucker, Andreas H., Schneider, Gerold, Taavitsainen, Irma & Breustedt, Barb. 2008. Fishing for compliments: Precision and recall in corpus-linguistic compliment research. In *Speech Acts in the History of English*, Andreas H. Jucker & Irma Taavitsainen (eds), 273–294. Amsterdam: John Benjamins.

Kachru, Braj B. 1985. Standards, codification and sociolinguistic realism: The English language in the outer circle. In *English in the World: Teaching and Learning the Language and Literatures*, Randolph Quirk & Henry G. Widdowson (eds), 11–30. Cambridge: Cambridge University Press.

Kallen, Jeffrey L. 2005. Politeness in Ireland: 'In Ireland, it's done without being said'. In *Politeness in Europe*, Leo Hickey & Miranda Stewart (eds), 130–144. Clevedon: Multilingual Matters.

Kalocsai, Karolina. 2011. The show of interpersonal involvement and the building of rapport in an ELF community of practice. In *Latest Trends in ELF Research*, Alasdair Archibald, Alessia Cogo & Jennifer Jenkins (eds), 113–137. Newcastle upon Tyne: Cambridge Scholars.

Kecskes, Istvan. 2007. Formulaic language in English lingua franca. In *Explorations in Pragmatics: Linguistic, Cognitive and Intercultural Aspects*, Istvan Kecskes & Laurence R. Horn (eds), 191–218. Berlin: Mouton de Gruyter.

Keenan, Edward L. & Comrie, Bernard. 1977. Noun phrase accessibility and universal grammar. *Linguistic Inquiry* 8(1): 63–99.

Keevallik, Leelo. 2005. Politeness in Estonia: A matter-of-fact style. In *Politeness in Europe*, Leo Hickey & Miranda Stewart (eds), 203–217. Clevedon: Multilingual Matters.

Kelly-Holmes, Helen. 2005. *Advertising as Multilingual Communication*. Basingstoke: Palgrave Macmillan.

Kharraki, Abdennour. 2002. The distribution of compliments in men's and women's speech in Eastern Morocco. *Langues et Linguistique* 9: 49–68.

Kiesling, Scott F. 2013. Flirting and 'normative' sexualities. *Journal of Language and Sexuality* 2.1: 101–121.

Kirkpatrick, Andy. 2006. Which model of English: Native-speaker, nativized or lingua franca? In *English in the World. Global Rules, Global Roles*, Rani Rubdy & Mario Saraceni (eds), 71–83. London: Continuum.

Kirkpatrick, Andy. 2011. English as an Asian lingua franca and the multilingual model of ELT. *Language Teaching* 44(2): 212–224.

Kiss-Gulyás, Judit. 2004. *The Acquisition of English Restrictive Relative Clauses by Hungarian Learners of English*. Budapest: Akadémiai Kiadó.

Kissling, Elizabeth Arveda. 1991. Street harassment: The language of sexual terrorism. *Discourse & Society* 2(4): 451–460.

Klimpfinger, Theresa. 2007. 'Mind you, sometimes you have to mix' – The role of code-switching in English as a lingua franca. *Vienna English Working Papers* 16(2): 36–61.

Klimpfinger, Theresa. 2009. 'She's mixing the two languages together' – Forms and functions of code-switching in English as a lingua franca. In *English as a Lingua Franca: Studies and Findings*, Anna Mauranen & Elina Ranta (eds), 348–371. Newcastle upon Tyne: Cambridge Scholars.

Knapp, Karlfried. 2002. The fading out of the non-native speaker. A case study of unco-operative lingua franca communication. In *Lingua Franca Communication*, Karlfried Knapp & Christiane Meierkord (eds), 217–244. Frankfurt: Peter Lang.

Knapp, Mark L., Hopper, Robert, Bell, Robert A. 1984. Compliments: A descriptive taxonomy. *Journal of Communication* 34(4): 12–31.

Kordon, Kathrin. 2006. 'You are very good' – Establishing rapport in English as a lingua franca: The case of agreement tokens. *Vienna English Working Papers* 15(2): 58–82.

Kramer, Cheris. 1977. Perceptions of female and male speech. *Language & Speech* 20: 151–161.

Kramsch, Claire. 1993. *Context and Culture in Language Teaching*. Oxford: Oxford University Press.

Kraus, Peter A. 2004. *Europäische Öffentlichkeit und Sprachpolitik. Integration durch Anerkennung*. Frankfurt: Campus.

Krzyżanowski, Michał. 2010. *The Discursive Construction of European Identities: A Multi-Level Approach to Discourse and Identity in the Transforming European Union*. Frankfurt: Peter Lang.

Kulick, Don. 2003. No. *Language & Communication* 23(2): 139–151.

Kurzová, Helena. 1981. *Der Relativsatz in den indoeuropäischen Sprachen*. Praha: Academia.

Lakoff, Robin. 1975. *Language and Woman's Place*. New York: Harper & Row.

Lapadat, Judy & Seesahai, Maureen. 1977. Male versus female codes in informal contexts. *Sociolinguistics Newsletter* 8(3): 7–8.

Leech, Geoffrey, Hundt, Marianne, Mair, Christian & Smith, Nicholas. 2009. *Change in Contemporary English: A Grammatical Study*. Cambridge: Cambridge University Press.

Lehmann, Christian. 1986. On the typology of relative clauses. *Linguistics* 24(4): 663–680.

Lehmann, Hans Martin. 1997. Automatic retrieval of zero elements in a computerised corpus. In *Corpus-Based Studies in English. Papers from the Seventeenth International Conference on English Language Research on Computerized Corpora (ICAME 17)*, Magnus Ljung (ed.), 179–194. Amsterdam: Rodopi.

Levey, Stephen. 2006. Visiting London relatives. *English World-Wide* 27(1): 45–70.

Lewandowska-Tomaszczyk, Barbara. 1989. Praising and complimenting. In *Contrastive Pragmatics*, Wieslaw Oleksy (ed.), 73–100. Amsterdam: John Benjamins.

Lichtkoppler, Julia. 2007. 'Male. Male.' – 'Male?' – 'The sex is male.' The role of repetition in English as a lingua franca conversations. *Vienna English Working Papers* 16(1): 39–65.

Locher, Miriam A. & Watts, Richard J. 2005. Politeness theory and relational work. *Journal of Politeness Research* 1(1): 9–33.

Love, Nigel & Ansaldo, Umberto. 2010. The native speaker and the mother tongue. *Language Sciences* 32(6): 589–593.

Lubecka, Anna. 2000. *Requests, Invitations, Apologies and Compliments in American English and Polish: A Cross-Cultural Communication Perspective*. Kraków: Ksiegarnia Akademicka.

Lüdi, Georges. 2002. Braucht Europa eine lingua franca? *Basler Schriften zur europäischen Integration* 60: 7–29.

MacKenzie, Ian. 2012. English as a lingua franca in Europe: Bilingualism and multicompetence. *International Journal of Multilingualism* 9(1): 83–100.

Mahootian, Shahrzad. 2006. Code switching and mixing. In *Encyclopedia of Language & Linguistics*, Vol. II, Edward K. Brown (ed.), 511–527. Amsterdam: Elsevier.

Maíz-Arévalo, Carmen. 2012. 'Was that a compliment?' Implicit compliments in English and Spanish. *Journal of Pragmatics* 44(8): 980–996.

Makoni, Sinfree & Pennycook, Alastair. 2007. Disinventing and reconstituting languages. In *Disinventing and Reconstituting Languages*, Sinfree Makoni & Alastair Pennycook (eds), 1–41. Clevedon: Multilingual Matters.

Makoni, Sinfree & Pennycook, Alastair. 2012. Disinventing multilingualism: From monological multilingualism to multilingua francas. In *The Routledge Handbook of Multilingualism*, Marilyn Martin-Jones, Adrian Blackledge & Angela Creese (eds), 439–453. London: Routledge.

Manes, Joan. 1983. Compliments: A mirror of cultural values. In *Sociolinguistics and Language Acquisition*, Nessa Wolfson & Elliott Judd (eds), 96–102. Rowley, MA: Newbury House.

Manes, Joan & Wolfson, Nessa. 1981. The compliment formula. In *Conversational Routine: Explorations in Standardized Communication Situations and Prepatterned Speech*, Florian Coulmas (ed.), 115–132. The Hague: Mouton.

Markus, Manfred. 2007. Maltese English in its multicultural setting. In *Tracing English Through Time: Explorations in Language Variation*, Ute Smit, Stefan Dollinger, Julia Hüttner, Gunther Kaltenböck & Ursula Lutzky (eds), 203–218. Wien: Braumüller.

Matsuoka, Rieko. 2003. Gender variation in explicitness of proffering compliments. *Proceedings of the Annual JALT Pan-SIG Conference* 2: 37–45.

Mauranen, Anna. 2012. *Exploring ELF. Academic English Shaped by Non-Native Speakers*. Cambridge: Cambridge University Press.

McEntee-Atalianis, Lisa J. 2004. The impact of English in postcolonial, postmodern Cyprus. *International Journal of the Sociology of Language* 168: 77–90.

McMillan, Julie R., Clifton, A. Kay, McGrath, Diane & Gale, Wanda S. 1977. Women's language: Uncertainty or interpersonal sensitivity and emotionality? *Sex Roles* 3(6): 545–559.

Meierkord, Christine. 1996. *Englisch als Medium der interkulturellen Kommunikation. Untersuchungen zum non-native-/non-native-speaker-Diskurs*. Frankfurt: Peter Lang.

Meierkord, Christiane. 2002. 'Language stripped bare' or 'linguistic masala'? Culture in lingua franca conversation. In *Lingua Franca Communication*, Karlfried Knapp & Christiane Meierkord (eds), 109–133. Frankfurt: Peter Lang.

Meinhof, Ulrike Hanna & Galasiński, Dariusz. 2005. *The Language of Belonging*. Basingstoke: Palgrave Macmillan.

Mesthrie, Rajend. 2010. New Englishes and the native speaker debate. *Language Sciences* 32(6): 594–601.

Milinkovic, Tihana. 2010. Compliments on possessions in Australian English. *Griffith Working Papers in Pragmatics and Intercultural Communication* 3(2): 83–91.

Mills, Sara. 2011. Discursive approaches to politeness and impoliteness. In *Discursive Approaches to Politeness*, Linguistic Politeness Research Group (eds), 19–56. Berlin: De Gruyter Mouton.

Mironovschi, Lilia. 2009. *Komplimente und Komplimenterwiderungen im Russischen und im Deutschen. Ein interkultureller Vergleich*. Frankfurt: Peter Lang.

Modiano, Marko. 1996. The Americanization of Euro-English. *World Englishes* 15(2): 207–215.

Modiano, Marko. 2006. Euro-Englishes. In *The Handbook of World Englishes*, Braj B. Kachru, Yamuna Kachru & Cecil L. Nelson (eds), 223–239. Malden, MA: Blackwell.

Modiano, Marko. 2007. Euro-English from a 'deficit linguistics' perspective? *World Englishes* 26(4): 525–533.

Modiano, Marko. 2009. Inclusive/exclusive? English as a lingua franca in the European Union. *World Englishes* 28(2): 208–223.

Møller, Janus Spindler & Jørgensen, J. Normann. 2009. From language to languaging: Changing relations between humans and linguistic features. *Acta Linguistica Hafniensia* 41: 143–166.

Mollin, Sandra. 2006. *Euro-English. Assessing Variety Status*. Tübingen: Gunter Narr.

Mollin, Sandra. 2007. New variety or learner English? Criteria for variety status and the case of Euro-English. *World Englishes* 28(2): 167–185.

Mortensen, Janus. 2013. Notes on English used as a lingua franca as an object of study. *Journal of English as a Lingua Franca* 2(1): 25–46.

Motschenbacher, Heiko. 2006. *'Women and Men Like Different Things'? – Doing Gender als Strategie der Werbesprache*. Marburg: Tectum.

Motschenbacher, Heiko. 2007. Can the term 'genderlect' be saved? A postmodernist re-definition. *Gender and Language* 1(2): 255–278.

Motschenbacher, Heiko. 2010. The discursive interface of national, European and sexual identities: Preliminary evidence from the Eurovision Song Contest. In *Intercultural Europe: Arenas of Difference, Communication and Mediation*, Barbara Lewandowska-Tomaszczyk & Hanna Pułaczewska (eds), 85–103. Stuttgart: Ibidem.

Motschenbacher, Heiko. 2011. Taking Queer Linguistics further: Sociolinguistics and critical hetero-normativity research. *International Journal of the Sociology of Language* 212: 149–179.

Motschenbacher, Heiko. 2012a. 'I think Houston wants a kiss right?': Linguistic constructions of het-erosexualities at Eurovision Song Contest press conferences. *Journal of Language and Sexuality* 1(2): 127–150.

Motschenbacher, Heiko. 2012b. Negotiating sexual desire at the Eurovision Song Contest: On the verge of homonormativity? In *Let's Talk About (Texts About) Sex. Sex and Language*, Marietta Calderón & Georg Marko (eds), 287–299. Frankfurt: Peter Lang.

Motschenbacher, Heiko. 2013. 'Now everybody can wear a skirt': Linguistic constructions of non-heteronormativity at Eurovision Song Contest press conferences. *Discourse & Society* 24(5): 590–614.

Motschenbacher, Heiko. forthcoming. *Language and European Identity Formation. A Discourse Analysis of Linguistic Practices at the Eurovision Song Contest*.

Mukherjee, Joybrato. 2008. English as a global pidgin (EGP) in academia: Some prolegomena. In *English in Academia: Catalyst or Barrier?*, Claus Gnutzmann (ed.), 107–115. Tübingen: Gunter Narr.

Mulac, Anthony. 1999. Perceptions of women and men based on their linguistic behaviour: The gender-linked language effect. In *Perceiving and Performing Gender*, Ursula Pasero & Friederike Braun (eds), 88–104. Opladen: Westdeutscher Verlag.

Mulac, Anthony, Seibold, David R. & Farris, Jennifer Lee. 2000. Female and male managers' and professionals' criticism giving. Differences in language use and effects. *Journal of Language and Social Psychology* 19(4): 389–415.

Mulo Farenkia, Bernard. 2005. Kreativität und Formelhaftigkeit in der Realisierung von Kompli-menten: Ein deutsch-kamerunischer Vergleich. *Linguistik Online* 22(1): 33–44.

Murata, Kumiko & Jenkins, Jennifer (eds). 2009. *Global Englishes in Asian Contexts: Current and Future Debates*. Basingstoke: Palgrave Macmillan.

Naglo, Kristian. 2006. Sprachgruppen und die Rolle von Sprachen in Identitätsbildungs-prozessen. In *Romanische Sprachen in Europa. Eine Tradition mit Zukunft?*, Michael Frings & Andre Klump (eds), 29–40. Stuttgart: Ibidem.

Nakamura, Momoko. 2009. How metalinguistic comments suppress subversive practices. In *Proceedings of the 5th Biennial International Gender and Language Association Conference IGALA 5, Wellington 2008*, Julia de Bres, Janet Holmes & Meredith Marra (eds), 1–13. Wellington: Victoria University of Wellington.

Nekvapil, Jiří & Neustupný, Jiří V. 2005. Politeness in the Czech Republic: Distance, levels of expression, management and intercultural contact. In *Politeness in Europe*, Leo Hickey & Miranda Stewart (eds), 247–262. Clevedon: Multilingual Matters.

Nevalainen, Terttu. 2012. Reconstructing syntactic continuity and change in early Modern English regional dialects: The case of *who*. In *Analysing Older English*, David Denison, Ricardo Bermúdez-Otero, Chris McCully & Emma Moore (eds), 159–184. Cambridge: Cambridge University Press.

Nic Craith, Máiréad. 2006. *Europe and the Politics of Language. Citizens, Migrants and Outsiders*. Basingstoke: Palgrave Macmillan.

Nicolaysen, Sünje. 2007. *Das Kompliment als Höflichkeitsstrategie: Ein Vergleich am Beispiel des Schwedischen und des amerikanischen Englischen*. Saarbrücken: VDM Verlag Dr. Müller.

Niedzielski, Nancy A. & Preston, Dennis R. 2000. *Folk Linguistics*. Berlin: Mouton de Gruyter.

Nikolaeva, Irina. 2006. Relative clauses. In *Encyclopedia of Language & Linguistics*, Vol. X, Edward K. Brown (ed.), 501–508. Amsterdam: Elsevier.

Nixdorf, Nina. 2002. *Höflichkeit im Englischen, Deutschen, Russischen: Ein interkultureller Vergleich am Beispiel von Ablehnungen und Komplimenterwiderungen*. Marburg: Tectum.

Norrick, Neal R. 1980. The speech act of complimenting. *The Nordic Languages and Modern Linguistics* 4: 296–304.

Olofsson, Arne. 2009a. The gift of the gap: A study of Dutch and Swedish learners' use of the English zero relativizer. *English Studies* 90(3): 333–344.

Olofsson, Arne. 2009b. In search of nothing in particular. A cross-linguistic study of advanced learners' use of the English zero relativizer. In *Corpora and Discourse – and Stuff: Papers in Honour of Karin Aijmer*, Rhonwen Bowen, Mats Mobärg & Sölve Ohlander (eds), 233–242. Gothenburg: University of Gothenburg.

Otsuji, Emi & Pennycook, Alastair. 2010. Metrolingualism: Fixity, fluidity and language in flux. *International Journal of Multilingualism* 7(3): 240–254.

Pakir, Anne. 2009. English as a lingua franca: Analyzing research frameworks in international English, world Englishes, and ELF. *World Englishes* 28(2): 224–235.

Papapavlou, Andreas N. 2001. Linguistic imperialism? The status of English in Cyprus. *Language Problems & Language Planning* 25(2): 167–176.

Parisi, Christopher & Wogan, Peter. 2006. Compliment topics and gender. *Women and Language* 29(2): 21–28.

Park, Joseph Sung-Yul & Wee, Lionel. 2009. The three circles redux: A market-theoretic perspective on World Englishes. *Applied Linguistics* 30(3): 389–406.

Pedrazzini, Luciana & Nava, Andrea. 2011. Researching ELF identity: A study with non-native English teachers. In *Latest Trends in ELF Research*, Alasdair Archibald, Alessia Cogo & Jennifer Jenkins (eds), 269–283. Newcastle upon Tyne: Cambridge Scholars.

Pennycook, Alastair. 2003. Global Englishes, rip slyme, and performativity. *Journal of Sociolinguistics* 7(4): 513–533.

Pennycook, Alastair. 2004. The myth of English as an international language. *English in Australia* 139: 26–32.

Pennycook, Alastair. 2007a. The myth of English as an international language. In *Disinventing and Reconstituting Languages*, Sinfree Makoni & Alastair Pennycook (eds), 90–115. Clevedon: Multilingual Matters.

Pennycook, Alastair. 2007b. *Global Englishes and Transcultural Flows*. London: Routledge.

Pennycook, Alastair. 2011. Global Englishes. In *The Sage Handbook of Sociolinguistics*, Ruth Wodak, Barbara Johnstone & Paul Kerswill (eds), 513–525. London: Sage.

Penz, Hermine. 2011. 'What do we mean by that?': Metadiscourse in ELF project discussions. In *Latest Trends in ELF Research*, Alasdair Archibald, Alessia Cogo & Jennifer Jenkins (eds), 185–201. Newcastle upon Tyne: Cambridge Scholars.

Peters, Hans. 1992. Zur Entwicklung der englischen Relativpronomina: Typologische und soziolinguistische Aspekte. *North-Western European Language Evolution* 20: 89–142.

Peterson, V. Spike. 1999. Sexing political identities/Nationalism as heterosexism. *International Feminist Journal of Politics* 1(1): 34–65.

Phillipson, Robert. 1998. Globalizing English: Are linguistic human rights an alternative to linguistic imperialism? *Language Sciences* 20(1): 101–112.

Phillipson, Robert. 2003a. *English-Only Europe? Challenging Language Policy*. London: Routledge.

Phillipson, Robert. 2003b. English for whose purposes in the new world order: Going beyond national and corporate linguistic imperialism. In *Wessen Sprache – lernen. Beiträge zu Autonomie und Sprachpolitik*, Thomas Fritz (ed.), 173–197. Wien: Verband Wiener Volksbildung.

Phillipson, Robert. 2008a. Lingua franca or lingua frankensteinia? English in European integration and globalisation. *World Englishes* 27(2): 250–267.

Phillipson, Robert. 2008b. Is there any unity in diversity in language policies national and supranational? English as an EU lingua franca or lingua frankensteinia? In *National and European Language Policies: Contributions to the Annual Conference 2007 of EFNIL in Riga*, Gerhard Stickel (ed.), 145–154. Frankfurt: Peter Lang.

Phillipson, Robert & Skutnabb-Kangas, Tove. 1997. Linguistic human rights and English in Europe. *World Englishes* 16(1): 27–43.

Piette, Adam. 2004. Communication, culture, community and the idea of Europe. *European English Messenger* 13(1): 18–23.

Platzack, Christer. 2002. Relativization in the Germanic languages, with particular emphasis on Scandinavian. In *Relativisation on the North Sea Littoral*, Patricia Poussa (ed.), 77–96. München: Lincom.

Pölzl, Ulrike & Seidlhofer, Barbara. 2006. In and on their own terms: The 'habitat factor' in English as a lingua franca interactions. *International Journal of the Sociology of Language* 177: 151–176.

Pomerantz, Anita. 1978. Compliment responses: Notes on the co-operation of multiple constraints. In *Studies in the Organization of Conversational Interaction*, Jim Schenkein (ed.), 79–112. New York: Academic Press.

Poussa, Patricia (ed.). 2002. *Relativisation on the North Sea Littoral*. München: Lincom.

Preston, Dennis R. 2004. Folk metalanguage. In *Metalanguage: Social and Ideological Perspectives*, Adam Jaworski, Nikolas Coupland & Dariusz Galasiński (eds), 75–101. Berlin: Mouton de Gruyter.

Probst, Julia. 2003. Ein Kompliment in Ehren… Aspekte eines 'höflichen' Sprechaktes in mehreren Sprachen. *Zeitschrift für Interkulturellen Fremdsprachenunterricht* 8(2–3): 210–225.

Prodromou, Luke. 2008. *English as a Lingua Franca: A Corpus-Based Analysis*. London: Continuum.

Quirk, Randolph. 1985. The English language in a global context. In *English in the World: Teaching and Learning the Language and Literatures*, Randolph Quirk & Henry G. Widdowson (eds), 1–6. Cambridge: Cambridge University Press.

Quirk, Randolph, Greenbaum, Sidney, Leech, Geoffrey & Svartvik, Jan. 2003 [1985]. *A Comprehensive Grammar of the English Language*. Harlow: Longman.

Rampton, Ben. 1999. Crossing. *Journal of Linguistic Anthropology* 9(1/2): 54–56.

Rees-Miller, Janie. 2011. Compliments revisited: Contemporary compliments and gender. *Journal of Pragmatics* 43(11): 2673–2688.

Reichelt, Melinda. 2006. English in a multilingual Spain. *English Today* 22(3): 3–9.

Rose, Kenneth R. 2001. Compliments and compliment responses in film: Implications for pragmatics research and language teaching. *International Review of Applied Linguistics in Language Teaching* 39(4): 309–326.

Rosenberger, Lukas. 2009. *The Swiss English Hypothesis*. Tübingen: Francke.

Ruhi, Şükriye. 2002. Complimenting women in Turkish. Gender identity and otherness. In *Us and Others. Social Identities Across Languages, Discourses and Cultures*, Anna Duszak (ed.), 401–427. Amsterdam: John Benjamins.

Ruhi, Şükriye & Doğan, Gürkan. 2001. Relevance theory and compliments as phatic communication: The case of Turkish. In *Linguistic Politeness Across Boundaries. The Case of Greek and Turkish*, Arin Bayraktaroğlu & Maria Sifianou (eds), 341–390. Amsterdam: John Benjamins.

Sandvoss, Cornel. 2008. On the couch with Europe: The Eurovision Song Contest, the European Broadcast Union and belonging on the old continent. *Popular Communication* 6(3): 190–207.

Saraceni, Mario. 2008. English as a lingua franca: Between form and function. *English Today* 24(2): 20–26.

Saraceni, Mario. 2010. *The Relocation of English: Shifting Paradigms in a Global Era*. Basingstoke: Palgrave Macmillan.

Schmied, Joseph. 1993. Qualitative and quantitative research approaches to English relative constructions. In *Corpus-Based Computational Linguistics*, Clive Souter & Eric Atwell (eds), 85–96. Amsterdam: Rodopi.

Schneider, Klaus P. & Schneider, Iris. 2000. Bescheidenheit in vier Kulturen: Komplimenterwiderungen in den USA, Irland, Deutschland, China. In *Ethische Konzepte und mentale Kulturen 2. Sprachwissenschaftliche Studien zu Höflichkeit als Respektverhalten*, Mariann Skog-Södersveld (ed.), 65–80. Vaasa: Vaasan Yliopisto.

Schreiner, Patrick. 2006. *Staat und Sprache in Europa. Nationalstaatliche Einsprachigkeit und die Mehrsprachenpolitik der Europäischen Union*. Frankfurt: Peter Lang.

Schweiger, Wolfgang & Brosius, Hans-Bernd. 2003. Eurovision Song Contest – Beeinflussen Nachrichtenfaktoren die Punktevergabe durch das Publikum? *Medien & Kommunikationswissenschaft* 51(2): 271–294.

Seidlhofer, Barbara. 2002. The shape of things to come? Some basic questions about English as a lingua franca. In *Lingua Franca Communication*, Karlfried Knapp & Christiane Meierkord (eds), 269–302. Frankfurt am Main: Peter Lang.

Seidlhofer, Barbara. 2003. Englisch: Adoptiert und adaptiert. In *Wessen Sprache – lernen. Beiträge zu Autonomie und Sprachpolitik*, Thomas Fritz (ed.), 198–211. Wien: Verband Wiener Volksbildung.

Seidlhofer, Barbara. 2004. Research perspectives on teaching English as a lingua franca. *Annual Review of Applied Linguistics* 24: 209–239.

Seidlhofer, Barbara. 2005a. Standard future or half-baked quackery? Descriptive and pedagogic bearings on the globalisation of English. In *The Globalisation of English and the English Language Classroom*, Claus Gnutzmann & Frauke Intemann (eds), 159–173. Tübingen: Gunter Narr.

Seidlhofer, Barbara. 2005b. Language variation and change: The case of English as a lingua franca. In *English Pronunciation Models: A Changing Scene*, Katarzyna Dziubalska-Kołaczyk & Joanna Przedlacka (eds), 59–75. Bern: Peter Lang.

Seidlhofer, Barbara. 2006. English as a lingua franca in the expanding circle: What it isn't. In *English in the World. Global Rules, Global Roles*, Rani Rubdy & Mario Saraceni (eds), 40–50. London: Continuum.

Seidlhofer, Barbara. 2007. English as a lingua franca and communities of practice. In *Anglistentag 2006 Halle. Proceedings*, Sabine Volk-Birke & Julia Lippert (eds), 307–318. Trier: Wissenschaftlicher Verlag Trier.

Seidlhofer, Barbara. 2009a. Common ground and different realities: World Englishes and English as a lingua franca. *World Englishes* 28(2): 236–245.

Seidlhofer, Barbara. 2009b. Orientations in ELF research: Form and function. In *English as a Lingua Franca: Studies and Findings*, Anna Mauranen & Elina Ranta (eds), 37–59. Newcastle upon Tyne: Cambridge Scholars.

Seidlhofer, Barbara. 2009c. Accommodation and the idiom principle in English as a lingua franca. *Intercultural Pragmatics* 6(2): 195–215.

Seidlhofer, Barbara. 2010. Lingua franca English. The European context. In *The Routledge Handbook of World Englishes*, Andy Kirkpatrick (ed.), 355–371. London: Routledge.

Seidlhofer, Barbara. 2011. *Understanding English as a Lingua Franca*. Oxford: Oxford University Press.

Seidlhofer, Barbara. 2012. Anglophone-centric attitudes and the globalization of English. *Journal of English as a Lingua Franca* 1(2): 393–407.

Seidlhofer, Barbara & Widdowson, Henry. 2007. Idiomatic variation and change in English. The idiom principle and its realizations. In *Tracing English Through Time: Explorations in Language Variation*, Ute Smit, Stefan Dollinger, Julia Hüttner, Gunther Kaltenböck & Ursula Lutzky (eds), 359–374. Wien: Braumüller.

Sewell, Andrew. 2013. English as a lingua franca: Ontology and ideology. *ELT Journal* 67(1): 3–10.

Sifianou, Maria. 2001. 'Oh, how appropriate!': Compliments and politeness. In *Linguistic Politeness Across Boundaries. The Case of Greek and Turkish*, Arin Bayraktaroğlu & Maria Sifianou (eds), 391–430. Amsterdam: John Benjamins.

Sifianou, Maria & Antonopoulou, Eleni 2005. Politeness in Greece: The politeness of involvement. In *Politeness in Europe*, Leo Hickey & Miranda Stewart (eds), 263–276. Clevedon: Multilingual Matters.

Sigley, Robert. 1997. The influence of formality and channel on relative pronoun choice in New Zealand English. *English Language and Linguistics* 1(2): 207–232.

Skutnabb-Kangas, Tove & Phillipson, Robert 2003. Can languages other than English benefit from globalisation and Europeanisation? Language policy and language rights challenges. In *Linguistic Cultural Identity and International Communication. Maintaining Language Diversity in the Face of Globalization*, Johann Vielberth & Guido Drexel (eds), 79–92. Saarbrücken: AQ.

Smit, Ute. 2010. *English as a Lingua Franca in Higher Education: A Longitudinal Study of Classroom Discourse*. Berlin: De Gruyter Mouton.

Smits, R.J. 1989. *Eurogrammar: The Relative and Cleft Constructions of the Germanic and Romance Languages*. Dordrecht: Foris.

Sowden, Colin. 2012. ELF on a mushroom: The overnight growth in English as a lingua franca. *ELT Journal* 66(1): 89–96.

Stenström, Anna-Brita. 1999. He was really gormless – She's bloody crap. Girls, boys and intensifiers. In *Out of Corpora. Studies in Honour of Stig Johansson*, Hilde Hasselgard & Signe Oksefjell (eds), 69–78. Amsterdam: Rodopi.

Stewart, Miranda. 2005. Politeness in Britain: 'It's only a suggestion…'. In *Politeness in Europe*, Leo Hickey & Miranda Stewart (eds), 116–129. Clevedon: Multilingual Matters.

Suárez-Gómez, Cristina. 2008. Strategies in competition: Demonstratives and interrogatives as relativizers in the history of English. *English Studies* 89(3): 339–350.

Sung, Chit Cheung Matthew. 2013. English as a Lingua Franca and English language teaching: A way forward. *ELT Journal* 67(3): 350–353.

Szmrecsanyi, Benedikt & Kortmann, Bernd. 2011. Typological profiling: Learner Englishes versus indigenized L2 varieties of English. In *Exploring Second-Language Varieties of English and Learner Englishes: Bridging a Paradigm Gap*, Joybrato Mukherjee & Marianne Hundt (eds), 167–188. Amsterdam: John Benjamins.

Taavitsainen, Irma & Jucker, Andreas H. 2008. 'Methinks you seem more beautiful than ever': Compliments and gender in the history of English. In *Speech Acts in the History of English*, Andreas H. Jucker & Irma Taavitsainen (eds), 195–228. Amsterdam: John Benjamins.

Tagliamonte, Sali A. 2006. *Analysing Sociolinguistic Variation*. Cambridge: Cambridge University Press.

Tagliamonte, Sali, Smith, Jennifer & Lawrence, Helen. 2005. No taming the vernacular! Insights from the relatives in northern Britain. *Language Variation and Change* 17(1): 75–112.

Temperley, David. 2003. Ambiguity avoidance in English relative clauses. *Language* 79(3): 464–484.

Thomson, Rob & Murachver, Tamar. 2001. Predicting gender from electronic discourse. *British Journal of Social Psychology* 40(2): 193–208.

Tottie, Gunnel. 1995. The man Ø I love: An analysis of factors favouring zero relatives in written British and American English. In *Studies in Anglistics*, Gunnel Melchers & Beatrice Warren (eds), 201–215. Stockholm: Almqvist & Wiksell.

Tottie, Gunnel. 1997a. Literacy and prescriptivism as determinants of linguistic change: A case study based on relativization strategies. In *Anglistentag 1996 Dresden. Proceedings*, Uwe Böker & Hans Sauer (eds), 83–93. Trier: Wissenschaftlicher Verlag Trier.

Tottie, Gunnel. 1997b. Overseas relatives: British-American differences in relative marker usage. In *Studies in English Language and Teaching. In Honour of Flor Aarts*, Jan Aarts, Inge de Mönnink & Herman Wekker (eds), 153–165. Amsterdam: Rodopi.

Tottie, Gunnel. 1997c. Relatively speaking: Relative marker usage in the British National Corpus. In *To Explain the Present: Studies in the Changing English Language in Honour of Matti Rissanen*, Terttu Nevalainen & Leena Kahlas-Tarkka (eds), 465–481. Helsinki: Société Néophilologique.

Trudgill, Peter. 1980. Acts of conflicting identity: A sociolinguistic look at British pop songs. *York Papers in Linguistics* 9: 261–277.

Trudgill, Peter. 1997. Typology and sociolinguistics: Linguistic structure, social structure and explanatory comparative dialectology. *Folia Linguistica* 31(3/4): 349–360.

Trudgill, Peter. 2000. *Sociolinguistics. An Introduction to Language and Society*, 4th edn. Harmondsworth: Penguin.

Trudgill, Peter. 2005. Native-speaker segmental phonological models and the English lingua franca core. In *English Pronunciation Models: A Changing Scene*, Katarzyna Dziubalska-Kołaczyk & Joanna Przedlacka (eds), 77–98. Bern: Peter Lang.

Ushioda, Ema. 2006. Language motivation in a reconfigured Europe: Access, identity, autonomy. *Journal of Multilingual and Multicultural Development* 27(2): 148–161.

van den Doel, Rias & Quené, Hugo. 2013. The endonormative standards of European English: Emerging or elusive? *English World-Wide* 34(1): 77–98.

van Els, Theo J.M. 2001. The European Union, its institutions and its languages: Some language political observations. *Current Issues in Language Planning* 2(4): 311–360.

van Els, Theo J.M. 2006. An update on the European Union, its institutions and its languages: Some language political observations. In *Language Planning and Policy in Europe, Vol. 2. The Czech Republic, the European Union and Northern Ireland*, Richard B. Baldauf & Robert B. Kaplan (eds), 252–256. Clevedon: Multilingual Matters.

Virkkula, Tiina & Nikula, Tarja. 2010. Identity construction in ELF contexts: A case study of Finnish engineering students working in Germany. *International Journal of Applied Linguistics* 20(2): 251–273.

VOICE Project. 2007. *VOICE Transcription Conventions [2.1]*. ⟨http://www.univie.ac.at/voice/voice.php?page=transcription_general_information⟩ (20 October 2013).

Walker, James A. 2010. *Variation in Linguistic Systems*. New York: Routledge.

Walker, Robin. 2010. *Teaching the Pronunciation of English as a Lingua Franca*. Oxford: Oxford University Press.

Warnke, Ingo H. & Spitzmüller, Jürgen. 2008. Methoden und Methodologie der Diskurslinguistik – Grundlagen und Verfahren einer Sprachwissenschaft jenseits textueller Grenzen. In *Methoden der Diskurslinguistik. Sprachwissenschaftliche Zugänge zur transtextuellen Ebene*, Ingo H. Warnke & Jürgen Spitzmüller (eds), 3–54. Berlin: Walter de Gruyter.

Watts, Richard J. 2003. *Politeness*. Cambridge: Cambridge University Press.

Watts, Richard J. 2005. Linguistic politeness research: Quo vadis? In *Politeness in Language. Studies in its History, Theory and Practice,* 2nd edn, Richard Watts, Sachiko Ide & Konrad Ehlich (eds), xi–xlvii. Berlin: Mouton de Gruyter.

Weber, Tilo. 1997. The emergence of linguistic structure: Paul Hopper's Emergent Grammar Hypothesis revisited. *Language Sciences* 19(2): 177–196.

Weinert, Regina. 2004. Relative clauses in spoken English and German – Their structure and function. *Linguistische Berichte* 197: 3–51.

Wenger, Etienne. 1998. *Communities of Practice: Learning, Meaning, and Identity*. Cambridge: Cambridge University Press.

Werthwein, Daniela Christina. 2009. *Already Got a Compliment Today? Wie Australier und Deutsche verbal auf Komplimente reagieren*. St. Augustin: Asgard.

White, Goodith. 2006. Standard Irish English as a marker of Irish identity. In *The Sociolinguistics of Identity*, Tope Omoniyi & Goodith White (eds), 217–231. London: Continuum.

Widdowson, Henry G. 1994. The ownership of English. *TESOL Quarterly* 28(2): 377–389.

Widdowson, Henry G. 1997. EIL, ESL, EFL: Global issues and local interests. *World Englishes* 16(1): 135–146.

Widdowson, Henry G. 2012. ELF and the inconvenience of established concepts. *Journal of English as a Lingua Franca* 1(1): 5–26.

Wieland, Molly. 1995. Complimenting behavior in French/American cross-cultural dinner conversations. *French Review* 68(5): 796–812.

Wilton, Antje & Stegu, Martin. 2011. Bringing the 'folk' into applied linguistics. *AILA Review* 24: 1–14.

Wodak, Ruth. 2004. National and transnational identities: European and other identities constructed in interviews with EU officials. In *Transnational Identities. Becoming European in the EU,* Richard K. Herrmann, Thomas Risse & Marilyn B. Brewer (eds), 97–128. Lanham, MD: Rowman & Littlefield.

Wodak, Ruth, de Cillia, Rudolf, Reisigl, Martin, Liebhart, Karin, Hofstätter, Klaus & Kargl, Maria. 1998. *Zur diskursiven Konstruktion nationaler Identität*. Frankfurt: Suhrkamp.

Wodak, Ruth & Weiss, Gilbert. 2005. Analyzing European Union discourses. Theories and applications. In *A New Agenda in (Critical) Discourse Analysis. Theory, Methodology, and Interdisciplinarity*, Ruth Wodak & Paul Chilton (eds), 121–135. Amsterdam: John Benjamins.

Wolf, Hans-Georg & Polzenhagen, Frank. 2006. Intercultural communication in English: Arguments for a cognitive approach to intercultural pragmatics. *Intercultural Pragmatics* 3(3): 285–321.

Wolfson, Nessa. 1981. Compliments in cross-cultural perspective. *TESOL Quarterly* 15(2): 117–124.

Wolfson, Nessa. 1983. An empirically based analysis of complimenting in American English. In *Sociolinguistics and Language Acquisition*, Nessa Wolfson & Elliott Judd (eds), 82–95. Rowley, MA: Newbury House.

Wolfson, Nessa. 1984. Pretty is as pretty does: A speech act view of sex roles. *Applied Linguistics* 5(3): 236–244.

Wolfson, Nessa. 1989. The social dynamics of native and nonnative variation in complimenting behavior. In *The Dynamic Interlanguage: Empirical Studies in Second Language Variation*, Miriam R. Eisenstein (ed.), 219–236. New York: Plenum.

Wolfson, Nessa & Manes, Joan. 1980. The compliment as a social strategy. *Papers in Linguistics* 13(3): 391–410.

Wright, Sue. 2000. *Community and Communication: The Role of Language in Nation State Building and European Integration*. Clevedon: Multilingual Matters.

Wright, Sue. 2011. Language and nation building in Europe. In *The Languages and Linguistics of Europe: A Comprehensive Guide*, Bernd Kortmann & Johan van der Auwera (eds), 775–788. Berlin: De Gruyter Mouton.

Xiao, Richard & Tao, Hongyin 2007. A corpus-based sociolinguistic study of amplifiers in British English. *Sociolinguistic Studies* 1(2): 241–273.

Yamashita, Junko. 1994. An analysis of relative clauses in the Lancaster/IBM Spoken English Corpus. *English Studies* 75(1): 73–84.

Yano, Yasukata. 2009. English as an international lingua franca: From societal to individual. *World Englishes* 28(2): 246–255.

Ylänne-McEwen, Virpi. 1993. Complimenting behaviour: A cross-cultural investigation. *Journal of Multilingual and Multicultural Development* 14(6): 499–508.

Young, Richard & Bayley, Robert. 1996. VARBRUL analysis for second language acquisition research. In *Second Language Acquisition and Linguistic Variation*, Robert Bayley & Dennis R. Preston (eds), 253–306. Amsterdam: John Benjamins.

Zabor, Lech. 1998. VARBRUL analysis for studies of variation in interlanguage. *Anglica Wratislaviensia* 33: 137–146.

Zifonun, Gisela. 2001. *Grammatik des Deutschen im europäischen Vergleich: Der Relativsatz*. Mannheim: Institut für Deutsche Sprache.

Index